To Irene Miluski
as a memento for ou

Finnish Art

OVER THE CENTURIES

MARKKU VALKONEN

Finnish Art

OVER THE CENTURIES

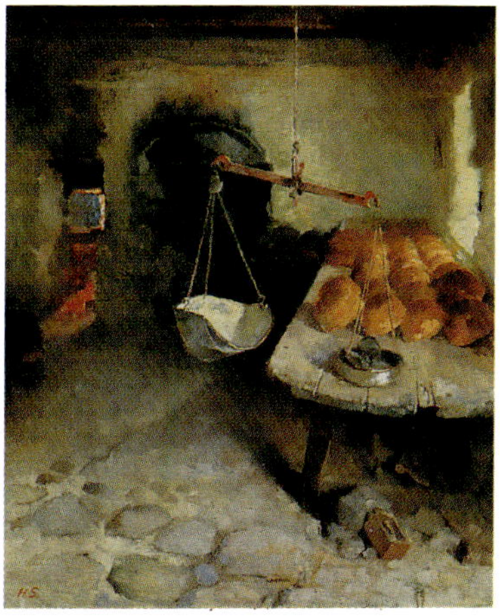

OTAVA PUBLISHING COMPANY LIMITED HELSINKI

Photographs:
Toimituskuva Oy, Matti Ruotsalainen.
Central Art Archives, Helsinki, p. 7,
Seppo Hilpo pp. 13, 15 (left) 40, 46, 53, 65 (above),
78, 81 (left), 83 (below) 87 (left), 93 (above), 99, 104,
105 (left), 111, 116, 118, (right), 121 (below), 132 (right),
144, 145, 147 (above), 153 (left), 154, 155, 156 and
Petri Virtanen p. 158.
Salvatore Licitra p. 157
Pirje Mykkänen p. 159 (below)
Esko Männikkö p. 160
Markku Alatalo p. 162 (above)
Pertti Kekarainen p. 162 (below)
Pia Paldanius p. 163
Ulla Hassinen p. 164
Screenshot: Marita Liulia p. 159
KUVASTO

2nd revised edition

Graphic design:
Markku Reunanen and Sinikka Lindfors
Translated by:
Martha Gaber Abrahamsen and Malcolm Hicks

Printed by the Otava Book Printing Company
Keuruu 1999

ISBN 951-1-16080-X

Contents

Foreword 7
On the borders of different cultures 9
Once the ice sheet had receded 9
From the advent of Christianity to the Reformation 10
Peaceful coexistence between Renaissance and Baroque 13
From Rococo to Gustavian Neo-antique 18

The achievements of autonomy 22
The czar and the Hellas of the north 22
The art world takes shape 26
Finnishness 28
What does a Finn look like? 30
Holmberg and Düsseldorf 34
The culmination of Romanticism and the challenge of Paris 39
From dreams of an academy to a "palace of industry" 44
The move away from historical painting 46
Air, light, and wind 49
A politicized review of sculpture 52
From Neo-classicism to Realism 54
Women make a breakthrough 58
The soul and the eye's testimony 60
Subjects lose ground 63
The Kullervo of painting 67
The search for atmosphere 69
The end of the Arts Society's power 71

The dream of Renaissance in the north 72
Myths and their bards 72
The search for a national identity 74
Slaves or the masters of their own destiny 77
Symbolism 78
The preachers of a new Renaissance 82
The romance of the Kalevala 85
The tamer of frost and death 87

Upheavals in society and art 89
Artists and the first period of Russification 89
Creating a synthesis 90
Monumentalism and national melancholy 92
A maid rising from the Baltic 98
Turbulent society, benumbed art 100
Theory and the liberation of color 101
The lesson of the Autumn Salon 102
The battles over Sallinen 107
Septem and the November Group 108
The intermezzo of Cubism 109
Reflections of the Civil War 110

Pride and prejudice in an independent land 114
Discordant harmony 114
The radicals of the Red Room 118
The Torch-bearers 119
The battle of the spirits 122
From regression to new heights 123
From the depths of the mind 126
Opening up contacts 127
Allegories of the republic 128
War-time Karelianism 128

Longing for internationalization 131
The frenzy and metaphysics of expression 131
The prism of structures 132
The rejected angel 136
Informalism 138
The return of the figure 142
Down the last stretch 143
The power of the grid 146
Art's triangle drama 148
Stories change 156
International exchanges 156
Kiasma like a sculpture 158
The bitch and her puppy 158
Extrusion and space traps 161
The natures of a sculpture 164
Select bibliography 165
Index 166

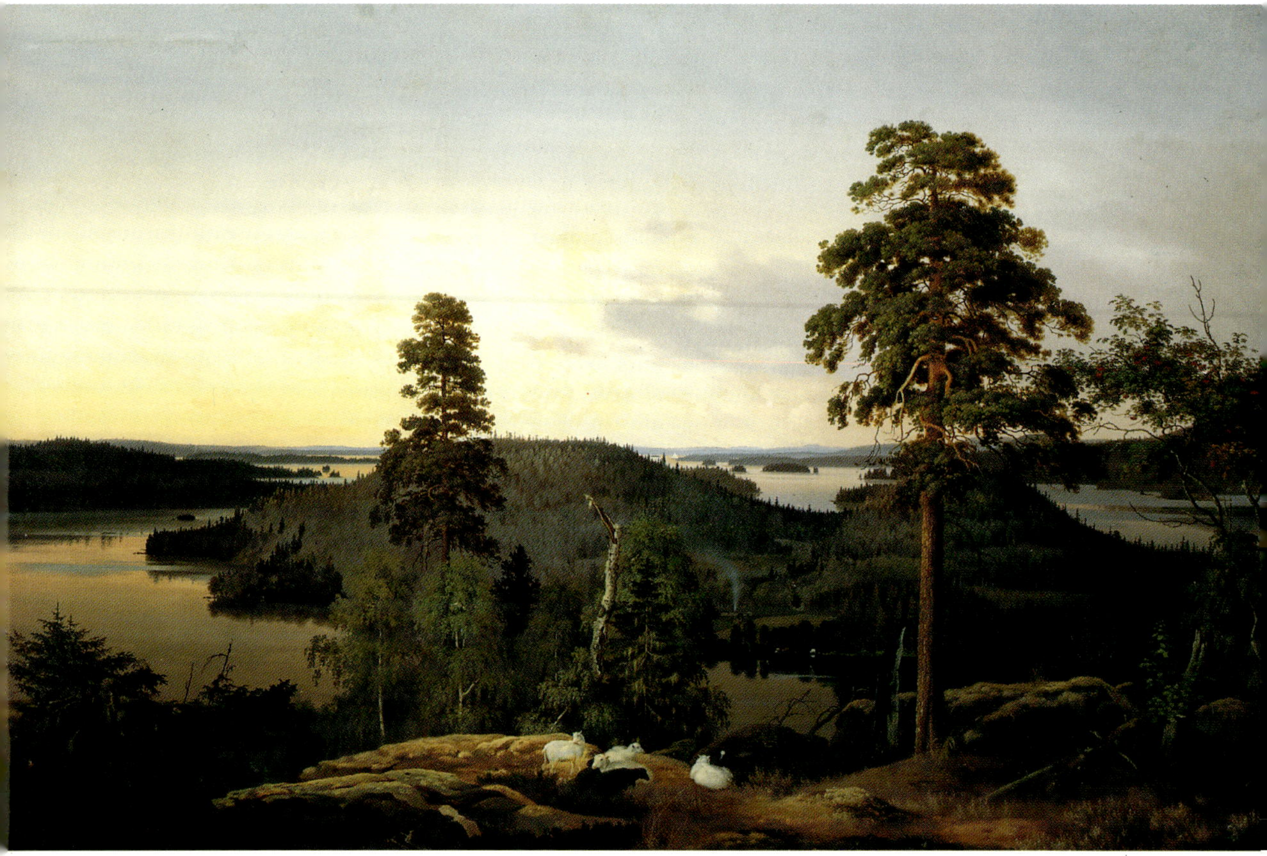

Foreword

How could a nationally distinctive art be created? This is the problem that has puzzled Finland's art world ever since the beginning of the 19th century. This book makes no attempt to revolve the conflicts passed on to us by history, but instead is intended to remind us that the prejudices of the past still affect the Finns' concept of art today. Why else would we have discussions at regular intervals about the "threat" of supranational culture or complaints that Finnish art is stagnating? The unification of Europe will increasingly bring new facets to these discussions.

Art's personal territory is greater today than ever before, but it was not so long ago that people accepted Frederik Cygnaeus's view: "It is possible with the brush, just as well as with the sword, to use immortal strokes to defend the loyalty and self-sacrifice that our homeland demands of its sons." These words were not referring to patriotic historical painting, as one might think, but to Ferdinand von Wright's gently idyllic landscape "Prospect of Hamina Bay" (1854). It was one of the day's greatest critical successes, since it was believed to show a true picture of the fatherland. The author Zachris Topelius sighed, "This painting is Finland," and an anonymous writer in the newspaper *Kuopio Tidning* claimed that "only an eye and artist's hand, trained by thousands of lakes, that not even in the smallest thing can be unfaithful to nature is able to create such a work on canvas..."

Books, even small ones, are not written without help. I would like to express my special thanks to Assistant Professor Eeva Maija Viljo, who took time from her many activities to read my manuscript and contribute valuable comments. My wife Kaija skillfully guided me in knotty questions of style and clarity.

MARKKU VALKONEN

On the borders of different cultures

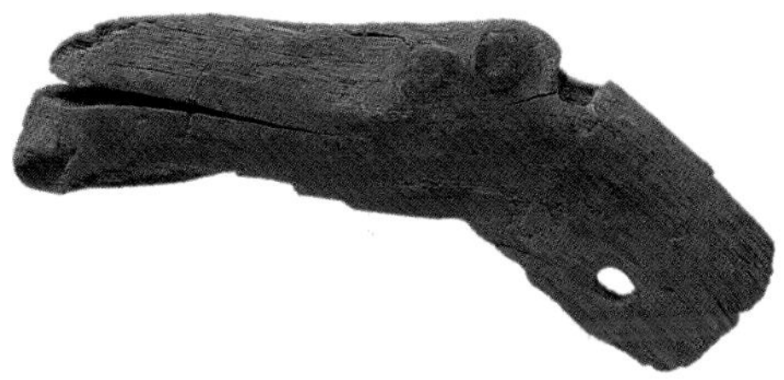

Elk head found at Lehtojärvi in Rovaniemi. C. 5000 B.C. Pine, length 37 cm.
NATIONAL MUSEUM OF FINLAND.

Once the ice sheet had receded

As our knowledge increases, history has a tendency to stretch farther back in time. Traces of human culture on Finnish soil cannot be followed back indefinitely, however, since we are confronted by an insurmountable barrier: the Ice Age.

The land was not suitable for settlement until the 8th–6th centuries B.C., when the ice sheet melted and the land rose from the waters. Finland's shoreline now looks very different since in those days, many large lakes, such as Näsijärvi and Päijänne, were bays of the Baltic Sea, actually what is known as the Ancylus lake.

It is impossible to know whether the first inhabitants of the land newly freed from the ice made pictures that could be called protoart. No finds have been made, and perhaps they never will be since organic substances decompose fairly quickly in Finland's soil. The earliest Stone Age finds, on the other hand, belong to what is called the late Suomusjärvi culture (c. 6500–4200 B.C.). Its people made finely fashioned round-headed clubs and decorated them with incised lines. Objects of this kind have not been found anywhere else.

The settlements of the Suomusjärvi culture were located in the south, but one of Finland's earliest "works of art," a wooden elk head, comes from Lapland, from Lehtojärvi in Rovaniemi. This unique piece, made of pine, is 37 cm long. The elk's lower jaw is missing, but we can still get a fairly good idea of its no-nonsense realism.

The elk head from Lehtojärvi is about 7000 years old. The hole pierced through the neck leads us to assume that the head was attached to a stick. It might have been a scepter or an object used for shamanistic rituals. Another guess is that the elk head decorated the prow of a boat, just as dragon heads graced the ships of later seafarers, the Vikings.

The elk and bear were hunted and also considered cult animals, and as such were of key importance to the Finns of the Stone Age, if we can call them Finns at all, since we know almost nothing of their origins. It seems as if Stone Age man and today's Finns are linked by a genetic bridge, since instead of completely displacing the original inhabitants, the East Baltic wave of settlement during the Iron Age absorbed the local population.

The earliest known stone sculptures depict the elk. Beautiful animal-head weapons from Huittinen and Säkkijärvi were not really weapons, in spite of the designation, and neither were they utilitarian articles: they were symbols of the owner's rank and might. The elk head from Huittinen is dated to the 5100s B.C.

In the later stage of the Stone Age (3000 B.C. to the beginning of the Christian era), the elk appears on nearly all known petroglyphs. These pictures were usually painted on steep cliffs rising from lake shores. The pigments were made from red ocher, which was also used to decorate pottery and graves. Red has been interpreted as the color of life. The first petroglyph

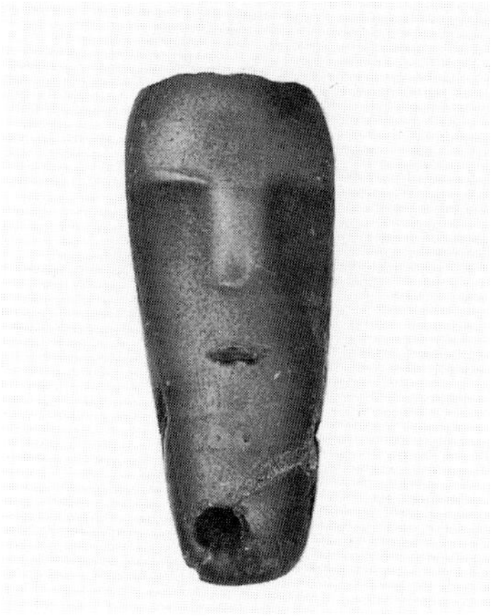

Amber pendant from Metsäpirtti. Comb ceramic culture, 3300–2800 B. C. Height 5.3 cm.
NATIONAL MUSEUM OF FINLAND.

was incidentally found by the composer Jean Sibelius in 1911 on the cliffs along the shore of Lake Hvitträsk.

Pottery was first made in Finland in about 4200 B.C. The first clay vessels bear witness to radical changes in living conditions. The level of the Atlantic ocean had risen, and salt water poured through the Danish straits into the Ancylus lake. A new water area was formed, the littorine stage of the Baltic.

Sea water brought with it new game animals, the most important being the Greenland seal. The pottery required by this hunter culture was first decorated with comb-like patterns imprinted in the clay, and later with cording. Most dating diagrams are still based on changes in ceramics styles.

The decorations on pottery and other objects give us no indication of whether the new way of life affected cult worship. The elk evidently maintained its dominant position in the Finnish pantheon.

Many of the finest pieces from the Stone Age were imported, Sculptures, jewelry, and idols in human form are among the rarest finds.

The fierce-looking amber pendant was dug up on the Karelian Isthmus, but it originally came from Jutland, in Denmark, where amber occurs naturally. The pendant was undoubtedly worn as an amulet to ward off the forces of evil.

The use of bronze spread to southern and western Finland in around 1500 B.C., to be supplanted about a thousand years later by iron. These "ages of metal" did not produce very many pictures or images. On the other hand, we do not know whether wooden objects might in fact have been richly embellished. Skill was primarily displayed in jewelry and weapons, with Germanic zoomorphic ornamentation.

From the advent of Christianity to the Reformation

The first traces of Christianity can be seen in the decorations on coins and crucifixes in the 11th century. The objects that have been found were usually imported, but even copies of Byzantine coins have been discovered. They are charmingly clumsy and were certainly made in Finland.

Finds naturally do not tell us whether the owners of these coins and jewelry understood the meaning of the new religion of the conquerors, or whether they had the same relation to these strange ornaments as they did to other magic charms. The latter seems most likely. Historical documents do, after all, tell us that as late as the 17th century, the Finns, rural and urban alike, enthusiastically practiced various forms of magic. In the north, people were not completely weaned away from them until this century.

Customs and cults often evolved at different tempos. As early as the Viking Age (800–1050 A.D.), the Finns gradually gave up cremating the dead and began to use the Christian custom of burial.

Christianity spread to Finland from two directions, the east and the west. In 1147, the

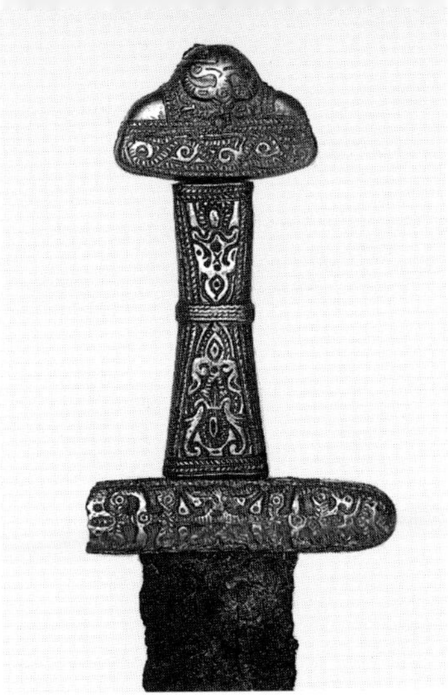

Double-edged sword with bronze hilt, decorated with Karelian ornamentation from Kekomäki, Kaukola. Iron Age.
NATIONAL MUSEUM OF FINLAND.

pope promised absolution to anyone who went off to convert the pagan peoples of the Baltic, and a number of years later, the pope's legate visited Sweden to encourage noblemen there to join the Crusades. Power politics and commerce nonetheless seem to have had more to do with these activities than religious fervor.

Sweden and Denmark were pitted against Novgorod, a trading power with interests to protect along the Finnish coast. The conflicts of the Viking Age were repeated, but took on a new form.

The eastern part of the country came under the religious influence of far-off Byzantium, while western Finland took its version of Christianity from Scandinavia. What is now known as Finland was not inhabited by a united people during the Crusades (1050–1150); it was not even a recognizable ethnic unit, simply a territory settled by contentious tribes.

The spread of Christianity drew the cultural map of the future, divided into two parts. The eastern parts of Finland were dominated by the Greek Orthodox Church, which was quite tolerant of the *Kalevala* way of life and beliefs of pagan times. Cultural changes took place more rapidly in the west.

The churchmen who went off to convert the Finns worked very diplomatically, though at times they also relied on their swords. Many churches were wisely built on the cult sites of pagan times.

The construction of churches considerably expanded the Finns' universe. The magnificence of the ceremonies, images, and sculptures, and the whole complex gallery of characters presented in the new religion also proved bewildering.

The first churches were built in the Åland archipelago. They were made of wood, and not a single one has survived. Churches made of red granite, in contrast, still stand to bear witness to the early stages of Christian architecture. The earliest stone church on the Åland Islands is St. Olaf's at Jomala, believed to have been built in the latter half of the 13th century.

Considerable power was concentrated in Turku. Construction on both the castle and the cathedral was begun at the end of the 13th century. By the end of the Middle Ages, the cathedral had become one of the grandest exemples of northern cathedral Gothic.

The interiors of these churches were decorated with *al secco* paintings. Pigments mixed with limewater were spread on the dry plaster surface, in contrast to the method favored in farther south in Europe, the more durable *al fresco* technique: painting on plaster that was still wet.

Very few medieval Finnish church murals have survived; they can be seen today in only about forty sanctuaries. The decorations in Hattula Church have been preserved most extensively.

It is so difficult to differentiate between Romanesque and Gothic styles in church murals that cut and dry "periods" lose much of their importance. Local variations were very great, and many churches were decorated primitively, something that explains their immense charm

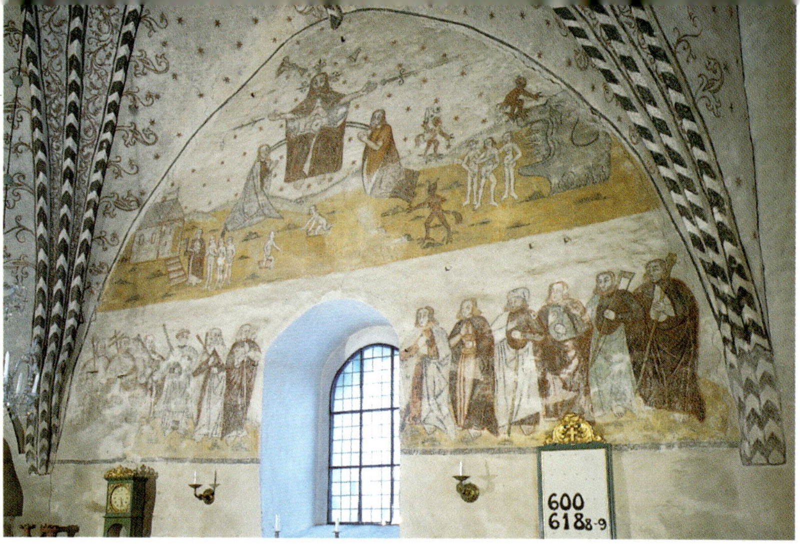

The Last Judgement. Choir of St. James's Church, Rymättylä. 1520–1521. Restored in 1928.

in the eyes of the modern beholder.

Pictures were intended to teach the central dogmas of the new religion and to recount the holy lives of its heroes. The didactic effectiveness of the murals seems doubtful, however, since the churches' small windows and poor lighting left large segments of the varied panorama in the dark.

Most of the church sculptures were imported. However, since master craftsmen traveled around carrying out commissions, some of the sculptures were also made on the spot. The mobility of these craftsmen has made it difficult to determine their origins. The much-admired master from Lieto is usually called a Finn, but no documentation has been found on the background of this fine sculptor, who might have learned his skills in Gotland.

How were the church's pictures understood? Let us take an example from farther south. The Bishop of Paris complained in the 1230s that his parishioners were "simple peasants who not even in our own time know how to separate the saints' pictures from the saints themselves in their prayers; and so when they should be appealing to the saints, they direct their prayers at the saints' images."

The same situation prevailed in Finland, and probably lasted much longer than on the Continent. Former beliefs were mixed with new ones, and many pagan images and signs were painted on the walls of churches. Influences were not just one-directional, either. Kaarle Krohn, the folklorist, calculated last century that some fifty saints had been incorporated in the people's incantations.

Most of the churches were consecrated to specific saints, who thus assumed an exceptionally powerful place or were credited with magical powers in the minds of the people.

One of the most important medieval festivals was Corpus Christi, in honor of the transformation of the Eucharist and Communion Wine into the body and blood of Christ. A miracle of this kind made pictorial representations even more important. It is true that the congregation was given the sacramental wafer at a side altar, but it was perhaps easier for the people to experience the material presence of their deity in the form of a picture.

In addition to Christ on the cross, Finnish churches have preserved many other types of sculpture, such as stages in the Passion of Christ and Christ in his coffin, an effigy that was taken out at Easter. Their significance should not be underestimated. Mikael Agricola, the reformer and father of written Finnish, retained the festival of Corpus Christi unaltered, along with many other Catholic practices. Agricola felt that the Reformation should be carried out without needlessly interfering with forms of piety that had become rooted in the customs of the people.

Reformers have often been accused of being enemies of imagery and destroyers of medieval church murals and other pictures. Much of this criticism is unjust. Clumsy restoration and changes made to the structure of churches, for example enlarging windows, have caused greater

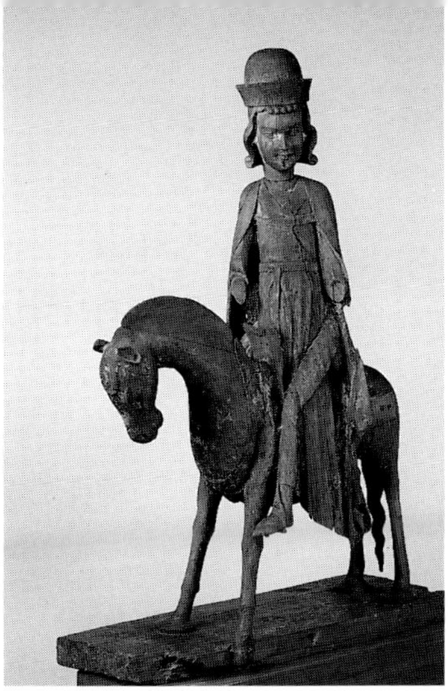

The Master from Lieto:
St. Martin, 316–397.
Raisio. C. 1340.
Oak, 125 cm.
NATIONAL MUSEUM OF FINLAND

damage. Negative attitudes towards the external manifestations of the deposed doctrine did not begin to appear until the 17th century, when Luther's teachings began to reach Finland, but not even the most orthodox wanted to touch the people's beloved St. Christopher, who protected them from an untimely death and ensured travelers a safe journey. Sculptures of Christ being borne by St. Christopher were made as late as the 18th century.

By the end of the Middle Ages, a firm economic foundation had been laid for a flowering of the arts. During bishop Magnus II Tavast's time, the Finnish church was granted the right to sell indulgences to raise funds to decorate its sanctuaries. Many a holy image, chalice, and liturgical garment lightened its giver's burden of sins and shortened his time in purgatory.

But the new age impoverished the church. Its property was reformed more rapidly than its doctrines. The Diet of Västerås in 1527 did away with the bishops' political might and their palaces were made over to the Crown. Most of the church's tithes had already been earmarked for the Crown treasury the year before.

The emphasis in art in fact shifted in the 16th century from ecclesiastical circles to secular spheres, castles and manors. The largest construction project was carried out in Turku (Åbo in Swedish). Between 1556 and 1563, under Duke John, its old castle was transformed into a court the likes of which had never before been seen in Finland. The necessary artisans were brought in from abroad, especially from Germany and the Netherlands. Two painters known by name came from Sweden, Henrik and Sigfrid Staffanson.

During the Renaissance in Finland, greater power and more luxury being acquired by the nobility. Changes could be seen in dress and everyday possessions, but one could hardly speak of a rebirth in art. Very few examples have even been preserved.

One of the few Renaissance programs in church art was carried out in 1560, in the medieval church in Isokyrö. We know little about the painter who did the work; he was probably German. The man who commissioned the project, Dean Jacob Sigfridsson Geet, on the other hand, was one of the famous churchmen of his day. He was known as "The Grand Duke of Kyrö," obviously with good reason. He paid for the church's murals out of his own pocket.

Peaceful coexistence between Renaissance and Baroque

Sweden rose to the ranks of the great powers of Europe in the 17th century. It waged several wars under Gustavus II Adolphus (1594–1632), the longest of which lasted thirty years. The war's ideological goal was to ensure the position of the Protestant religion in Central Europe, but actually power and economic interests were at stake. Sweden expanded to its

Peter Schultz: Monument to Marshal Åke Tott and his second wife, Christina Brahe. 1678. Chapel of St. Laurence, Turku Cathedral.

Anonymous: Epitaph for the family of Hartikka Speitz from Sääksmäki Church. 1619. Oil on wood, 90 x 105 cm.
NATIONAL MUSEUM OF FINLAND.

greatest size under Charles X Gustavus, after the Danes seceded territory in accordance with the Treaty of Roskilde.

Gustavus II Adolphus and his skillful chancellor Axel Oxenstierna (1583–1654) devised a domestic reform program that divided the country into provinces and created an all-encompassing bureaucracy. The program was aimed at unifying all the parts of the country under the central administration, both provinces stolen from neighboring lands and Finland, which had been Swedish for centuries, but was still very different from the mother country.

Competent men were needed for the bureaucracy to work. This led to an improvement in education. The church gained a new role: it was to make the people more civilized, literate, and obedient. Johan Gezelius the Elder was one of the bishops of Turku who dreamed of founding elementary schools in every parish. In 1640, during the term of office of Governor General Per Brahe (1602–80), Finland's first university was opened in Turku. Its founding was part of the program to standardize education under which the University of Tartu (Dorpat, in what was then Livonia) was founded in 1632 and the Academia Carolina, in Lund, Sweden, in 1668.

The university in Turku educated a small group in Finland in science and art. Scientific work also made it necessary for the country to produce its own books. And so an official printer, Petrus Waldin, was hired by the university in 1642. His assistants undoubtedly included draftsmen, since the books he published were graphically advanced and often illustrated.

The aristocracy became wealthier during Sweden's period as a great power and learned the fine art of civilized ostentation, disguised as "virtue" and "honor." War required money, and it was obtained by selling the Crown's lands and granting the aristocracy the right of taxation. Finally, two-thirds of the government's accumulated taxes went to the nobility.

Continental Europe had entered the Baroque era, and it gradually made its appearance in Finland as well. The center of the arts was naturally the Swedish court. Queen Christina gathered around her important scholars, compiled an art collection from the magnificent booty of Prague, and hired one Dutchman and three Frenchmen as court painters.

But the stylistic features of the Renaissance remained on the periphery of the kingdom for quite some time. Finnish art, as well as architecture and town planning, relied on Renaissance models for years to come. Not even fashions in painting immediately complied with new forms, as shown by the church interiors decorated by the German-born Christian Hendhersson Willbrandt, who worked in Ostrobothnia between 1637 and 1677. The most famous are the rich paintings found in the churches of Saloinen, Hailuoto (both destroyed by fire), and Pyhämaa, covering all the walls and ceilings.

Emphasis on the individual grew among the nobility and high clergy. Portraits became more common, and many itinerant portrait painters earned

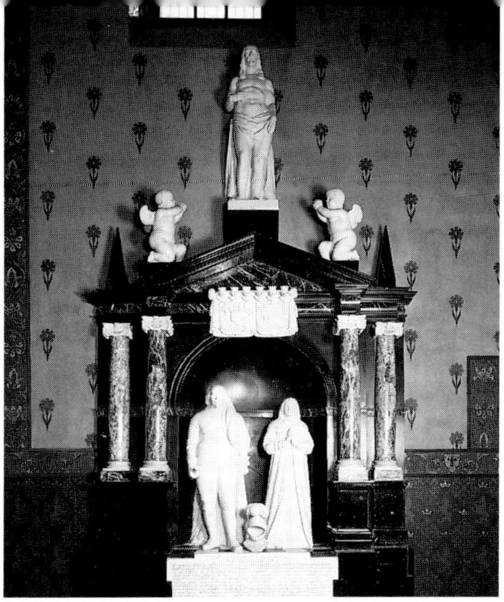

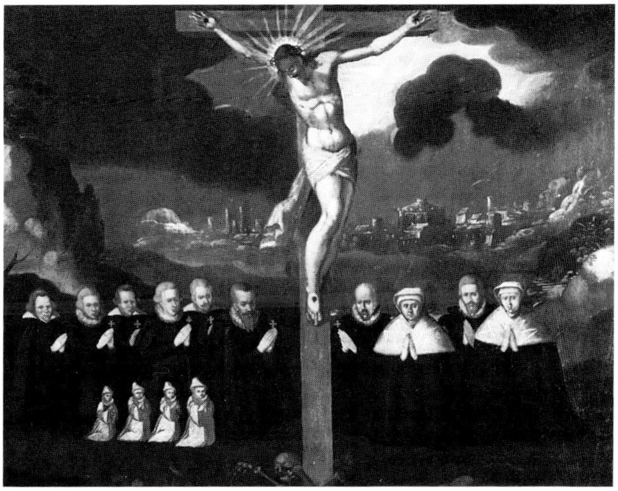

their living from them. But the churches were the true scenes of the nobility's display of power. The congregation sat according to rank, and the decorations of the churches also followed society's hierarchy.

The wealthy nobility commissioned large tombs for their churches. Instead of entrusting the work to the bereaved family, the subject himself commissioned it while he was in the best of health. Those of smaller means had epitaphs painted, a testimony to their dignity and that of their family.

Monuments were imported from abroad, since Finnish artisans were not yet able to make such fine pieces as the tomb of Åke Tott and Christina Brahe at Turku Cathedral. It was sculpted in 1678 by a German, Peter Schultz.

Church decorations were mostly financed through donations. The greatest patrons included Henrik Fleming (1584–1650), who presented several pulpits to Turku churches and a whole portal to St. James's Church in Stockholm. The imposing monument to Fleming and his wife in Mynämäki Church was probably made by the Dutch master Aris Claeszon in 1632.

The Baroque favored allegories. In fact, many altarpieces did not illustrate the words of the Bible: they developed them into allegorical presentations with many levels of meaning.

Adam and Eve stand on the altarpiece of Pöytyä Church in front of a tribunal consisting of the Holy Trinity. But in fact, their judges include not only God, Jesus, and the Holy Spirit (a dove with a human face), but also female personifications of Justice, Truth, Mercy, and Peace. The texts painted on the altarpiece explain who each figure is, and they also reveal the picture's fundamental purpose. The tablet in Jesus's hand reads, "I do not wish for the godless to perish, but for the godless to change his ways and live..."

Patrons were fond of having themselves depicted in the forefront of great events in the history of the redemption. The donors of commemorative paintings are often shown kneeling together with their whole family at the foot of the cross on Calvary. A typical example is the epitaph of the Speitz family in Sääksmäki Church.

The central figure is Hartikka Speitz (1591–1651), a cultured lawyer who translated laws into Finnish, whose unfortunate penchant for getting embroiled in quarrels and even committing lese majesty almost earned him a death sentence. He had the painting made in memory of his father, mother, and siblings. All those who had already died when the painting was made are shown holding a red cross.

A large number of artists from Sweden's days as a great power are known by name. Jochim Neiman (c. 1600–1673) was Finland's first itinerant portrait painter. This artist, perhaps German by birth, became a respected citizen of Finland.

Neiman immortalized not only the faces of numerous pastors, but also the forbidding features of Turku's influential bishop, Isak Rothovius. Rothovius in fact seems to have been the man responsible for bringing Neiman to Finland

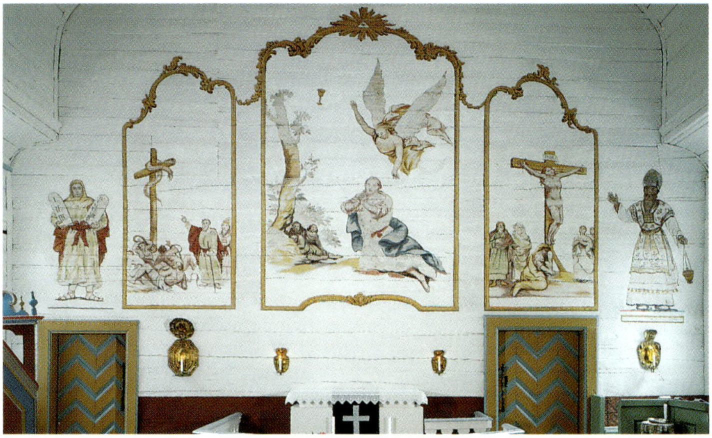

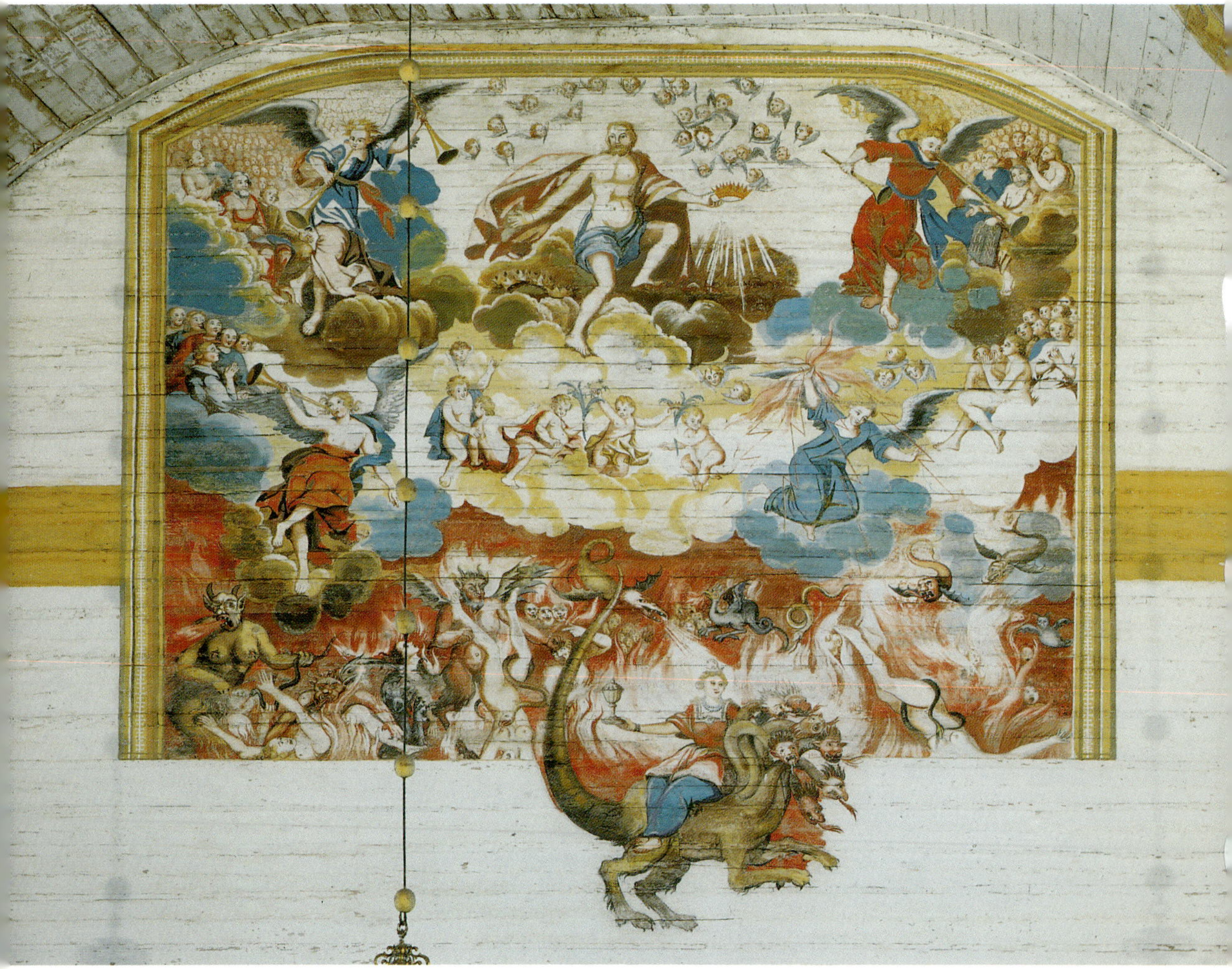

Mikael Toppelius:
Serpent, Gethsemane, and Jesus on the cross. Kiiminki Church altar triptych. After 1779.

Emanuel Granberg:
The Last Judgement. 1778–1781. Paltamo Old Church, Paltaniemi. The hell shown in the painting was so frightening to the congregation that the lower part was covered, but The Revelation's Beast and Whore of Babylon were kept.

from Stockholm. Later portrait painters include the Dane Diedrich Møllerum (1641–c. 1702), who arrived in Finland in 1684 to take part in the restoration work following one of Turku's many fires.

The most successful of the Finnish painters was Elias Brenner (1647–1717), born in Isokyrö in Ostrobothnia. He became court miniaturist in Stockholm, and Charles XII raised him to the aristocracy. Brenner is still remembered as an important numismatist and collector of medieval treasures.

The most conspicuous achievements of the Finnish Baroque are the gilded wood carvings, pulpits and altarpieces, found in a number of churches. The frames of these altarpieces often overshadowed the paintings themselves. The most famous wood-carver known by name is Matias Reiman, who was active in the second half of the 17th century.

Most buildings were made of wood during this period. They fell easy prey to fire, and the wooden structures and their furnishings which have survived from this time are cherished rarities. Most of them are found in Ostrobothnia, which grew wealthy from ship building and tar exports.

The lushness of the Baroque made its advent, though in clumsy fashion, in the church paintings of Ostrobothnia in the latter half of the 17th century. The paintings in the buttressed church in Tornio made by Lars Gallenius (né Kukko, c. 1658–1753) from Oulu are a graphic example of how stylistic influences made their way to the north.

The idiom dating from the 16th century lived on tenaciously alongside the Baroque, and did not disappear in the following century, either. Model books helped maintain continuity in tradition. The Ostrobothnian church painter Johan Backman (1706–1768) relied on such things as woodcuts by Jacob Moss (c. 1588), illustrations from Gustavus II Adolphus's Bible (c. 1618), and Mathäus Merian's biblical pictures (c. 1630). If we can imagine an ordinary Finn in the 18th century, his concept of a suitable artistic style would have been formed mostly by woodcuts and engravings, in addition to church paintings.

Wars plagued Sweden, especially its eastern regions, during the 18th century. The "Hero King" Charles XII's martial foreign policy eroded Sweden's power and proved Finland's bane.

Russia became a great power under Peter I. His army invaded Finland and won the southeastern part of the country in the Peace of Nystad in 1721.

No wonder little can be said of Finnish art in the early 18th century. Late Baroque continued, however, as the situation stabilized. The work of Finland's first woman painter, Margareta Capsia (1682–1759), is among the best achievements of the day. She painted portraits and several altarpieces whose costumes and feel for materials had a magnificence never before seen in Finland. The influence of Rubens has also been noted in Capsia's paintings, but their most important models were found closer: in the style of Martin Mitjens the Elder, a Dutchman who worked in Stockholm.

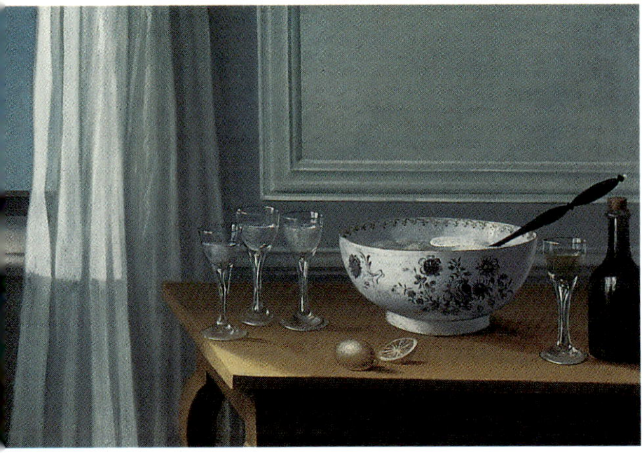

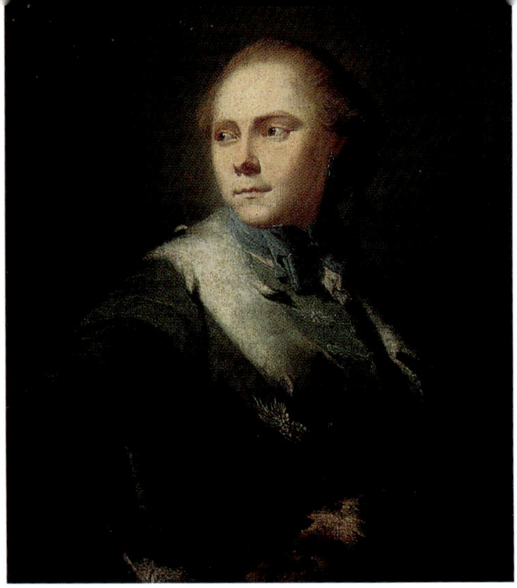

Nils Schillmark: Still-life with Bowl. C. 1795. Oil, 77 x 107.5 cm.
ART MUSEUM OF THE ATENEUM.

Isak Wacklin: Dorothea Maria Losch. C. 1755. Oil, 71 x 56 cm.
ART MUSEUM OF THE ATENEUM.

Carl August Ehrensvärd and Johan Tobias Sergel: Monument to Augustin Ehrensvärd. Courtyard on Susisaari Island, Suomenlinna. Gustavus III approved C. A. Ehrensvärd's drafts in 1783, but the work was not completed until 1807, when the bronze ornaments cast by F. L Rung from models by Sergel were installed.

From Rococo to Gustavian Neo-antique

In around the middle of the 18th century, the airy decorativeness of the Rococo began to arrive in Finland, still recovering from the ravages of war. Construction picked up and interior decoration along with it. Large wall paintings made on canvas, their motives idyllic landscapes, romantic couples, and hunting scenes, were bought for manors. The panels at Jakkarila Manor, painted in the 1760s, are the best example.

The wars had resulted in major changes in Swedish (and Finnish) society. Political power was transferred from the king to the estates, the position of the civil service aristocracy was strengthened, and the importance of society's economic movers, the bourgeoisie, increased. The period before Gustavus III's absolute monarchy is, in fact, called the Era of Liberty (1719–1772).

The ideologies of exploitation and enlightenment spread. The government favored mining, which created a new kind of factory community surrounding the refined manors of the owner. Fashions came from France, following the example of the court.

Economic growth expanded the social circles reached by art. In addition to the nobility, the bourgeoisie also began to decorate their homes as best they could. Even northern church painters were employed in interior decoration. Emanuel Granberg (1754–before 1791) is known to have painted landscapes for merchants, and an allegory depicting the five senses for the parsonage in Oulainen.

An important step was taken in art education in 1735, with the founding of what is now the Royal Swedish Academy of Fine Arts. It became the seat of learning that had long been dreamed of, but it took quite some time before the academy's influence was felt in Finland. The guilds trained most artists within the limits of their own modest resources. The academy's "liberal artists" rose above their artisan colleagues not only because of their better training, but because they no longer had to heed the limitations of the guilds.

The role of bishops as patrons of fine art seems to have been just as important as it had been during Sweden's days as a major power. C. F. Mennander, bishop of Turku, owned a large art collection that is said to have included at least one genuine Roman marble sculpture. In keeping with the spirit of the times, Mennander commissioned the painter Johan Georg

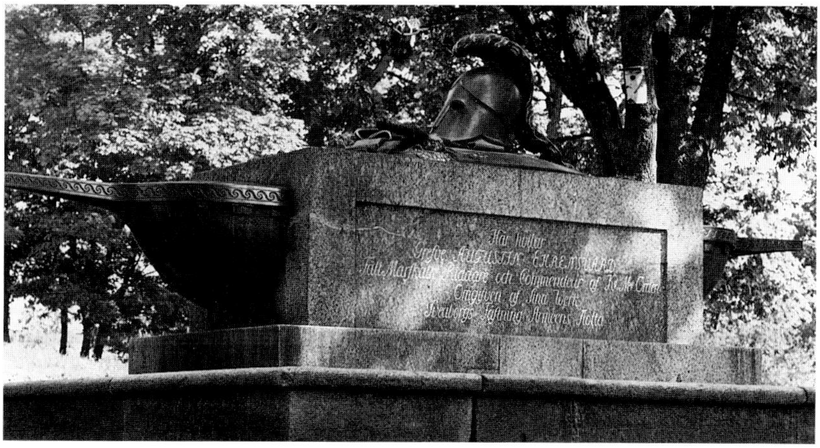

Geitel (1683–1771), who had settled in Turku, to paint three large allegorical paintings, Faith, Hope, and Charity.

Graphics gradually developed, nourished by the university. Illustrations were increasingly needed for dissertations, and the university in Turku had to establish a special position for a master draftsman at the beginning of the 18th century.

At the end of the century, attention was also focused on the study of national subjects. The Aurora Society was founded in 1770 for precisely this purpose. Its moving force, Henrik Gabriel Porthan (1739–1804), professor of oratory, wrote, "Even though the society deals primarily with Swedish literature, it nonetheless delves into several other sciences, especially the Finnish language, this country's past and history, and the liberal arts, especially music."

The study of Finnish folklore was to have a decisive influence on Finland's national awakening and create important thematic material for the pictorial arts.

Porthan was a man of many interests; in 1796–1797, he delivered Finland's first lectures on the archeology and art history of antiquity. These lectures largely followed the ideas presented by the German art historian Johann Winckelmann, but Porthan supplied his own footnotes. He believed even more firmly than his mentor in the good taste and artistic mastery of the Greeks of antiquity. Porthan suggested that the Finnish cruciform church be abandoned, to be replaced by an oval or round floor plan.

It is difficult to say how much Porthan's work actually influenced art in practice. He tried to get the university to hire a good master draftsman, but the artist that was chosen proved an expressionless hack. The new horizons opened up by Porthan did, however, lay the basis for the idea of creating a distinctive Finnish culture, on the noble foundations of antiquity, of course.

Conditions in the province of Finland in the 18th century did not yet tempt skilled artists to remain where they were. Many left their homeland entirely. Finland's most important Rococo painter, Isak Wacklin (1720–1758), spent most of his life abroad, as did G. W. Finnberg (1784–1833), though he was not especially successful.

Alexander Lauréus (1783–1823) settled down permanently in Sweden. He might have been forgotten entirely in his homeland if a large number of his creations had not been shown in Finland in exhibitions and "given our public the best example of genre painting," as the art historian Eliel Aspelin wrote at the end of last century.

Artistic creativity in Finland especially flourished in the architecture and paintings of the churches of Ostrobothnia. Dozens of works of art by Mikael Toppelius (1734–1821) and Emanuel Granberg bear witness to the vigor and vibrancy of church art in the north.

Toppelius finished off his artistic training in Stockholm under the court painter Johan Pasch, but for some unknown reason, perhaps a shortage of money, he discontinued his studies. Toppelius's provincial Rococo displays a bold overall concept, but its details are clumsy. His style nonetheless has expression and his ideas humor. In painting wall panels for one of his friends, Toppelius created Paradise covered with snow, with Adam and Eve – without a stitch – skating on the ice of a lake.

The official Neo-antique style of the Gustavian period, 1772–1809, was unable to put a damper on the obstinate creativity of the church painters of Ostrobothnia. The authorities in Stockholm only inspected the drawings for public buildings; they were not concerned with their decorations.

Finland benefitted only sporadically from developments in Sweden in the 18th century. Recurrent times of crisis wreaked havoc especially with this eastern province of the kingdom. The unrealistic war against Russia started by the "Hat Government" (the Hats and Caps were two opposing parties) in 1741 was naturally fought and lost on Finnish soil.

After the war, a new sentiment emerged in government circles of Stockholm: feelings of guilt towards ravaged Finland. The exalted phrases favored in the period about virtue and honor were now taken seriously. In spite of good intentions, measures aimed at economic recovery were rather ineffective, but military build-ups proved a boon.

In 1748, construction began on an island fortress consisting of a system of bastions: Sveaborg (originally Finnicized as Viapori, now called Suomenlinna). It was one of the largest – if not the largest – construction projects in the kingdom, and great pains were taken to make its architecture impressive. Sveaborg was to become the final barricade against the threat from the east.

Carl Hårleman, highly placed at the Swedish court, designed the ceremonial entrance to the fortress, the King's Gate. His ideas are also reflected in the French-inspired design of the courtyards. The courtyard on Susisaari Island, with its false perspective, has been compared to Les Écuries at Versailles.

Lieutenant-Colonel Augustin Ehrensvärd (1710–1772) was put in charge of the construction work. In addition to having other talents, he had exceptional artistic gifts. Thanks to him, Sveaborg became one of Sweden's most active art centers in the first half of the 1760s. Its enlightened efforts nonetheless had little effect on the Finns' way of life and art, though the use of stone foundations and the planting of lilacs did spread from the fortress to the mainland.

The Swedish painter Elias Martin (1739–1818) sailed to Sveaborg to work as a decorator at the request of Frederik Henrik af Chapman, the builder of the archipelago fleet. Martin captured Sveaborg's landscape and construction work on paper for two years, but above all he was employed teaching the fortress's officers how to draw. Art was part of an officer's education, but draftsmanship also had military uses when landscape panoramas for maps were to be made. Ehrensvärd's son Carl August was a member of Sveaborg's young artist community. When the "Caps" came to power in Sweden, the fortress's commander was discharged and the artist community disbanded.

Sveaborg's reputation and work opportunities in Finland attracted others from abroad. Nils Schillmark (1745–1804) came to Finland and stayed. He was a busy portraitist, and has been called the father of Finnish landscape painting, perhaps a bit artificially, since other candidates for the title were available, beginning with Ehrensvärd. The same kind of pioneering status was also accorded to Schillmark in the field of still-lifes, which he painted in overdoors. Schillmark's importance as a representative of Gustavian art has only been properly acknowledged in recent years.

On King Gustavus III's orders, Ehrensvärd was buried in the courtyard on Susisaari Island.His monument was erected to sketches made by the king himself, though Ehrensvärd son's Carl August was probably the actual designer. Work on the project was delayed, and it was not completed until the order was given by Gustavus III's successor, Gustavus IV Adolphus. The work was entrusted to Sweden's best sculptor, the German-born Johan Tobias Sergel (1740–1814), a personal friend of C. A. Ehrensvärd's.

Sergel spent his best years in Rome, and returned there in 1783–1784 with that great dilettante, Gustavus III, who embraced the ideals of Neo-antiquity more fervently than any other ruler.

Gustavian Classicism was found in many ways in the public buildings of Finland. Examples are the main building of the university in Turku, designed by Carl Christoffer Gjörwell in 1801, and Carl Frederik Adlercrantz's Court of Appeal Building in Vaasa (completed in 1786). Finland's public buildings had to be made of stone in Gustavian times, since the law enacted on Adlercrantz's recommendation applied to the whole kingdom without exception, but in practice wood was widely used.

Carl August Ehrensvärd was an even more enthusiastic admirer of antiquity than his king. He gave his esthetic literary form in numerous travelogues and his book *De fria konsters philosophi* (the philosophy of the liberal arts). Ehrensvärd was also the father of a notion with which the Finns had to come to grips in the 19th century. Adapting Montesquieu's theory of climate, he vehemently declared that art could never be created in northern climes.

Even some Finns made pilgrimages to the birthplaces of antiquity. They included Sergel's pupil, Erik Cainberg (1771–1816), and Alexander Lauréus.

When the bronze segment of the Ehrensvärd monument was attached to its granite base in autumn 1807, the bells were tolling for the union between Sweden and Finland. Only a short time before, the French Emperor Napoleon I and the Russian Czar Alexander I had signed the Treaty of Tilsit and had agreed upon a new political order for Europe. Alexander was to persuade Sweden to join the blockade against England.

But Sweden could not be persuaded, and threats were followed up by deeds. Russia invaded Finland in the merciless war of 1808–1809.

The achievements of autonomy

Erik Cainberg: Väinämöinen Playing his Kantele. The first of six reliefs for the auditorium of the University of Turku. 1814. Plaster, 130 x 285 cm.

The czar and the Hellas of the north

When weapons fell silent, the Finns received their new master fairly calmly. Conditions in the country stabilized rapidly. On March 29, 1809, Czar Alexander I gave his Act of Assurance to the Porvoo Diet, and guaranteed Finland extensive autonomy. The Czar declared that Finland had been "placed henceforth in the rank of nations."

The liberal policy of Alexander and his advisor Mihail Speranski was not completely new. In her manifesto of 1742, the Russian Czarina Elizabeth had tried to tempt the Finns to join sides with Russia if Finland wanted to be "like a free country under no other power."

The military defeat was a contributing factor to the end of the absolute monarchy in Sweden. Gustavus IV Adolphus was deposed in 1809 while the war was still in progress. The Gustavian period continued almost unabated in Finland, however, since the Grand Duchy of Finland was permitted to keep its laws, its estate privileges, and its old constitution. Finland only had to build up its own central government. After various delays, it was transferred in 1819 from Turku to Helsinki, which had become the country's new capital.

State borders were redrawn. "Old Finland," the eastern parts that had belonged to Russia, were joined with the provinces that had been conquered from Sweden. The Åland Islands were also annexed.

Alexander's pet projects included building a monumental center for Helsinki. Its design was entrusted to Carl Ludvig Engel (1778–1840), the Neo-classicist architect from Berlin who had been in the service of the Russians for years. Alexander's successor, Nicholas I (ruled from 1825 to 1855) and his Finnish Minister Secretary of State, R. H. Rehbinder, inspected each little detail in the plans, to the architect's dismay.

In the words of the Finnish historian Matti Klinge, the Neo-classical buildings that surround Helsinki Senate Square expressed Finland's political and ideological identity, its "imperial Greekness," which was to reflect the wisdom of the administration, the moral and esthetic importance of learning and science, the enlightenment and expansiveness of religion.

This "trinity" embodied by Senate Square was very concrete indeed. The Cathedral rises at the highest point in the square, surrounded by the university and the senate.

Neo-classicism captured Finland's architecture and art in a kind of pincer movement. Gustavianism, which brought to mind links to Sweden, represented continuity and the Finns' own profile vis à vis Russia, while the Neo-classical style of St. Petersburg brought an unprecedented outer magnificence to Finland's new status.

Construction on the university in Turku continued after the war, and the old plans to commission a series of reliefs to decorate the auditorium were revived. Erik Cainberg was asked to make the reliefs,

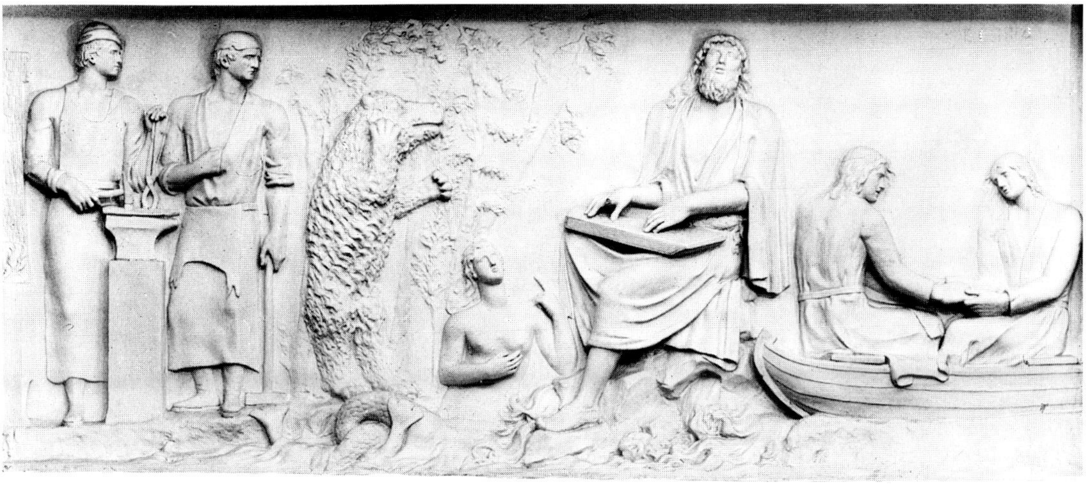

against the wishes of the architect, Carl Christoffer Gjörwell. Cainberg had graduated from the Royal Swedish Academy of Fine Arts and by Finnish standards was highly trained.

Cainberg's choice showed patriotic consistency, since educated circles in Turku had paid for the Rome education of the artist, born in Ostrobothnia.

The kindly Sergel wrote a recommendation for Cainberg, even though he was not satisfied with the achievements and habits of his colleague, who had just returned from Rome.

The original program for the reliefs had been outlined in 1807 by Franz Michael Franzén, professor at the university. He felt that the relief should present the progress of enlightenment and science in Finland.

The poetic idea that the roots of enlightenment reached back to pagan times had been developed during Porthan's day: Väinämöinen, the Mercury and Orpheus of the Finns, discovered fire, the boat, and the lyre, and enchanted even the animals of the forest with his music.

The Swedish academy of science, history, and antiquities felt that Franzén's plans were too Finnish, but the changes it proposed under Louis Masreliuz were never carried out because of the war.

The university was now able to decide itself on the content of its relief, naturally following the obligations of loyalty. Professor Johan Frederik Wallenius, an expert in classical archeology and numismatics, revised Franzén's idea to correspond better to the situation at hand. The figure of Gustavus III, for example, was replaced by Alexander I, in the guise of Apollo Musagetes.

The greatest significance of Cainberg's work lay in its visualization of the figures of Finnish mythology for the first time. They were given the forms of Greek heroes. Material that emphasized Finland's national distinctiveness was clothed in a style that sought to achieve universal validity. Hellas, with its own heroes, was to be found in the north.

Two forms of Classicism, from St. Petersburg and from Stockholm, joined forces in the decorations for the university in Turku. The plaster cast for Cainberg's reliefs and the stucco decorations for the building were made by Jakov Shelesnov of St. Petersburg, and another St. Petersburg artist, Ivan Martos, was commissioned to make the bust of the czar, crowned with the laurel wreath of Apollo and depicted as a Roman emperor.

The cult of the imperial Apollo continued later on in the plans for Helsinki University. A statue of Apollo was to have been placed at the top of the pediment on the facade of the main building, but evidently it was impossible to find a sculptor skilled enough to fashion it, and the plans were abandoned.

No effort was made to disguise public dissatisfaction when the reliefs were completed in Turku in 1816. The future archbishop, Jakob Tengström, described his disappointment by saying that Cainberg's work showed "clearly either indifference or an inability to do any better."

Ideals were repeatedly com-

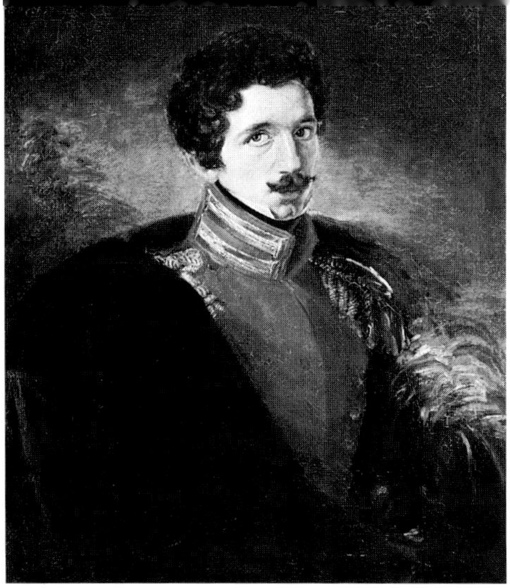

Gustaf Wilhelm Finnberg: Portrait of Rabbe Fabian Gustaf Wrede. C. 1831. Oil, 83 x 65.5 cm.
ART MUSEUM OF THE ATENEUM.

promised by the skills and training of Finnish artists. Without a broad cultural foundation, it was difficult to carry out Neo-classicism's requirement that nature's imperfections be overcome by presenting the best forms and combining them into a harmonious entity dominated by noble simplicity.

Romanticism, the counterforce to the Neo-antique, went about its revolutionary work in Sweden in the beginning of the 19th century, but new concepts of art were not welcome in Finland. Adapting Matti Klinge's idea, we could see this as the loyal parallel to imperial policies. Common sense, order, and knowledge were important, while emotions, chaos, and mysticism were reprehensible, especially if they were combined with political dreams of freedom. The ideal can also be seen as a demonstration that the czar and the Finnish bureaucracy had the same interests.

Artists quickly found their places in the new political system. St. Petersburg attracted them, and Emanuel Thelning (1767–1831), who originally came from Sweden, painted his most important work, "The Porvoo Diet," immediately following the event, between 1809 and 1812.

Thelning moved to St. Petersburg and sold his historical painting to the czar. Not bad for a man who had kept busy painting the Swedish officers of Sveaborg just before the war. Thelning was also given a 600-rouble pension from the czar's treasury.

The academy in Stockholm remained the most important goal of Finnish artists, but artists trained in St. Petersburg began to appear as well. One of them was Berndt Abraham Godenhjelm (1799–1881), from Mäntyharju in "Old Finland." He abandoned the law for art, received an imperial grant, and attended the six-year academy in St. Petersburg.

Godenhjelm was commissioned to paint a large number of altarpieces in the 1840s. Together with the work of Robert Wilhelm Ekman (1808–1873), they significantly raised the level of Finnish church art. Among the most important achievements of Godenhjelm's Biedermeier-like Classicism are a number of tranquil interiors and paintings based on themes from the poems of Johan Ludvig Runeberg (1804–1877).

One can get a good idea of how sensitive questions of style were from the fate of Gustaf Wilhelm Finnberg (1784–1833). After studying at the academy in Stockholm and trying his luck in Sweden, Finnberg arrived in Finland, made a series of paintings for the gallery of the church in Kemiö, and executed numerous portraits of Turku's elite. Finnberg's training had been dominated by Classicism, but his work was already influenced by Romanticism.

Finnberg infuriated his patrons by using colors that were brighter than usual and by leaving their portraits "unfinished." He felt an artist should know when to stop, before he ruined the portrait.

For Finnberg, painting was a matter of feelings and intuition, even though he would have preferred to do historical paintings. They were most prestigious, since according to the theory of the times, the historical painter touched on universal concepts in his work, while a portrait painter dabbled with imperfect individuality. From this point of view, Finnberg can hardly be called a Romantic, but his best portraits show that that is just what he was. They endeavor to capture the model's natural, true-to-life features. One more reason why his subjects grumbled.

The quick rhythm of Finnberg's brush strokes and his skill at composition can be seen best in his landscape wash drawings. Their basic technique, with powerful contours, is as Classical as that of Elias Martin and Carl August Ehrensvärd, but Finnberg had already achieved a sketch-like, dynamic result.

Turku burned in early September 1827. The fire spread inexorably across the city, destroying all of Finnberg's possessions, and both completed and unfinished work. The artist went into debt, moved to Sweden, and lived in abject poverty, in spite of a number of good commissions. Finnberg's best-known work among the public at large, and among his contemporaries, is a colored lithograph of the Turku fire.

Alexander Lauréus did not have much influence on Finnish art during his lifetime. After going off to study in Sweden, on a grant raised by the gentlefolk of Turku, he never returned to his native land. Lauréus became a successful genre painter and was given a Swedish state travel grant in 1817.

Lauréus painted his best pictures in Rome, the artists' Mecca of the period. His favorite subjects included the romantic robber tales favored by the day and the effects of bonfires at night, but he succeeded best of all in his subdued, picturesque tavern scenes.

Finnish art in the early 19th century was almost always described in pathetic, somber terms, and the tone survived even into this century. Take this example:

"Cainberg had died the victim of evil ways; Lauréus, whose successful work was done in Sweden, ended his days in Rome in 1823; and Finnberg had left his homeland for ever. The background against which Finland's budding art was limned was truly mournful," wrote Axel Haartman in 1945.

The writer Zachris (Zacharias or Sakari) Topelius (1818–1898) looked at matters in a lighter vein from Helsinki, and reminded his contemporaries that "in the 1830s the new capital of Finland was still in an immature state, like Jeppe, son of Nils, when he woke up a fine gentleman," a reference to the hero of Holberg's comedy *Jeppe of the Hill.*

The world of art was not completely desolate, however. When the job of master draftsman at Helsinki University was declared open in 1830, four artists applied for it: Fredrik Ekman, Pehr Adolf Kruskopf (1805–1852), Johan Erik Lindh (1793–1865), and C. A. Linning (1781–1843). Kruskopf, a lawyer who had been born in St. Petersburg and had studied art under F. F. Sedmigradski, was chosen for the job. Lindh, a well known portraitist, would certainly have been the most competent artistically, but his application was late.

Kruskopf's most important

achievement was the little collection of landscape lithographs *Finska vyer tecknade efter naturen* (Finnish views, drawn from nature,1837–1838), which provided a basis for later landscape art. Kruskopf also helped arrange Finland's first art exhibition in 1845.

Nils Abraham Gyldén (1805–1888), the young classical philologist, became interested in classical archeology and in the 1830s began to work on acquiring a collection of plaster copies of antique sculptures for Finland. Collecting money was a slow process, and the students' enthusiasm and generosity were needed. Charles Rappo, an Italian athlete who arranged "tableaux vivants" of the sculptures of antiquity, also supported the project. His work sparked off a true passion for antiquity, with misconceptions and erotic overtones playing an important role.

When the "Apollo Belvedere," the "Versailles Diana," and "Laocoon" arrived in Finland and were put ceremoniously on exhibit, people began to doubt the value of all these effects, "since what good does just wondering do if it does not engender the desire to do independent work, or even follow the example set?"

A great deal was said and written about the need for cultivating the mind, but this usually meant written culture. Not very many people believed that art, least of all sculpture, would succeed in Finland. Even Gyldén's hopes were dashed.

For nearly two hundred years, the Finns had complained that the fruits of art, "the flowers of the south," would have difficulty in thriving in the north. This complaint was actually a remnant of the favorite theory of the Gustavian era (cf.p. 21, C. A. Ehrensvärd) that had taken root in Finnish soil.

Especially in the middle of the 19th century, artists were awarded the mantle of "genius" and given a hero's aura, since they were making the impossible possible, bringing the muses of Greece to *ultima Thule*.

The art world takes shape

The artist's social status in Finland in the first half of the 19th century was nothing to brag about. But in 1830, a new entry was found in the censuses: the designation "artists" was added to the population tables. They were placed before servants but after doctors, barber-surgeons, and architects.

Those who had attended the academy were naturally more highly respected than the painters and stone- and wood-carvers trained by the guilds. Art training was reorganized, though with only modest changes, in 1830. The master of the Turku painters' guild, Carl Gustaf Söderstrand, had proposed that an art school be founded in the city, and his proposal was approved. Landscape drawing was included in its program from the beginning, and later a class concentrating on antiquity was established. Painting was not taught at all initially; those who wanted it had to take private lessons.

Plans were being made to improve the state of affairs in art education in Helsinki, too. The Saturday Society, a discussion group, outlined a cultural program for Finland in the beginning of the 1830s. The university had been transferred from Turku to the new capital after the fire, and the gentlemen of this informal society (even women were known to have participated) developed Turku's romantic ideology, though in more subdued form. They especially stressed the importance of history, the Finnish language, and literature. The other arts were not forgotten, either.

The first offspring of this cultural program, the Finnish Literature Society, was born in 1831. Three years later, a Finnish Senator, Baron O. W. Klinckowström, was the first and most influential person to sign the appeal to establish an arts society. His co-signers included a key figure in the Saturday Society, the poet Johan Ludvig Runeberg.

Their dream came true in 1846. In his history of the society, J. J. Tikkanen writes that educated circles did not begin to believe in the success of art in Finland until Robert Wilhelm Ekman arrived in Turku from Stockholm in 1845 to teach at the art school.

One of the stories told about the slow start of the Finnish Arts Society was how the approval given by the Senate lay forgotten for years on the desk of an absent-minded professor. On the other hand, people in the capital were accustomed to the bureaucracy in the time of Nicolas I. Even plans of little importance had to be approved by the czar's system, and excessive initiative was by no means rewarded. The muses had to be kept in harness. The czar, who adored order, was even shown in military uniform in his official portraits.

It is interesting that the Senate approved the statutes of the Finnish Arts Society in the early 1840s, but waited three years to allocate even a single rouble to carry out the Society's goals. Efforts were finally made to increase its reserves by selling shares in the Society to individuals, entitling the owners to tickets for the art lottery held once a year.

The Finnish Arts Society founded an art school in Helsinki in 1848, but its importance should not be exaggerated, since only a single teacher worked there in its early years, B. A. Godenhjelm. The Society also awarded grants, and in 1858 founded a prize for young Finnish artists.

One of the active participants in the Society was Zachris Topelius, historian, journalist, and author. He described the Society's finances during its early years as fairly good. Its first grants were awarded in 1847. But major frustrations were unavoidable, since "more than two thirds of the first fledglings were lost, some by death, others due to broken wings."

Finland's Grand Duke Alexander, the Heir Apparent, in practice his father the czar, had generously agreed to serve as patron of the Society and bought Baron Klinckowström's art collection, donating it to the Society in 1851. The recipient was required to exhibit the works of art. After tabling the

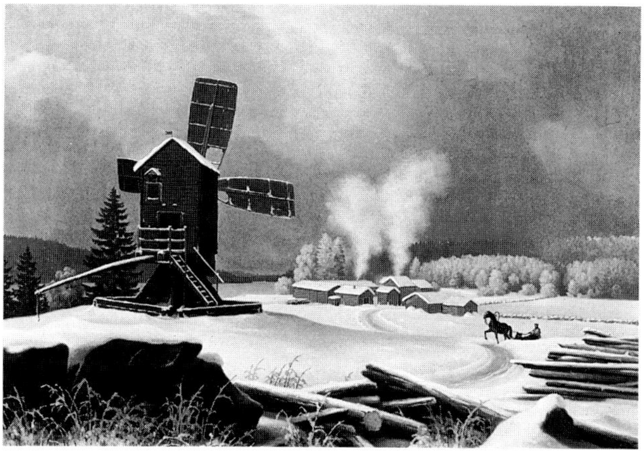

Ferdinand von Wright:
Old Hamina Bay in Winter. 1858.
Oil, 49.5 x 67 cm.
PRIVATE COLLECTION.

matter for eight years, the Society's board decided to have its permanent collection on display "here in the Society's premises on days and at hours publicly notified."

There was not much in the capital in the way of an art world, and the lack of demand undoubtedly slowed down developments. Supply was only ensured by the enlightened members of the upper class, but their ideological idealism was still not reflected in larger circles. The basic reason, the lack of education, was acknowledged, as shown by the start of drawing instruction in a number of Helsinki schools back in the 1830s. One of the teachers was Magnus von Wright (1805–1868), one of three artist brothers whose work had an incalculable effect on the nationalistic art of the 19th century.

Finnishness

A suitable portion of patriotism was a good thing for the Grand Duchy of Finland. This was the opinion of the czar and his bureaucracy. Their interest in Finnishness distanced the intellectuals from Sweden's sphere of influence and strengthened the young nation's ties to the empire.

Of course the Finns tried to see how far they could go. Adolf Ivar Arwidsson, who had studied in Sweden, wrote his dissertation on the influence of the Middle Ages on Romanticism. There was nothing suspicious in this, even though studying the Middle Ages was uncommon in a country that admired antiquity. Arwidsson drew "Jacobite" conclusions from Romanticism, however, and in his newspaper, *Åbo Morgonbladet*, increasingly criticized government officials and demanded that in addition to studying Finnish, the Finns begin to concern themselves with their own history, in other words to be politically active.

Rehbinder, the Minister Secretary of State, called Arwidsson's opinions "immature and revolutionary." Arwidsson was obliged to move to Sweden in 1823. Conflicts of this kind did not appear in art. It was still more or less impossible to imagine an artist who might try to rebel through his work.

Folklore was among the Finns' legal preoccupations. It taught the educated classes to understand the latent talents of the common people. But efforts were made to idealize the peasants, and they were only studied as decorative ethnographic material. Before the advent of Realism, national costumes in fact interested artists much more than individual representatives of the common people.

Modern Finland initially meant the landscape, and not its inhabitants. Runeberg's "Our Land," which became Finland's national anthem, describes the lake-filled landscape of the interior in all its versions, Finnish and Swedish. The third stanza reads:

We love the rush of our rivers
the running of our brooks,
the mournful rustle of the dark
forests,
our star-lit night, our summer light,
all, all that in visions and songs
once touched our hearts.

When Ferdinand von Wright exhibited his painting

"Prospect of Hamina Bay" in 1854, Zachris Topelius wrote in his review, "This painting is Finland."

Topelius saw love and soothing silence in the beauty of the landscape. The pantheistic experience of joy created by nature engendered a completely new concept of the Finns' fate. For example, J. J. Tengström had felt that the northern environment's effects on human nature (and physiognomy) were a barrier to progress. The love projected onto the landscape broke these deterministic chains and made the inescapable a national virtue.

Fredrik Berndtson dedicated an admiring poem to von Wright's painting, listing the most important features of the Finnish landscape: the shoreline, expanses of water, and hills. All of them radiated the gentleness of summer, but winter also had to be included in the magical circle of national beauty.

We should probably credit Ulrik Thersner (1779–1828) with making winter acceptable among the great subjects of painting. In 1828, Thersner published the little book *Om landskapmålning* (on landscape painting) in Sweden, where he had worked for some years. He explained that the artist must not forget the worst of the seasons, since "winter, no matter how cold, is often no less charming than the other seasons; the Nordic countries, especially, offer great subjects for artists."

Thersner was a practical man and not a brilliant theoretician, but his writings seem to have been reflected in the production of the von Wright brothers. They created the Finnish winter landscape as a genre.

The interplay of literature and art should not be ignored. Winter often formed the background for events in poetry, and that scourge of winter, frost, was made the heroes' adversary and the touchstone for Finnish fortitude, *sisu*.

Nationalists were of course not unanimous when it came to nature. The Hegelian philosopher and statesman Johan Vilhelm Snellman (1806–1881) condemned all manner of pastoral idyll, but the Finnish educated classes and finally the ordinary people preferred to listen to their poets instead of unpleasant common sense, and worshipped their painters and their idyllic creations.

The foundation for the Finnish landscape as a concept was laid by artists and writers. *Finland framställdt i teckningar* (Finland in pictures) was published between 1845 and 1852 in booklets, a common practice at the time. The texts were written by Topelius and H. A. Reinholm, with P. A. Kruskopf, Johan Knutson (1816–1899), Lennart Forstén (1817–1896), and Magnus von Wright making the illustrations. The work was printed in Dresden.

The publication's 120 pictures illustrated the period's landscape ideals. Nature in its wild, virgin state was not yet appreciated; the landscape as it was shaped by man was considered most beautiful. An industrial community erected on the shores of the rapids was just as admirable as fields of grain and pastoral idylls.

Tremors were felt even in Finland when Europe experienced its great year of upheavals. On Flora Day, May 13th, Topelius's poem "Spring 1844" was printed in *Helsingfors Tidningar*.

It is coming, it is coming across the
 land,
the spring storm raging;
And the clouds are transformed;
the shadows start to flee;
The spirit of the storm envelopes
 the land,
and the skies are gory.
It is not only the spring of the
meadow, the valley;
the lands of the spirit are verdant.
The earth grows bright; the
 heavens rise,
Our hearts once again may hope.

Readers understood Topelius's allegory without any difficulty. The landscape was no longer just a patriotic matter; it had now become politicized.

The same day, students staged a long procession. Fredrik Cygnaeus, a versatile humanist and one of the leading men behind the Finnish Arts Society, delivered his most famous speech. He addressed his fiery words to Finland's name, which he declared was warmed by the farmer behind his plow and by the scientist burning his midnight oil. "Our Land" was sung on this occasion for the first time. Tears welled in the eyes of the participants. Finland's "revolution" had ended.

The fact that the Finns were anything but susceptible to revolt did not impress leading government officials, and in 1850, Governor General Menshikov recommended that an even more restrictive law on censorship be enacted. It was aimed at the "Fennomen," the adherents of the Finnish movement, since it permitted the publication of only religious and financial literature in Finnish. The law, which had been watered down in practice, was rescinded in 1860 at the instigation of Snellman.

Increasing censorship does not seem to have been the policy of only the Russians since it was also a good way for the Finnish authorities to repress the Finnish-language movement. The historian Heikki Ylikangas has interpreted this to mean that the Fennoman movement among the lower-ranking civil servants was trying to gain power, while the higher-ranking civil servants tried to ward off this threat to Swedish-language ideology. It was a question of the rights of the majority. Should the language it spoke be used as the language of public administration and culture? Legislation that granted the same status to Finnish and Swedish was not enacted until 1902. The last battle over language was waged in the 1930s to make the University of Helsinki more Finnish. The language problem was reflected in art as well.

What does a Finn look like?

Genre pictures and landscapes dominated the Finnish Arts Society's exhibitions for its first two decades. The art historian Jukka Ervamaa has calculated that a full 60 percent of all the paintings represented these two main categories. Very few depictions of the actual life of the common people were exhibited, and there were also very few still-lifes, allegories, and mythological subjects.

Ervamaa considers one of the reasons for this state of affairs to be the infrequent participation of R. W. Ekman, the most important painter in the middle of the 19th century. He sold his work direct to private buyers, and demand was so great that the paintings were never shown to the public. Perhaps the artist also frowned upon the amateur level of the work initially exhibited.

Helsingfors Tidningar published a delighted and optimistic review of the Finnish Arts Society's first exhibition in 1847. According to the writer, Finland was, after all, a country "where hardly anyone speaks of paintings except those splashed down on wall paper and on shades.

"Mr. F. von Wright will probably attain a distinguished position as a painter: his birds are considered masterpieces and the exhibition included the portrait of an old woman that has an amazing likeness," raved the critic of *Helsingfors Tidningar*. He also predicted a successful career for E. J. Löfgren (1825–1884), but he was so critical of the popular portraitist J. E. Lindh that from then on, Lindh's paintings were rarely ever exhibited. The institution of art criticism had assumed its necessary but often merciless role.

The newspaper predicted a fine future for Miss Edla Jansson, but above all the critic mentioned Mr. Ekman, who was "generally known as the country's most skillful painter."

Ekman had studied in Stockholm under Professor J. G. Sandberg, had done well, and had applied for Swedish citizenship in order to get a travel grant. Ekman continued his studies in Paris and Italy. On his return, he surprisingly moved to Finland in 1845. Ekman had been offered a job – though in somewhat vague terms – that he found difficult to refuse: the frescos for Turku Cathedral.

The matter had not been settled at all in Turku, but Ekman started on other commissions and began to teach at the newly founded art school. He also went inland to collect material for depictions of peasant life.

On his travels, Ekman met the peasant poet Pentti Lyytinen and transformed him into the romantic hero of enlightenment for the masses in one of his major works of art. Later he found other ideal models, such as the kantele player Kreeta Haapasalo. Ekman usually depicted his main characters in the center of genre-like cabin interiors, arranging around them a group of devoted listeners. They generally represented different classes and reminded the beholder of the new spirit of equality.

The fresco commission was confirmed in 1847, but at that stage Ekman was painting the large altarpiece that is now in Helsinki's Old Church.

The work at Turku Cathedral proved a major endeavor. Ekman was given the job of decorating the whole choir of the church. Its most important frescos depict Bishop Henry baptising the Finns and Mikael Agricola presenting the first Finnish translation of the Bible to Gustavus Vasa. The paintings required a great deal of preliminary work, and Ekman had to

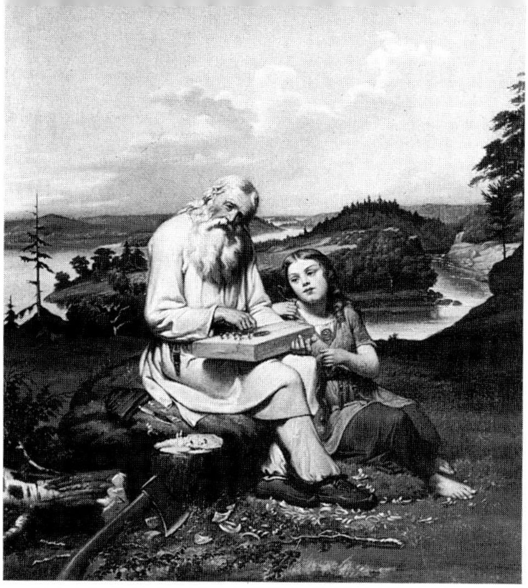

Johan Z. Blackstadius: Väinämöinen Stringing his Kantele. 1851. Oil, 81 x 65 cm.
KALEVALA SOCIETY.

search museums in both Stockholm and Copenhagen to find models for clothing and weapons.

The historical subject matter of the frescos created the basis for Ekman's paintings on themes from the *Kalevala*. This was actually a national endeavor, since the epic compiled by Elias Lönnrot (1802–1884) was considered Finland's most important literary monument. The *Kalevala* created a mythical history for Finland and justified the existence of the whole nation, even though the poems that made up the work had been collected from only one region, Karelia.

Lönnrot had studied the theory of the birth of the Greek epics according to which their songs had originally been separate creations. An entity had been compiled later from these stories. Lönnrot drew his own conclusions:

"As I compared them [the results of previous trips to collect poetry] with those known before, the desire was born in me to arrange them into a single entity in order to produce from the Finnish mythology something that corresponded to the Icelandic *Edda*."

The first version of the *Kalevala*, the *Old Kalevala*, reached the book stores for Christmas 1835. The *Kalevala* was well known even before it had been translated into Swedish, but it took quite some time before the material was transformed into pictures. The Swede Johan Z. Blackstadius made the first ambitious attempt by painting "Väinämöinen Stringing his Kantele" in 1851.

Ekman did not tackle themes from the *Kalevala* until the end of the 1850s. He was familiar with Blackstadius's painting and with the work with *Kalevala* themes done by Carl Eneas Sjöstrand (1828–1906), a Swedish sculptor who had settled in Finland.

The largest of Ekman's *Kalevala* paintings was "Väinämöinen Playing his Kantele," but its final version, made in Paris, proved hopelessly out of date by the time it had been completed in 1866. The painting had technical defects as well.

Sjöstrand was also criticized, but his supporter, Fredrik Cygnaeus, now professor of esthetics, staunchly defended him. The figures of Sjöstrand's frieze "Väinämöinen's Song," 1859–1866, were accused of being too Greek. Ekman's figures, in contrast, were considered too Finnish.

The fate of the Väinämöinen frieze showed just how deep the divisions were between Swedish-speaking and Finnish-speaking circles. The frieze was not put in what is now the Swedish Theater, as originally planned, but in the foyer of Helsinki University. Väinämöinen was considered a hero of the Fennomen; Cygnaeus had seen to this himself by calling the rune-singer in Ekman's "Fleeing Pagan" the first Fennoman.

Theories on race seem to have been brought into the debate at quite an early stage. The Swede August Sohlman demanded in 1855 that Finland be joined to its old fatherland, and wrote a pamphlet that deeply wounded the Finns. It stated that the Finns belong to a race that completely lacks a society and the ability to create a cul-

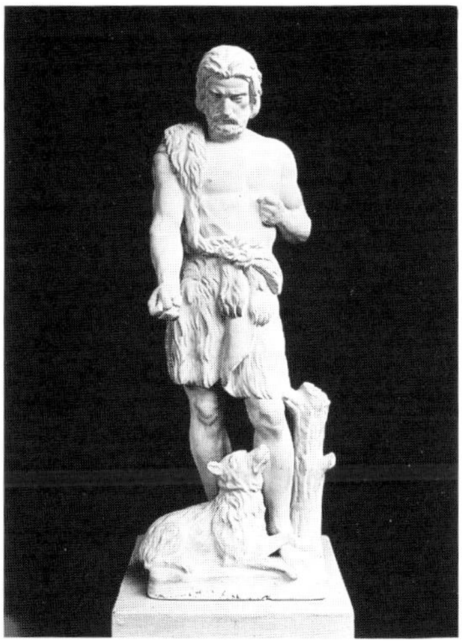

Carl Eneas Sjöstrand: Kullervo Speaking to his Sword. First draft 1860, plaster 1867. FINNISH NATIONAL GALLERY. *Bronze sculpture in the Helsinki City Gardens.*

ture. Sohlman's ideas were taken from Count Gobineau's book *Essai sur l'inégalité des races humaines* , in which the Aryans (the Germanic peoples) were considered the highest race. The theory suited the Svecomen as an ideological weapon, but its effects on the Finns' way of thinking was to be seen for decades, even after the battle over language had subsided.

The pseudonym Antti Barbarus gave an example of how the theory of race was applied to art. "The Finns and almost the whole tribe of Uralic peoples have the kind of appearance that art and artistic feeling do not accept as beautiful. Why should a Finnish artist have to start depicting this kind so faithfully?"

The Finns received crushing criticism at the Nordic exhibition in Stockholm in 1866. The Norwegian art theoretician Lorentz Dietrichson considered even Finnish mythology to be so nebulous that there was no reason at all to try to depict it in painting. Dietrichson's views should not be put down to just a "Scandinavian superiority complex." Finnish art had simply not reached the level achieved in the other Nordic countries, whether its creators spoke Swedish or Finnish.

Interest in themes from the *Kalevala* waned, though it never entirely disappeared. An enthusiastic dream conceived twenty years before was never carried out: "When will a giant statue of Väinämöinen, carved from marble from Ruskeala, decorate the National Museum in Helsinki?"

But Sjöstrand had done what Finnish cultural circles had expected of him, brought the "noble art" of sculpture to the country. Until then, with the exception of Cainberg, sculptors had been brought in from abroad to do specific commissions, while the work done by the Finns was very modest indeed.

It was typical of conditions in Finland that the heroes and heroines of the *Kalevala* sculpted by Sjöstrand were only executed in plaster during his lifetime. One of Sjöstrand's best known pieces portrays the child Kullervo like a muscleman from antiquity in "Kullervo Breaks out of his Swaddling Clothes" (1858). Ten years later, the sculptor depicted the end of the story of Kullervo: the hero holds the sword given to him by Ukko, the chief god, and asks if the sword would like to "feast on guilty flesh, drink tainted blood." Sjöstrand had derived the Kullervo theme from Cygnaeus's study of the tragic features of the *Kalevala*. This professor of esthetics, enthralled by great ideals, is credited with much more. He conceived the idea of erecting a full-sized monument to Porthan, the father of Finnish history. It was the first of its kind, and Sjöstrand had originally been brought to Finland to execute it.

Porthan's monument was not an isolated idea: it was linked with the project to depict great national figures that was gradually taking shape. Lönnrot, Runeberg, and Snellman were made into "great men" on the spot, and Cygnaeus firmly believed that he would join them. The first phase of the project, however, was intended to honor a great man who was already deceased.

Sjöstrand was a sculptor who had been trained in the spirit of

Robert Wilhelm Ekman: Lemminkäinen's Mother. 1862. Oil, 77 x 62 cm.
CYGNAEUS GALLERY.

Werner Holmberg: Storm on Lake Näsijärvi. 1860. Oil, 36 x 50 cm.
ART MUSEUM OF THE ATENEUM.

Werner Holmberg: Kyröskoski Rapids. 1854. Oil, 110 x 102 cm.
ART MUSEUM OF THE ATENEUM.

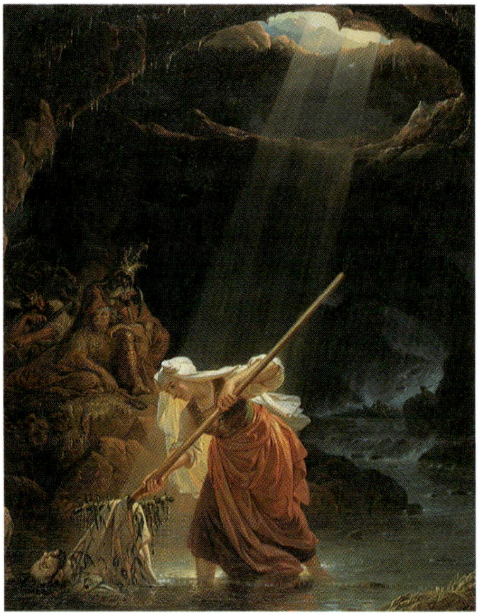

Danish Classicism. When he rounded out his studies in Copenhagen he was largely guided by Herman Vilhelm Bissen (1798–1868), whose reputation as a teacher was well known. But Sjöstrand distanced himself from pure Classicism, and his art began to show signs of romantic expression and plastic coarseness, as shown by "Kullervo Speaking to his Sword."

Finnish stylistic ideals were so steeped in tradition that, when Sjöstrand displayed the first version of his statue of Porthan – seated, not standing – in 1857, the librarian Sven Gabriel Elmgren noted angrily in his diary, "The only thing that can be criticized about it is the position, free or not free, but this is really nothing at all; a true work of art cannot be anything but a Greek god whose forms a traveling cloak neither covers nor effaces."

Elmgren was not just a neutral observer; he was one of the key figures in the Finnish Literature Society, which had commissioned the statue. He was not really able to stomach Romanticism's emphasis on the individual and its mundane approach to monuments honoring the glorious past.

Sjöstrand sculpted this prince of thought, holding a pen and stack of books, in Rome, where "the monument must be created for posterity," as Cygnaeus put it. A debate raged in Finland on Porthan's importance and the location of the statue, and money was collected so that the work could be completed.

The bronze parts of the monument had to be cast in Munich, and when nearly everything was finished, the authorities demanded a complete report on the project. Even though this was the time of Alexander II's liberal government, the Finnish bureaucracy was accustomed to looking into anything where even the smallest spark of separatism might be smouldering.

There was nothing to criticize in the plans, and Porthan's bronze figure, bigger than life, was cast together with the five medallions for its base and was unveiled with festive canon salutes, patriotic speeches, and the strains of "Our Land" in September 1864.

Holmberg and Düsseldorf

As R.W. Ekman's reputation reached its zenith at the end of the 1840s, he was readily compared to the country's best poet: "What Runeberg is to Finland as a poet, this is what Ekman can become in the field of the pictorial arts." Ekman was unable to live up to these great expectations. But Werner Holmberg (1830–1860), his assistant on the Turku frescos, did.

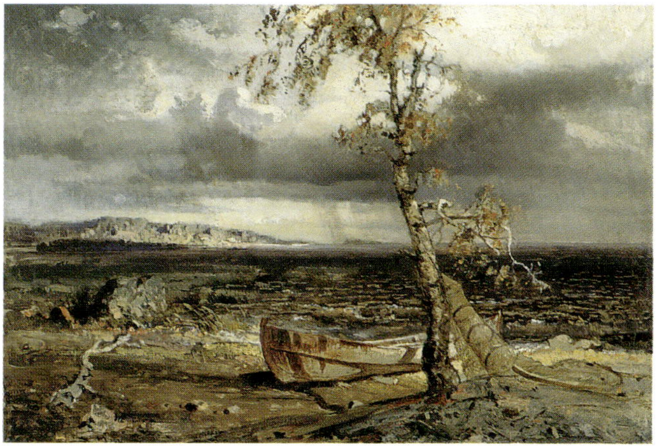

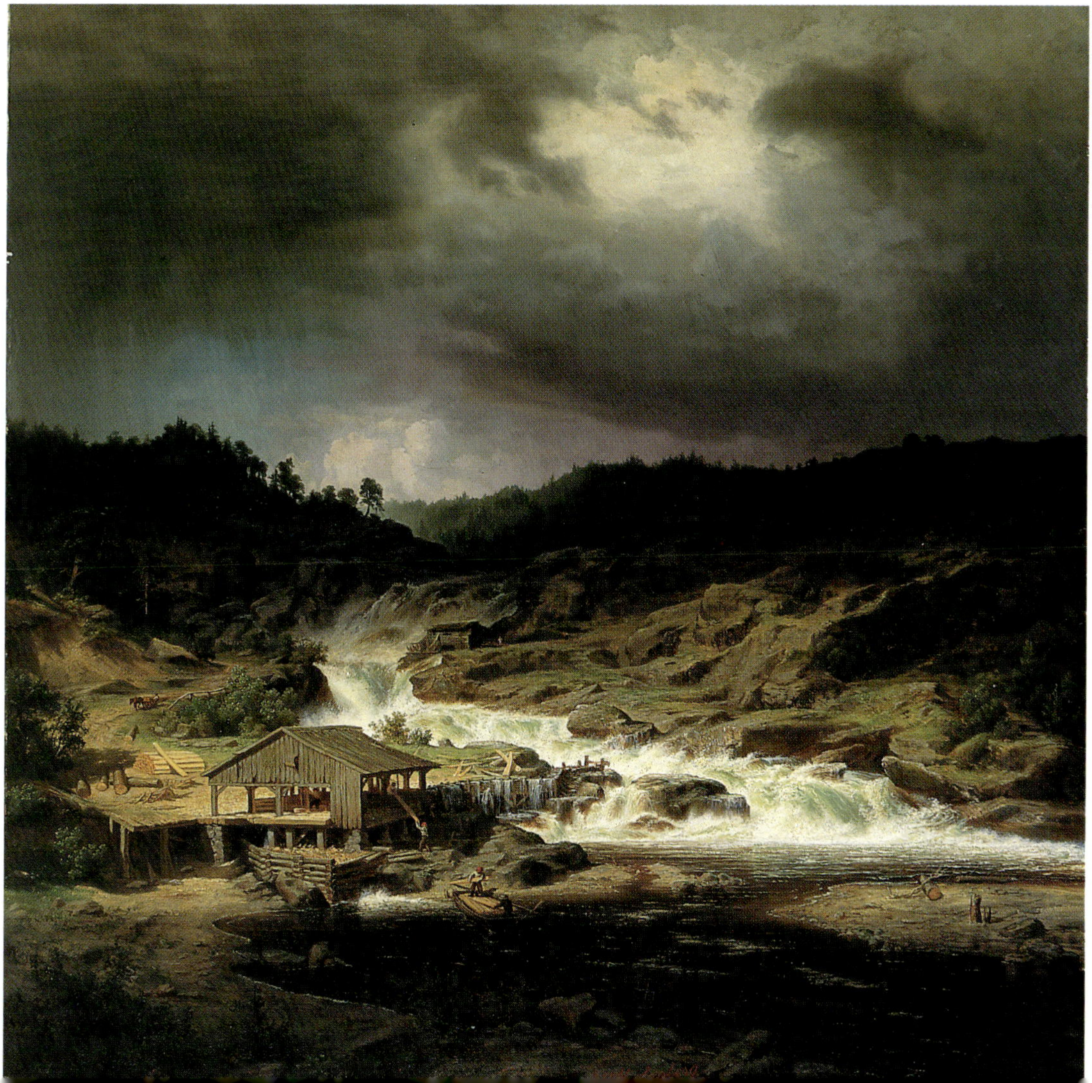

The young man was of two minds. He was well on his way to becoming an architect, even though painting attracted him more. Holmberg's father objected to his son's taking the more uncertain path of an artist, and the cautious bureaucrat was unconvinced when nearly the whole art world of the day, including Topelius, seemed to support Werner's art studies.

At around twenty years of age, Holmberg had received as much art training as Finland was able to provide. He painted, exhibited his work, and, according to the art historian Aimo Reitala, realized the effectiveness of the ideal topographic landscape seen from a high vantage point even before Ferdinand von Wright did. "Prospect of Lake Pielisjärvi," painted in 1851, is a good example.

The fame of the Düsseldorf school spread to Scandinavia in the middle of the century. The work done by Norwegian artists in Germany caused quite a stir at the Scandinavian exhibition in Stockholm in 1850. This exhibition helped convince Holmberg that he should head for the Rhineland as well.

Reitala, partly relying on studies by Wolfgang Hütt, believes that Düsseldorf's attraction lay in its democratic atmosphere and active art market. The artists of the town had taken part in the bourgeois revolution of 1848, and had buried both the old system and Berlin's Post-romanticism.

Holmberg arrived in Düsseldorf in summer 1853. He got acquainted with the artist community and discovered unexpected things. "I thought that I would come here just to paint glowing southern landscapes. But in fact people demand authenticity. At least this winter I plan to paint only Finnish prospects."

Holmberg quickly grasped the new ideology. "Naturalists make up the core of the painters' community, and I suppose I will join them. They say that nature must be our teacher, and that we should not copy pictures."

Holmberg was very independent in his studies. Though he did not attend the academy, he did receive some guidance from the Norwegian Erik Bodom. Later Holmberg sought more formal training; the famous Hans Gude, another Norwegian, taught him in 1855–1856.

In 1854, Holmberg completed his large painting of western Finland's most famous natural attraction, Kyröskoski Rapids. He intended to send it with a few other paintings to Finland, but the Crimean War cut sea links and Holmberg's work did not arrive in Finland until 1856. Critics expressed their open satisfaction when the pieces were exhibited. *Helsingfors Tidningar* wrote of Holmberg's work:

"They clearly show the budding master. They have power and control, vigor and reflectiveness. The Düsseldorf school demands cloudy skies and ponderous shadows … The largest painting, a subject from Kyröskoski Rapids, is a ruggedly magnificent painting. Shadowed by dark thunder clouds, the rapids rush down the cliffs in the midst of the wilderness. The colorful glimmer of the water can be seen above the stones. On the left, the sawmill is running … The shadows of the clouds upon the rapids are masterful and calculated so that the most light falls on the mill."

Finnish art had never before witnessed such a skillful, majestic scene with nature and little homo sapiens. Holmberg was becoming the Finnish "genius" that the gentlemen from the Arts Society had so often longed for.

Holmberg had never visited Kyröskoski himself. He had to rely on the wash drawing made ten years before by his former teacher, P. A. Kruskopf. It should be emphasized that open-air painting was not among Düsseldorf's doctrines. Sketches were made outdoors, but the actual work of painting was always done in the studio.

Many topographic pictures bear witness to the popularity of Kyröskoski as a subject. The scene, considered the equal of Imatra Rapids in the east, had been painted by A. F. Sköldebrandt ("Voyage pittoresque au Cap Nord, 1801), by Alexander I's personal painter, Carl von Kügelgen ("Vues pittoresque de la Finland," 1823–1824), and by Johan Knutson and Magnus von Wright.

Rapids were all the rage abroad, and many parallels can be found to Holmberg's painting. Johann Christian Dahl romanticized Norway's mountain waterfalls as early as the 1810s. The Germans found their own models in the Alps but also in Tivoli, whose waterfalls were combined with relics from antiquity to add a special touch. The Germans also sought out northern sites: Andreas Achenbach painted the surging falls of Trollhättan in 1835.

"A Mill Dam," painted by Holmberg's teacher Hans Gude in 1850, is one of the most idyllic depictions of rapids, but also one of the most realistic examples of the genre.

Kyröskoski did not yet make Holmberg the perfect master. The painting did not make much of a break with tradition, either. Ulrik Thersner's instructions for painters of heroic landscapes could just as well have been applied to it:

"A landscape painter should…examine wild nature in its gigantic forms – falls rushing down cliffs, boulders reaching for the skies, deep forests, monuments of eternity."

In the years to come, Holmberg painted a great many German themes, but his most important work was done depicting Finnish and Norwegian landscapes.

Holmberg spent the summer of 1858 in Norway, painting together with Gude. He studied atmosphere and worked towards more delicate lighting effects. The most important of these Norwegian landscapes is a skillful depiction of mist, "Autumn Morning in Ringerike." The enchantment of this saturated atmosphere became even more intense in "Forest in the Rain," painted in Finland in 1859. It is considered his true breakthrough.

"Subject from Toriseva," a kind of forest interior (1859), is the most romantic of Holmberg's Finnish landscapes. It raises the question of the relationship between conventions and personal symbolism in the period. The peace and quiet of the picture are tangible. The black eye of the pond, with its

Karl Emanuel Jansson:
The Sacristy. 1874.
Oil, 22 x 18.5 cm.
ART MUSEUM OF THE ATENEUM.

Hjalmar Munsterhjelm:
Landscape from Tuulos. 1899.
Oil, 26.5 x 53.5 cm.
ART MUSEUM OF THE ATENEUM.

boat, is hidden within the cliff and the shelter of the trees. It forms a temple in the wilds that can be reached only by the path on the right side of the painting.

The boat is the only element that signals the presence of man, but what does it signify? Is it a boat from Christian or Classical allegories, or the Finnish equivalent of Romanticism's sailboats that symbolize a longing for far-off places, a look into the other world, à la Caspar David Friedrich?

Or could the painting be interpreted as Holmberg's personal sentiments? The boat and the birch are repeated in much the same way, but given more prominence, in "Storm on Lake Näsijärvi," painted in 1860. It is a depiction of atmosphere, and even quite a realistic one, but it is extremely improbable that the boat and the lone birch were chosen at random.

Lone trees were an essential part of the landscape painting of Romanticism. They often represented man in the great outdoors. Crosses and church towers are found standing against the sky in the same way in the paintings of the Dresden Romantics.

We do not know what Holmberg's own intentions were, but he might have been expressing his fate as an artist, his increasing illness, and the anguish caused by financial uncertainty.

The landscape projections of Finnish poetry remind us that the boat was compared to man or man's presence. This was the case in Wilhelmina Nordström's poem *Erämaan poika* (Son of the Wilds), written in 1861.

O wilderness, I love you;
No roads meet me there,
No boat rows near,
No village disturbs my peace.

Yes, roads. They were among the themes in Holmberg's key works of art. "Mail Road" and "Hot Summer Day" might seem very idyllic today, but the wagons running along the roads signified dynamic progress in Holmberg's time. The country flourished under the financial reforms of "His Dreadfulness" Senator Lars Gabriel von Haartman. A network of routes into the interior was built to promote economic growth.

Holmberg's last important landscape, "Ideal Landscape," was a more conservative work than its many predecessors. The artist painted it to show his suitability as professor at the art academy in Weimar. To his utter dismay, Holmberg was not given the position, which instead was awarded to the Swiss Arnold Böcklin. Holmberg's tuberculosis quickly worsened after this disappointment.

The artist who raised Finnish painting to an international level died in Düsseldorf on September 24, 1860.

Holmberg's example attracted many Finnish artists to Düsseldorf. The first to go off to Germany in the footsteps of the master were Augusta E. Soldan (1826–1886), Viktoria Åberg (1826–1892), and Erik Johan Löfgren (1825–1884).

At the end of the 1850s, these artists were followed by Magnus von Wright (1805–1868), Adolf von Becker (1831–1909), and Alexandra

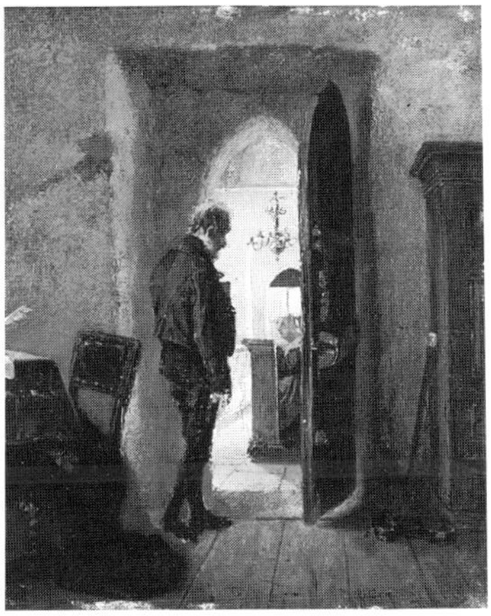

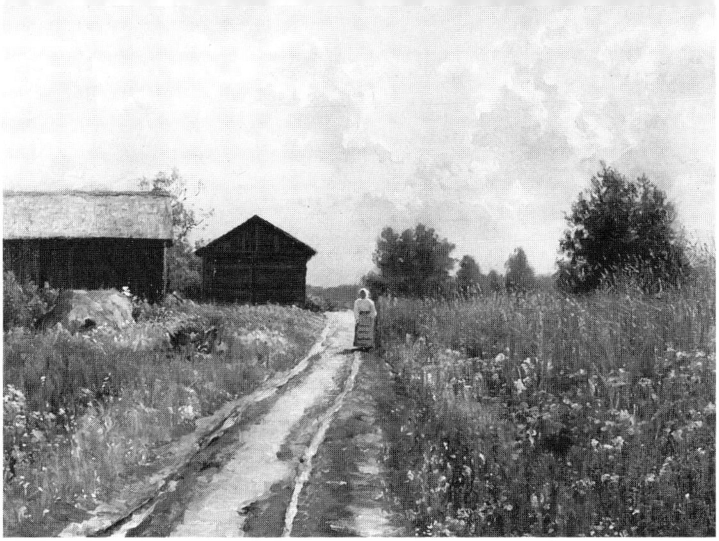

Frosterus-Såltin (1837–1916). Finns remained faithful students of Düsseldorf into the following decade, too. The most important, in order of arrival, were Berndt Lindholm (1841–1914), Hjalmar Munsterhjelm (1840–1905), Arvid Liljelund (1844–1899), Fanny Churberg (1845–1892), and Karl Emanuel Jansson (1846–1874).

Being a woman in Düsseldorf was probably a painful experience since only men were accepted by the academy. Private lessons were readily available, however.

Finnish artists sought guidance and inspiration according to their inclinations. Von Becker, Liljelund, and Jansson concentrated on genre painting. Lindholm, Munsterhjelm, and Churberg put landscape painting in the fore.

Jansson, who came from the Åland Islands, managed to become a member of the art academy in St. Petersburg during his brief career. He demonstrated his incomparable skill in interiors and portraits, and had a more realistic approach than his contemporaries.

As early as 1859, von Becker found the atmosphere in Düsseldorf unpleasant and criticized "the old rigidness of this little town, where people theorize, drink beer, and all paint with the same color." After leaving Düsseldorf, von Becker studied in Paris, for a time even under Gustave Courbet himself, but the aristocratic Finnish artist's approach remained more conventional than Jansson's. Liljelund, in contrast, developed into a diligent composer of ethnographically precise genre pictures and didactic anecdotal paintings.

There was a great deal of discussion about historical painting, but few embarked on depictions of the past in the 1860s. Löfgren's painting "Erik XIV and Karin Magnusdotter" from 1864 was a rare and unusually large (225 x 165 cm) endeavor. One of the painting's fine points is its warm colorism, but the style's naive sentimentality invited mockery even in its own day.

The culmination of Romanticism and the challenge of Paris

Ferdinand von Wright remained the popular favorite for decades, despite all the changes in style, or perhaps because of them. After all, Ferdinand and his brothers' approach proclaimed the permanence of the Finnish idyll. The extremely productive landscape painter Hjalmar Munsterhjelm did, however, become just as popular. Unlike Holmberg, he ended up an artist against his will.

His father, a cavalry officer, considered his son's choice of career much too dangerous – the boy wanted to become a sea captain – and suggested the safer profession of painter. The difference in opinion was settled by letting Hjalmar sail off to Spain, but making him start his art studies on his return.

Father and son traveled to Düsseldorf in 1860 to meet Holmberg. The master was already weakened by illness, but

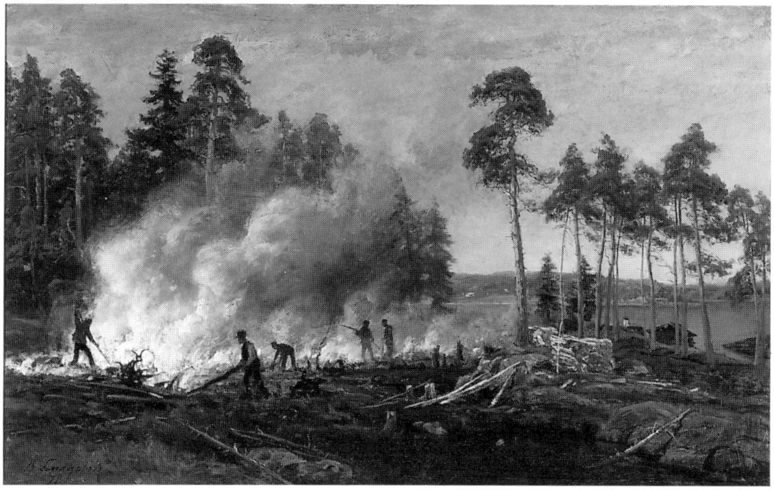

Berndt Lindholm: Clearing the Forest in Savo. 1872. Oil, 57 x 88.5 cm.
PRIVATE COLLECTION.

he agreed to take Hjalmar as his pupil, or actually as his assistant, to carry easels and other equipment on a sketching trip to Erkrath.

Munsterhjelm certainly knew that he would inherit Holmberg's mantle, though Gude, his teacher at the onset, doubted the youth's gifts. But there was nothing to be desired in the way Munsterhjelm learned techniques, and he became the first Finnish artist to complete the whole course in Düsseldorf.

While Munsterhjelm worked away in Germany, his future friend and rival Berndt Lindholm copied Holmberg's paintings in Helsinki. Lindholm received a grant from the Arts Society and used it to travel to Düsseldorf in 1863.

The differences between the two art students were soon clear. Lindholm did not adapt to Düsseldorf's teaching, and neither was he enthusiastic about Oswald Aschenbach's Italian-style landscapes. Lindholm was more captivated by the realistic approach taken by Johan Christian Lessing and Gude, who had moved to Karlsruhe, but not even that was enough for very long. When he moved to Paris, Lindholm became attracted to the "value party," and consciously undertook to reform Finnish landscape painting in the spirit of the masters of the Barbizon, Daubigny and Corot. Lindholm was unable to accept the art of Manet and Pissarro, in contrast.

The Finnish art world found Lindholm's French-inspired work unappealing, considering it too realistic, and made Munsterhjelm its new favorite. It found his atmospheric depictions of mist and moonlight enchanting, but the unevenness of his vast production and his lack of independence were criticized as early as the 1870s.

Reitala has noted that it was Lindholm who discovered the Finnish evergreen forest. The dark spruce, spruce ornamentation, gradually developed into the Finnish national symbol.

Lindholm became director of the Gothenburg Art Gallery in 1878, and his late production is generally remembered only for its seascapes, accented with massive, boulder-strewn shores. It is still difficult to get an overall idea of Lindholm's art since it has not yet been studied sufficiently in either of the two countries where he did his life's work. Lindholm himself emphasized that he was a representative of Finnish landscape painting, even though his late work mainly depicts Swedish scenes.

An excellent characterization of young Berndt Lindholm was given in a letter by his drawing student, Fanny Churberg (1845–1892): "Does not behave gallantly, but neither is he pompously distinguished and never tiring. Does not talk in class, but gives me a great deal of information (historical, so to speak), about what I am engaged in."

When Lindholm returned to Düsseldorf from Helsinki in autumn 1867, Fanny Churberg went with him. The Finnish colony there at the time included Thorsten Waenerberg (1846–1917), Oscar Kleineh (1846–1919), Arvid Liljelund, and Victorine Nordensvan (1838–1872).

Fanny Churberg: Landscape from Uusimaa. 1872. Oil, 54 x 85.5 cm.
ART MUSEUM OF THE ATENEUM.

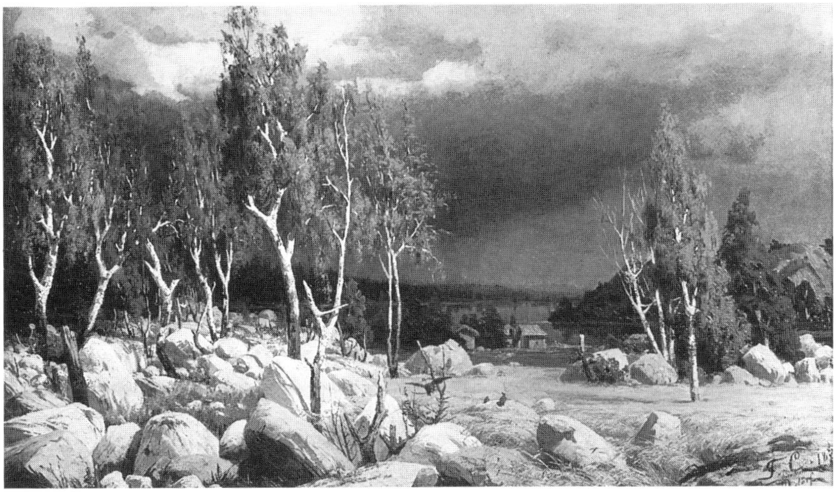

Churberg was annoyed by the discrimination against women practiced at the art academy and by a few other Düsseldorf features, but started her studies with Carl Ludwig, a Romantic landscape painter. His idea of picturesqueness took root in Churberg's painting from the very beginning. She felt that lone gnarled pines were an especially suitable subject.

The Franco-Prussian War, which broke out in 1870, delayed Churberg's studies, but Ludwig got his Finnish pupil back at the end of 1871. Churberg made rapid progress, something that was noted at the exhibition in Finland in 1872. The work she sent to the exhibition was found to have originality and vigor, but also strange natural forms. The critics did not really like the composition of her work, either.

Churberg's most important early painting is undoubtedly "Landscape from Uusimaa," completed in 1872. The painting's strong colors, the synthetic way in which she treated forms, and the dramatic lighting of the foreground had a boldness never before seen in Finnish art. Churberg had a good knowledge of the German painting of the day, but this depiction of the Finnish landscape was still found to have been influenced mostly by Düsseldorf. In her monograph on Churberg, Aune Lindström pointed out Lessing's "The Siege" from 1848 as the model.

The subject of the picture is an approaching thunderstorm. It can be seen in the darkness around the clouds and in the sharp delineation of light and shadow. The work has an expressive fierceness, but the artist herself noted that it made her homesick. "Now I am painting a clearing and approaching thunderstorm, a subject that seems to interest everyone who sees it – and as I paint it I have such a warm summery feeling, as if I were sitting there and could hear the whispering of the birches, smell the flowering fragrance of the rye, and the air would be so very, very light – and my heart, too" (a letter from Düsseldorf, 1871).

Churberg's emotional words did not just refer to the landscape. She was a rabid Fennoman, and Finnishness was an important ideological element in her life, one she had embraced at Topelius's university lectures.

"Landscape from Uusimaa" was given a mixed reception at the exhibition. Perhaps the conflicting opinions were best reflected in the review published by the Svecoman paper, *Vikingen* "One of her paintings on exhibit, especially, a landscape after a thunderstorm, seems to have been planned to have more a sensational effect than to achieve an impression of reality ..." No one doubted Churberg's gifts, however.

During the Franco-Prussian War, Churberg was an outspoken defender of all that was German, but her feelings during this period did not prevent her from leaving for Paris in 1876. Lindholm's example had a greater influence on Churberg than her admiration for the Prussians.

Several gifted young Finns were working in Paris at the time. Maria Wiik (1853–1928) had come to Paris with her sister

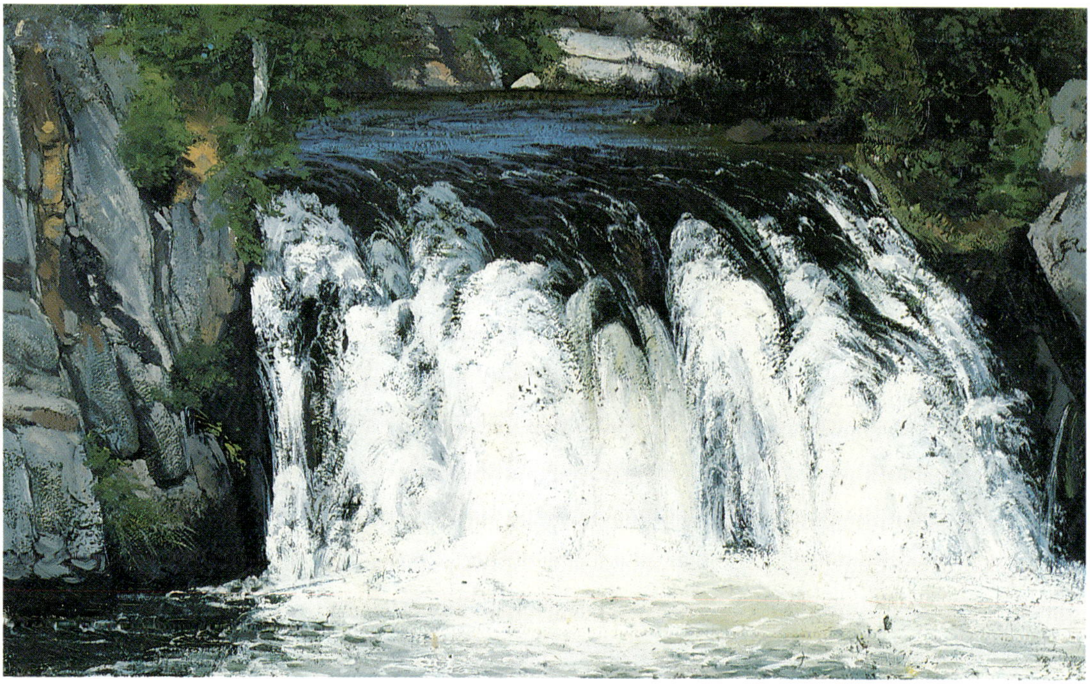

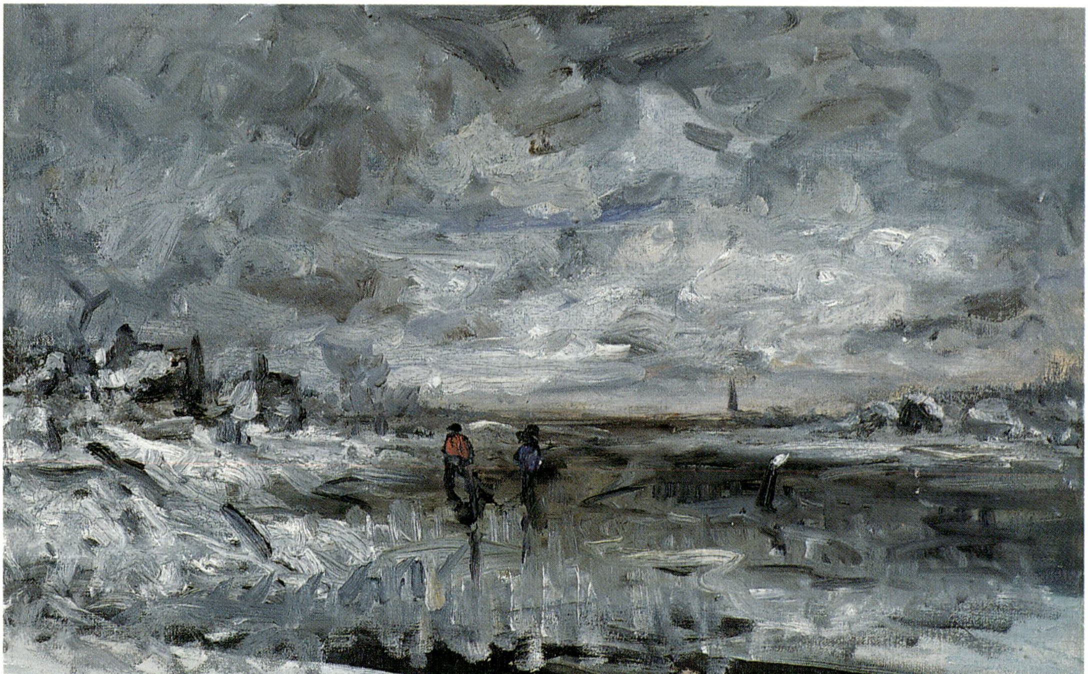

Fanny Churberg:
Waterfall. 1877.
Oil, 30.5 x 48.5 cm.
ART MUSEUM OF THE ATENEUM.

Fanny Churberg:
Winter Landscape. C. 1880.
Oil, 38 x 56 cm.
ART MUSEUM OF THE ATENEUM.

to study at the Académie Julian. Albert Edelfelt (1854–1905) had decided to leave Belgium and come to this metropolis of innovation in art.

Even in France, the academies proper treated women as second-class citizens, and Churberg became a pupil of the Swede Wilhelm von Gegerfelt, who, after studying in Düsseldorf, had developed his own approach as a pupil of Gustave Courbet.

Churberg made a careful study of both museums and salons, and got a fairly detailed picture of French art in the 1870s. Impressionism was a hot topic of debate, but Churberg was not inclined to it. She was more captivated by Chardin's still-lifes and the landscapes of Jules Dupré and Diaz de la Peña.

On her second trip to Paris in 1878, Churberg saw such paintings as Courbet's "The Waves" and a representative collection of paintings by Daubigny at the Universal Exposition. Churberg also took a look at what her fellow countrymen had achieved, since a dozen Finnish artists were represented at the Exposition: Edelfelt, von Becker, Jansson, Kleineh, Liljelund, Lindholm, Munsterhjelm, Julia Stigzelius, J. Ahrenberg, Walter Runeberg (1838–1918), and Johannes Takanen (1849–1885). The work of the Finns was shown at the Russian pavilion, but it was separated from the Russian exhibition by a partition. This eloquent partition attracted considerable attention.

Paris's annual Salon offered little in the way of surprises, since all efforts had been concentrated on the Exposition. But the Salon did contain a work that was important from a Finnish point of view, Edelfelt's historical painting "Duke Charles Insulting the Body of his Enemy Fleming, Governor of Finland." It did not make much of an impression on Paris; it was a competent though not distinctive example of academic painting. And Edelfelt knew it himself. He had said that he admired J. P. Laurens' painting "The Austrian General Staff by Marceau's Body." And the Frenchman that reviewed the Salon mostly admired the Swede C. G. Cederström's painting "The Body of Charles XII of Sweden Being Carried Home from Norway." Subjects that dealt with death were all the rage.

Edelfelt's painting encouraged Finland's art world since it fulfilled the hopes of the older generation of idealists for great Finnish historical painting. The work, which depicts the aftermath of the Peasant Revolt of 1596–1597, was awarded a state prize. Edelfelt had been taught by Jean-Léon Gérôme and had done considerable preliminary work for the painting. He studied costumes and weapons and even had the old coffins at Turku Cathedral opened in order to create the right impression of aristocratic funerals at the end of the 16th century.

The Finnish artist at the Universal Exposition most admired by the French critics was Lindholm. Churberg agreed, and Lindholm's influence can be found in her production in the ensuing years. In Paris, however, Churberg painted a moonlit landscape limned with energetic brush strokes. It is one of her most radical pieces.

Paris had attracted Churberg not only with its art, but also with its decorative art. The French pavilion at the exposition offered only period revivals, but Churberg considered Scandinavian crafts of major importance. She returned to Finland in July 1878 together with the young sculptor Ville Vallgren (1855–1940).

Churberg painted for only two more years after her return from Paris. Her work during that brief period was uneven but astounding. Churberg painted boldly simplified pieces that a later age would have called Expressionist. It seems as if Impressionism liberated Churberg from her Romantic outlook by giving her the right to use independent brush strokes and color.

The final culmination of Churberg's work was represented by such pieces as "Winter Landscape, Sunset" (1879) and "Winter Landscape" (1880?). The former is signed, while the artist's initials are missing from the latter. Considering her approach, it, too, can be considered completed. The fiery, criss-crossing brush strokes of "Winter Landscape" make the overall effect almost abstract. It is exciting to compare Churberg's paintings with the Swedish playwright and painter August Strindberg's visions of nature in the 1890s. The differences are clear, but the trend was the same: to break down the effects of nature into their painterly elements and combine them into a new synthesis.

Few people in Finland understood Churberg. Her work was found to have "abnormalities" and people were likely to comment to her that "no pine ever looked like that." The strong local color that originated in the landscapes of the Dresden Romantics was sometimes criticized as being hard, at others as being discordantly unbalanced. Churberg's art fell between two mainstreams: idyllic National Romanticism and its challenger, Parisian Naturalism.

People have often wondered why Churberg decided to leave painting and start working with the newly founded Friends of Finnish Handicraft. Perhaps her frustration as a painter made it easy for Churberg to move into another fascinating profession. It provided challenges that were not controversial, but also a modern field of battle – women's liberation.

Churberg's farewell to art can be read in her appeal, presented in 1879, to found a society to revive Finnish handicrafts, following the Swedish model.

"While the man sang the immortal verses of the *Kalevala* … the woman wove the colors of the rainbow into her cloth and created models with her own rich imagination. Unknowingly, she created a patriotic treasure."

From dreams of an academy to a "palace of industry"

The idea of founding Finland's very own academy of fine arts was born at the end of the

1850s at the same time as people began to speak in earnest of Finland as a state. The Porvoo Diet was now viewed as a true parliament. The change in attitude was also seen in art. The title of R. W. Ekman's painting (1858) depicting the opening ceremony in fact used the word for parliament.

The new parliament, or more correctly, the meeting of the Estates, was convened in 1863 as a result of political pressure, and once again Ekman painted the ceremony, adapting a form handed down by Thelning.

Founding an academy of fine arts was the great dream of Fredrik Cygnaeus, but the proposal had been made back in 1854 by Professor M. Akiander. Cygnaeus went to work on the project right after the end of the Crimean War in 1856. As he wrote of his plans to Baron Casimir von Kothen, he believed that about 10,000 roubles would be needed. Such a small sum would be enough to fulfill the "liberty's most noble demands."

The university's council supported the proposal for an academy of fine arts made in 1860 by the Finnish Arts Society, but the Senate found that the time was not yet ripe for the project. And it did not ripen later, either. Many people felt that the catastrophic famine in the 1860s did not give the idealists of the art world the moral right to demand money for major cultural undertakings.

Cygnaeus, who died in 1881, never saw the founding of a noble birthplace for historical painting. His plans were countered in the mid-1870s by a completely new proposal. The Swedish-speaking liberals, under the leadership of C. G. Estlander, began to work for an art school that would be linked with a new art museum. Instruction would not be limited to pictorial art; decorative art would be included on an equal footing. Estlander, who was the new arbiter in esthetic questions, justified his ideas by the unity of art. Decorative art was part of the "concept" of art in the sense meant by Hegel and Friedrich Theodor Vischer. The Senate's members in charge of industrial development were glad to hear talk of this kind.

The Senate rejected the Finnish Arts Society's proposal for a building for art and decorative art, but offered a solution of its own. Plans finally began to take shape, and an architecture competition was held for the "temple" that was to seal the unity of art. It was won by a Berliner, Arthur Walter. The awards committee did not recommend that the winning proposal be carried out, however, and the Senate handed over the planning to a Finnish architect, Theodor Höijer.

Estlander proposed that the Neo-renaissance building, completed in 1887, be called the Ateneum. Carved above the pediment on the facade are the words *Concordia res parvae crescunt* (concord makes even little things grow). The use of Latin bypassed Finland's language problems and emphasized the concept of the building as a temple.

The decorations initially intended for the facade of the Ateneum were extensive. The art historian Eeva Maija Viljo

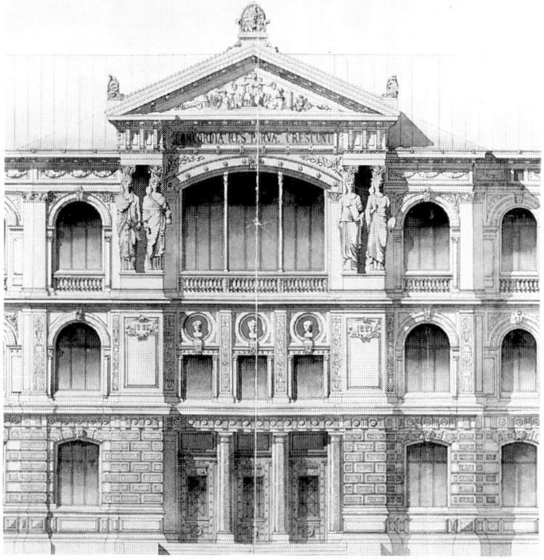

Carl Theodor Höijer: Facade of the Ateneum. Wash drawing.
FINNISH NATIONAL ARCHIVES.

found that Estlander in fact drew up a basic plan, but that the head of the Senate's finance committee, Leo Mechelin, already interfered at the planning stage. The program was truncated.

The models for the decorations were found on the facades of the Louvre and the École des Beaux-Arts, but Munich's triumvirate of museums – the *Glyptothek*, *Alte Pinakothek*, and *Neue Pinakothek* – also provided suitable material.

Sjöstrand's tympanum frieze was placed in the pediment of the Ateneum's ressaut. Its most important figure is a seated woman bearing a mural crown. Reitala has interpreted her as the Maid of Finland crowning art and decorative art.

For the third story, Sjöstrand sculpted four caryatids, whose attributes show that they represent painting, sculpture, architecture, and that new arrival, decorative art.

Three busts were placed on the Ionian-style second story. They, too, were made by Sjöstrand and represent Raphael, Phidias, and Bramante.

A pantheon of artists was also sculptured for the facade: sixteen portrait reliefs showing the classic figures in the history of pictorial art, architecture, and decorative art, from Michelangelo to Werner Holmberg, from Benvenuto Cellini to Carl Ludvig Engel. These portrait reliefs were made by Ville Vallgren.

Finland's art had thus been linked to the great lines of development in world art. If Cygnaeus had been alive, he would hardly have dared use his favorite derogatory expression for the building – "a palace of industry."

The move away from historical painting

Albert Edelfelt had painted his spectacle of insatiable hate, "Duke Charles," partly because he wanted to shed his reputation as a harmless portrayer of "petites femmes gentilles."

His artist friends taunted Edelfelt, but both the bourgeoisie that commissioned portraits from him and the public at large loved the sweetness of his art. "Queen Bianca," a historical anecdote painted in 1877, became one of the best-known works of its day in Scandinavia. But Edelfelt longed for greater subjects. After "Duke Charles," he painted "The Burned Village" (1879), depicting the Peasants' Revolt. The events are set outdoors in a snowy winter landscape, but although he had made sketches in Finland, Edelfelt was unable to achieve a natural outdoor atmosphere. Efforts to combine historical painting and *plein-air* painting proved fruitless. Edelfelt understood that he had to make a final decision in favor of *plein-air*.

Adolf von Becker's teenage pupil, Helene Schjerfbeck (1862–1945), began painting historical themes at the end of the 1870s in order to show doubters that the *grande manière* suited women, too. Schjerfbeck was interested in the sad fate of Karin Magnusdåtter and Erik XIV, but she was also fascinated by Runeberg's *Tales of Ensign Ståhl*, the heroic poems of the War of 1808–1809.

Helene Schjerfbeck:
Wounded Soldier in the Snow. 1880.
Oil, 38.5 x 59.5 cm.
ART MUSEUM OF THE ATENEUM.

Albert Edelfelt:
Duke Charles Insulting the Body of his Enemy Fleming, Governor of Finland. 1878.
Oil, 157 x 202 cm.
FINNISH NATIONAL GALLERY, TURKU CASTLE.

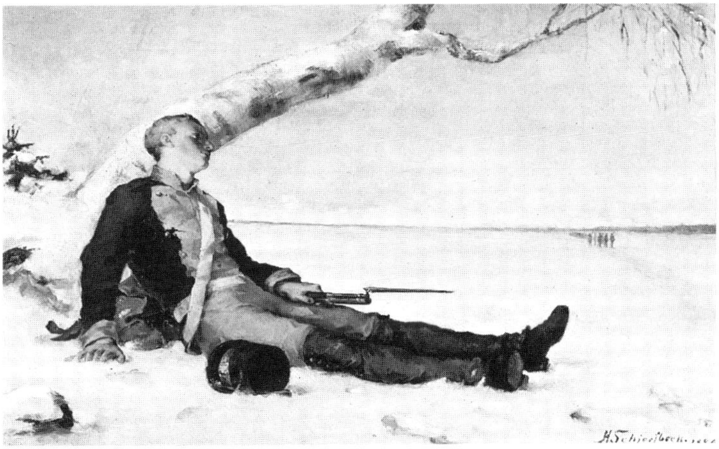

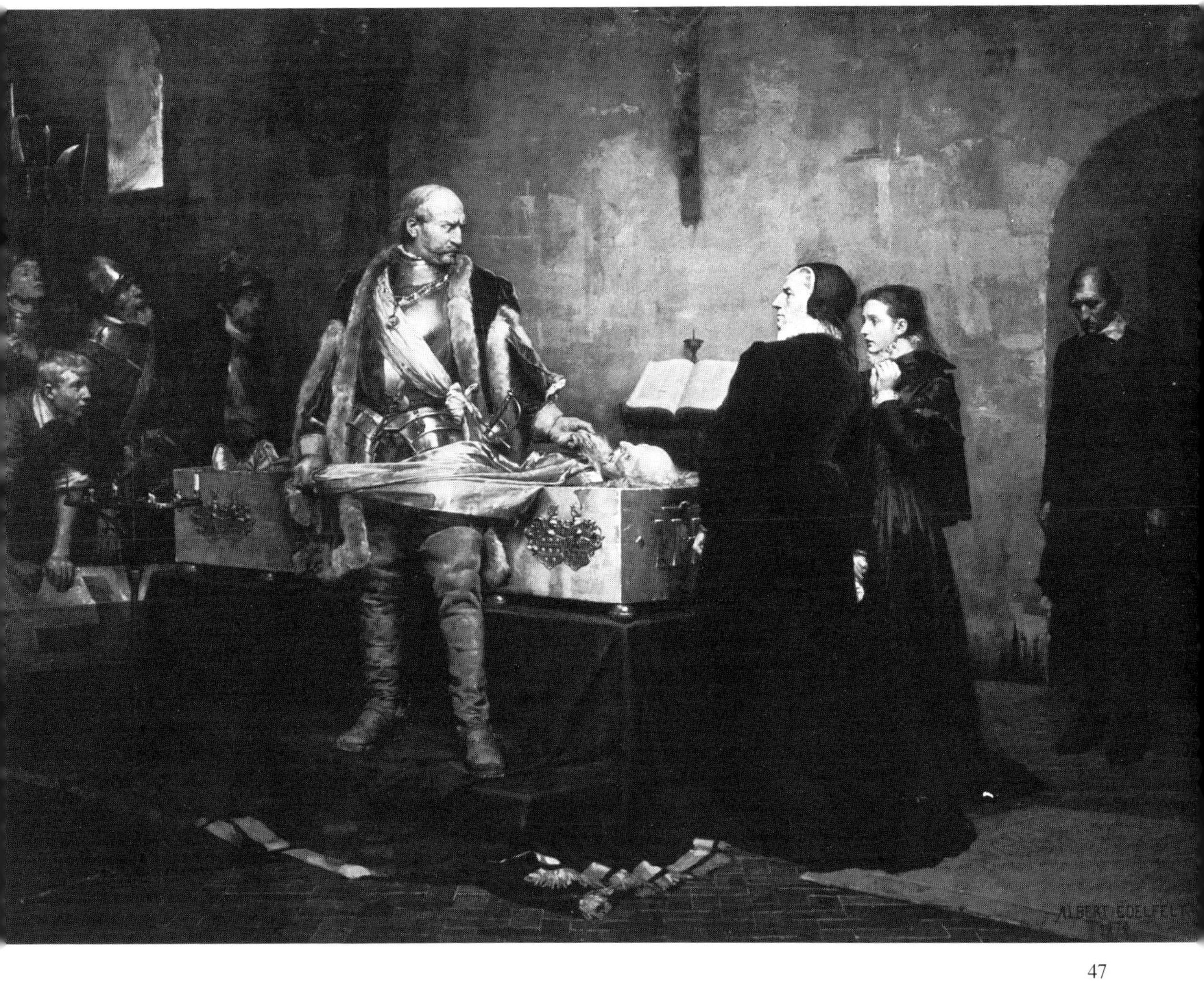

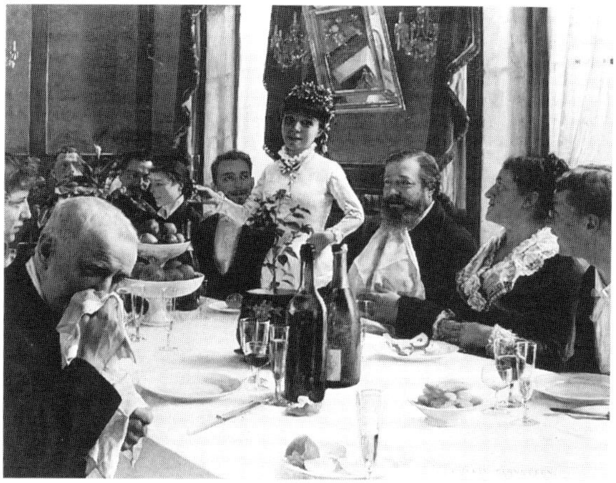

Gunnar Berndtson:
The Bride's Song. 1881.
Oil, 66 x 82.5 cm. Antell Collection,
ART MUSEUM OF THE ATENEUM.

The choice of Runeberg's verses for a painting was a patriotic gesture, at least superficially. Choosing war and death as themes did not just reflect a general point of view, but also enabled her to give vent to her personal emotions. For example "Wounded Soldier in the Snow" (1880) reflected the artist's loneliness and dejection as her friends left for France. In 1881, Schjerfbeck was given a travel grant to study in Paris, and the soldier's "wounds" healed.

Schjerfbeck's early major work, "The Death of Wilhelm von Schwerin" (1886) was a slightly stiff figure composition, but its melancholy atmosphere seems more plausible than the theatrical psychology of Edelfelt's "Duke Charles." Fanny Churberg, who had stopped painting, surprisingly criticized Schjerfbeck for her choice of subject. "We, in turn, although we do support the equality of the sexes, do not believe in female war painters."

The "students" in Paris delved into historical subjects in the late 1870s partly because of the demands of the Finnish Arts Society and partly because of personal preferences. Edelfelt's friend and contemporary Gunnar Berndtson (1854–1895) admired Jean-Léon Gérôme and Jules Bastien-Lepage, but his real model was Ernst Meissonier, with his meticulous style. Berndtson's first major work, "Art Connoisseurs in the Louvre" (1879), was well received in the salons. The painting's Rococo costumes were very skillfully reproduced, and the artist had shown a fine sense of humor in his treatment of the subject. A true salon painter had been born.

Berndtson reached the peak of his career at the Salon in 1881 when he showed "The Bride's Song," an anecdotal painting that demonstrated a delicate feel for values and skillful draftsmanship. The painting's well-to-do bourgeois atmosphere and its heartfelt though not profound psychology showed the best aspects and limitations of Berndtson's art. It is understandable that he never developed into a true historical painter. Orientalism, in contrast, suited his tastes and way of thinking. He even worked for a few months in Cairo, but had to return to Finland after falling ill.

Good teachers were needed at home, and in the end of the 19th century, Berndtson was the best and most professional. The public wanted him to depict the common people as well, but the role did not suit a painter like Berndtson in the least. He did his best work painting elegantly dressed women, glorified by the summer sun.

Severin Falkman (1831–1889) was still working on a large historical painting in the middle of the 1880s. Its exhausting title reflected the painting's ambitious dimensions: "Carl Knutson Leaves Viborg Castle for the Election of the King in Stockholm in 1448."

Like Edelfelt, Falkman tried to combine historical reconstructions with atmosphere, but the result was mediocre. One of the artist's most successful paintings, in contrast, was "Il Decamerone," made during his period in Rome, a skillfully composed anecdotal piece on whose costumes the artist used all his

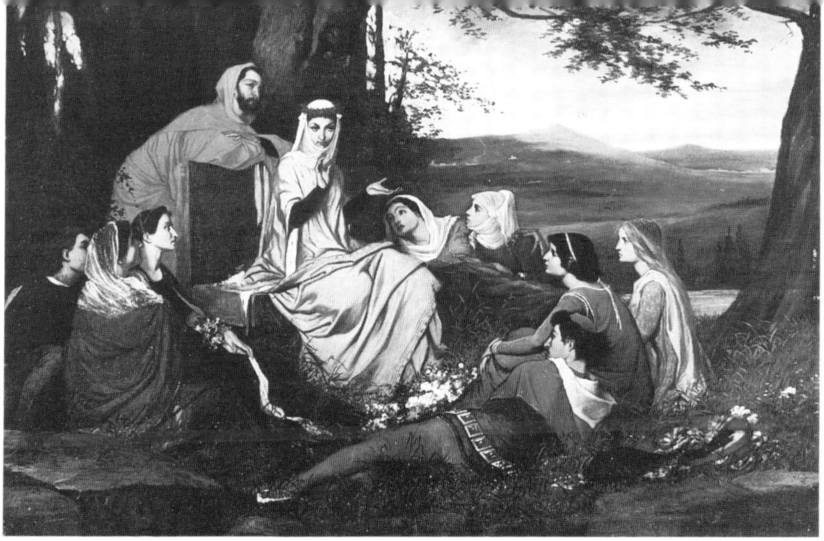

Severin Falkman:
Il Decamerone. 1870.
Oil, 84 x 112 cm.
PRIVATE COLLECTION.

skill and enthusiasm. Perhaps Falkman's career should be examined on the basis of the dozens of "tableaux vivants" he designed. Reitala points out that Falkman's tableaux are easily forgotten, even though they were the best ever conceived in Finland.

Historical painting lost the battle to *plein-air* painting. At least this is how the matter is usually viewed, but explanations have been oversimplified, since historical painting's own goals contained its seeds of destruction: the demand for documentary accuracy. A graphic example can be found in Edelfelt's work.

As he traveled to Karelia together with Adolf von Becker, Edelfelt sketched the common people in order to achieve an *aspect de verité*. One of the sketches was developed into a remorselessly naturalistic portrait, "One-eyed Karelian" (1877–1878). He transferred the face to the male figure in "The Burned Village," but by then it had lost its original effect and had been transformed into a kind of stage prop.

Air, light, and wind

In late summer 1879, Edelfelt worked at Haikko, near Porvoo on the south coast, and managed to sketch a group of fishermen rowing in their Sunday clothes. The people were on their way to a child's christening. The scene made an impression on Edelfelt, and he suddenly understood that this was something that had never been portrayed, the Finnish archipelago shimmering in the backlight.

Death was a more weighty subject than birth, at least in fashionable circles in Paris, and Edelfelt transformed the event into a child's funeral.

The painting had to be made outside, Edelfelt decided, and as he struggled in the autumn winds with his two meters of canvas and easel, he admitted, "I never believed that it would be so difficult to paint outdoors."

Despite all the *plein-airism*, Edelfelt's painting did not capture reality with the faithfulness of photography. It was selected, staged, and composed of separate parts right down to the subject itself. Edelfelt's painting nonetheless marked a radical move forward by Finnish standards. From a French viewpoint, it was a compromise: the artist had chosen as his style a middle ground between the Naturalism of the Academy and Impressionism.

Edelfelt had been influenced most profoundly by his mentor and friend Bastien-Lepage. Pissarro once noted acridly that Bastien-Lepage flirted with modern art, but remained completely estranged from it. No wonder Bastien-Lepage, who was enchanted by silvery-gray tones, criticized the bright colors in "A Child's Funeral."

The painting did so well in the Salon in 1880 that Edelfelt wrote to his mother, restraining his joy, "You know, Mother, that Dagnan [-Bouveret] received a first-class medal. Bastien, who hoped for a medal of honor, did not receive one, and is probably pretty humiliated."

Edelfelt was awarded a third-class medal. Evidently it was the only one given that year

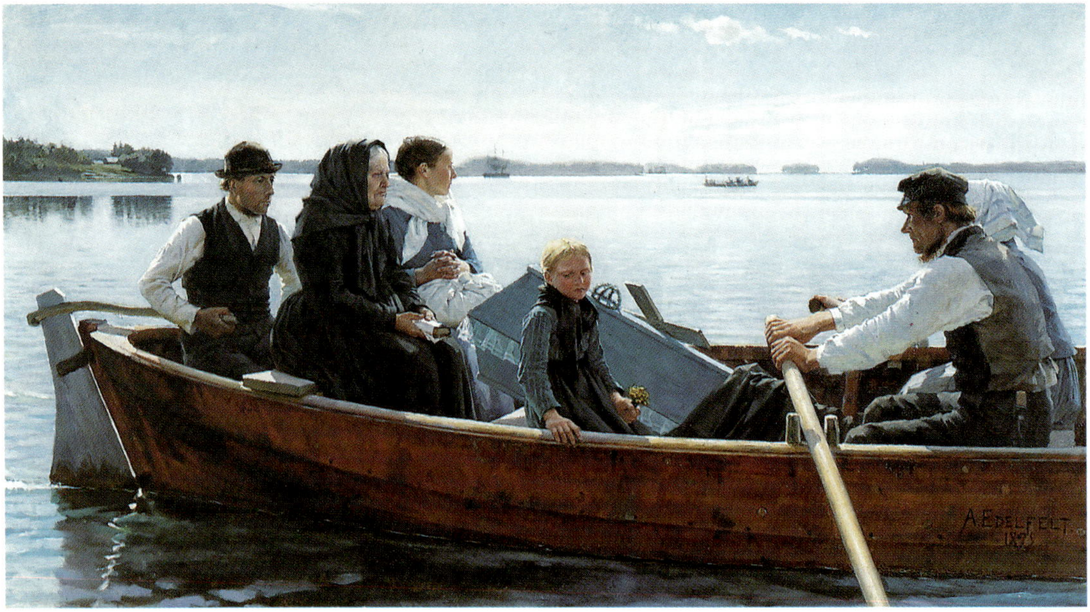
A.EDELFELT
1879

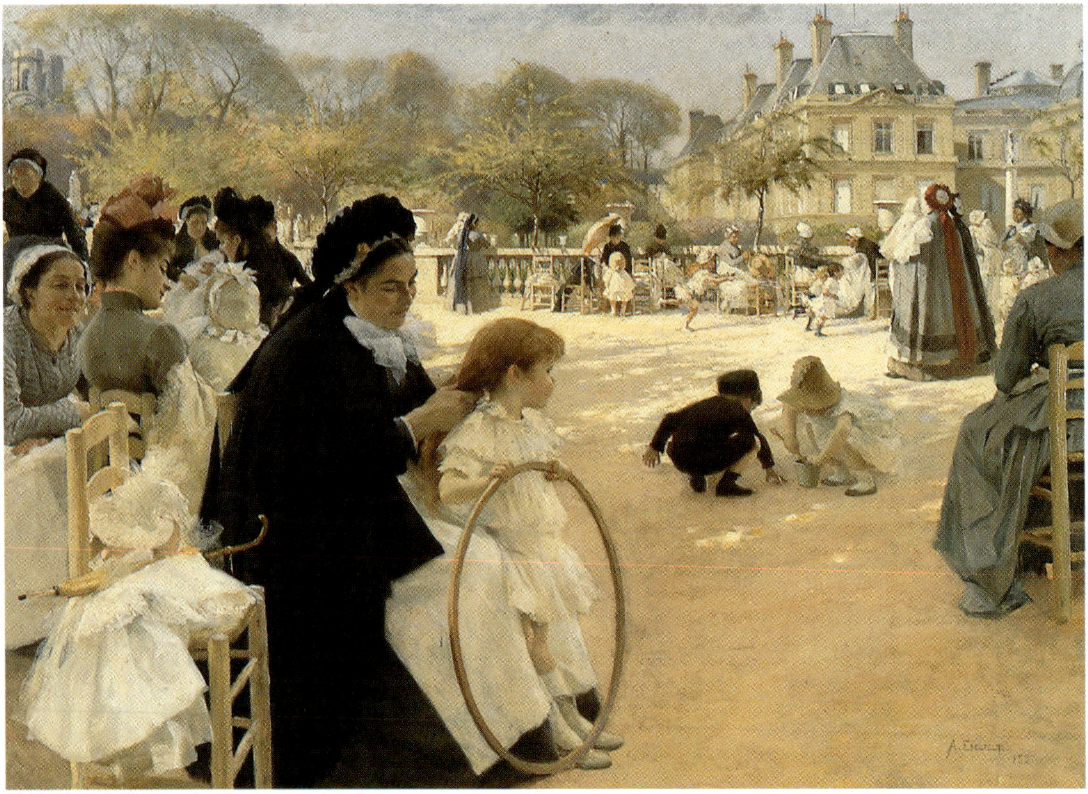

Albert Edelfelt:
A Child's Funeral. 1879.
Oil, 120 x 205 cm. Antell Collection,
ART MUSEUM OF THE ATENEUM.

Albert Edelfelt:
The Luxembourg Gardens. 1887.
Oil, 144 x 188 cm. Antell Collection,
ART MUSEUM OF THE ATENEUM.

Aukusti Uotila:
Fisherman's Hut in Brittany. 1881.
Oil, 32 x 42.5 cm.
COLLECTION OF THE REITZ FOUNDATION.

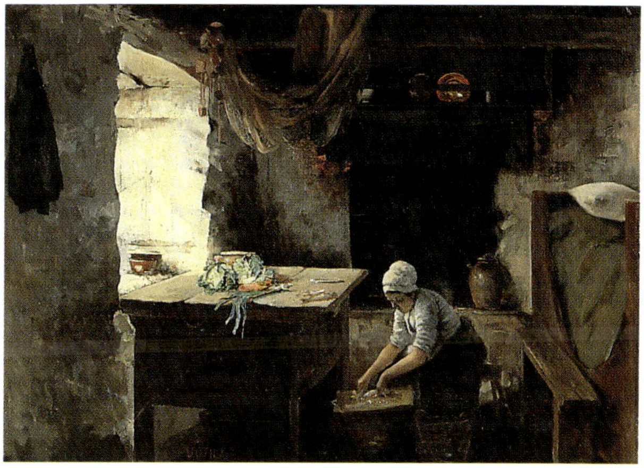

to a foreigner. Edelfelt's success piqued his Scandinavian colleagues somewhat, and even C. G. Estlander played down his protege's sudden success by saying that it was the cool shadow and not the sunlight that makes a larva grow into a butterfly.

The Finnish public's negative reaction was hardly a surprise to the artist. Observers found "A Child's Funeral" lacking in emotion and considered the diagonal position of the coffin offensive. They missed sympathy and profound sorrow, in other words, the sentimentality so familiar to them. But the work put a new angle on discussions. The fresh light found in landscape painting projected on human figures revealed something about reality that people initially refused to see.

Edelfelt's painting naturally had a forerunner. As early as the 1860s, Jules Breton had painted peasant subjects outdoors. Jean Cazin joined the *plein-air* painters later, but the most important influence from a Finnish point of view was exerted by Bastien-Lepage, the painter of the *juste milieu.* His "Haymaking" and "Digging Potatoes" had attracted considerable attention at the Paris Salon in 1878 and 1879.

The Impressionists continued their own battle against the Salon. Renoir made a useless attempt to reform the system in 1880, and Emile Zola wrote an article, "Le naturalisme au Salon," whose lifeless spirit of compromise did not in the least satisfy the Impressionists.

At first glance Edelfelt seemed to have rejected the Impressionists' style, but in the mid-1880s, his attitude changed, and he painted a great many Impressionistic pieces. Their coloristic boldness and the openness of their brush strokes varied considerably; the more important the work, the more likely Edelfelt was to heed conservative warnings.

The effect of external influences on the artist's personality can be seen by how he toned down the color scale in the painting that followed "A Child's Funeral," "Service in the Southern Archipelago" (1881), so that it resembled Bastien-Lepage's style.

When Edelfelt began to paint one of his most important works of art, "The Luxembourg Gardens" (1887), Gérôme came to warn him of Impressionism. Edelfelt believed that his debt to the past could clearly be seen in the fine values of the otherwise vibrant park scene.

Edelfelt attained an important position in Paris as a portraitist for the upper class. He experienced his finest triumph in 1886 when he exhibited his portrait of Louis Pasteur (1885) at the Salon.

There happened to be another portrait of Pasteur at the Salon, painted by an old and respected master, Léon Bonnat. The coincidence caused quite an uproar, and *Le Figaro* wrote that Edelfelt had "completely thrown master Bonnat out of the ring." The French government bought Edelfelt's portrait of the scientist and made the 30-year-old artist a member of the Legion of Honor.

Naturalism was becoming difficult for Edelfelt to accept. After reading Zola's works, he was appalled, wondering why Flaubert was an artist but Zola

Walter Runeberg: Memorial to Alexander II (1884–1894) at Senate Square, with Nicholas Church (now Helsinki Cathedral) in the background. Height of the Czar's figure 3.23 m; whole monument 10.7 m. "Lex" in the foreground.

was not. Later Edelfelt realized Zola's importance and also understood the Naturalistic, "true-to-life" painting of such young colleagues as Axel Gallén (1865–1831, called Akseli Gallen-Kallela from 1907).

Edelfelt tried Naturalism in a slightly aloof manner, but the innovations of the 1890s seemed rather strange to him. Edelfelt was open to new ideas, and we can see the flexibility of his talent in the way which his painting "Christ and the Magdalen" (1890) served as a landmark for this period of inter- nalization.

Aukusti Uotila (1858–1886) was the Finnish student in Paris who belonged to the same generation as Edelfelt. Uotila's gifts were largely wasted, since he was unable to continue his studies due to a lack of money. His most interesting works of art were the melancholy, dignified depictions of oyster fishermen, sketched in Brittany.

Uotila had to satisfy mundane tastes in his landscapes. In his own words, in his desperation he had to paint "moonlight scenes and seascapes, with or without reflections, because of the public's stupid taste." The depressed artist died in 1886 in Ajaccio, Corsica.

A politicized review of sculpture

Robert Montgomery, professor of law, and 21 other members of the nobility and aristocracy proposed at the convening of the Estates in 1882 that a collection be taken to finance a monument to Czar Alexander II, Finland's Grand Duke, who had been assassinated the previous year.

Alexander II was an important ruler from Finland's point of view since he had approved the country's parliamentary system in 1869. The monument's political message embodied the hope that this liberal policy would be continued.

The monument committee, headed by Topelius, started its work. A collection was taken throughout the country, and an open competition was arranged in 1883 to find a design for the monument. Proposals were to be submitted by September 1884.

It was decided to erect the monument on Senate Square, symbolically the most important spot in Helsinki.

Every major Finnish sculptor took part in the competition, and there were only five of them in all: C. E. Sjöstrand, Walter Runeberg, Johannes Takanen, Ville Vallgren, and Robert Stigell (1852–1907).

The committee's work did not go at all smoothly, since the animosity between the two language groups was reflected in the judges' opinions. Two proposals made it to the final round.

Dr. Eliel Aspelin supported the simple and dignified figure of the czar in the proposal marked "E" (Takanen). Messrs. Donner, Forsman, Löfgren, and Meurman concurred, while Edelfelt favored the proposal marked "C" (Runeberg).

Most of the judges' remarks dealt with the written content of the proposals and insignificant details that could easily be changed. Why was the left hand on Takanen's figure behind the

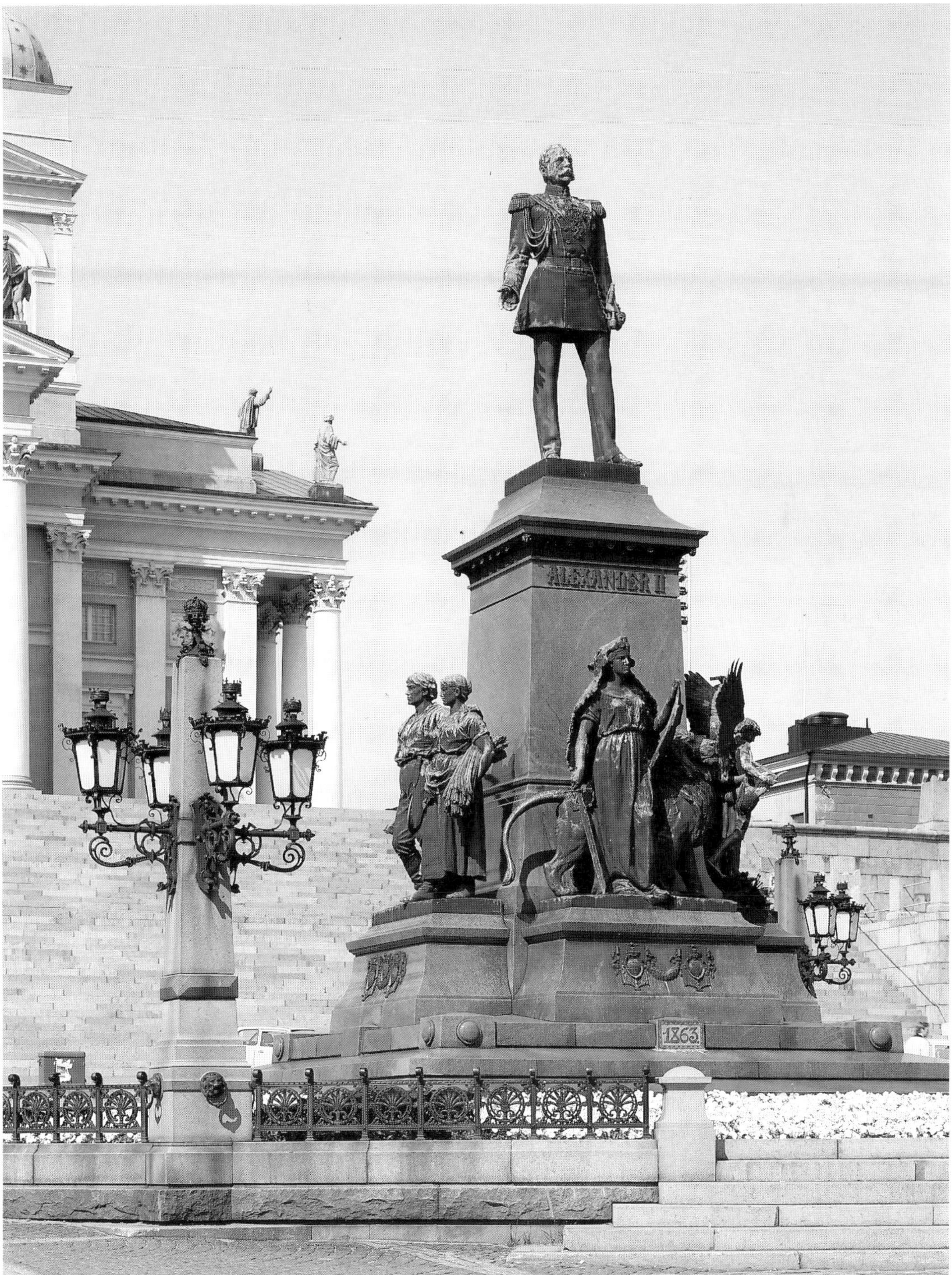
ALEXANDER II
1863

body if it was supposed to hold a roll of paper signifying the new parliamentary system? Or: Runeberg's proposals for secondary figures, "Lex," "Pax," "Lux," and "Labor", might give foreigners (!) the false impression that Finnish art and industry were the achievements of the czar.

Takanen's proposal won the secret ballot, eight to seven, but differences in opinion did not end here. Just before the Estates were was to deal with the question of the monument, Runeberg signed an appeal to divide the work among as many sculptors as possible. The matter was submitted to the general committee on education, which understood it to mean that the work should be divided between Takanen and Runeberg if "cooperation can be established between them."

The peasantry opposed dividing up the work and demanded that it be commissioned from Takanen alone. The other estates shared the committee's view, and the artists had to make do with a compromise. Takanen assured them that he accepted their decision. "I do not believe that the matter could have been settled any better, since in this way we reduce party criticism and doubts as to trustworthiness."

This is where the matter ended for Takanen. He came down with rheumatic fever in 1885 and died of complications within a few weeks. The monument was left to Runeberg. He sculpted the figure of the czar after Takanen's sketch, and developed his original proposal for subsidiary figures, trying to resolve the conflicting wishes of the judges.

From Neo-classicism to Realism

Takanen and Runeberg differed greatly as sculptors, despite their similar training. Both had initially studied at the Arts Society's art school as pupils of Sjöstrand, and later at the Royal Danish Academy of Fine Arts under Herman Vilhelm Bissen, Bertel Thorvaldsen's successor. Takanen also attended classes given by Bissen's son, Wilhelm.

Runeberg's career got off to a smooth start since he was the son of Finland's best known poet. No one considered his artistic gifts a matter of course, however, and J. L. Runeberg spoke unflatteringly of his "son running wild with [his] pictures."

Walter's future was to be decided by an impartial expert, the St. Petersburg sculptor P. Klodth von Jürgensburg. His evaluation was positive, and Walter was allowed to begin his training.

The Arts Society awarded Walter Runeberg a 500-rouble travel grant in 1863 since it was found that he had a "soft hand" and a "noble approach." The matter is worth mentioning since Walter's grant was the first one ever given to an artist by the Finnish state.

Runeberg remained a Neo-classicist throughout his life, his subject matter comprising mostly the mythology of antiquity and the Christian allegories of grave monuments. The first example of his work sent back to Finland was entitled "The Centaur Chiron Instructing

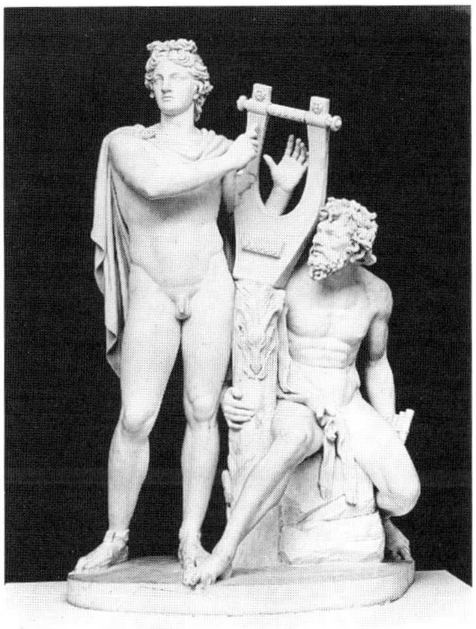

Walter Runeberg: Apollo and Marsyas. 1872. Marble, 200 cm.
ART MUSEUM OF THE ATENEUM.

Achilles in Javelin-throwing." It was finished in Rome in 1865.

The monument to Alexander II was not Runeberg's first monument; he had already made one to glorify his own great father. The standing figure represents the poet preparing a speech, clad in the simple garb of a secondary school teacher.

The statue was cast in bronze in 1882 and was unveiled with great ceremony in Helsinki's Esplanade Park in 1885. At the base of the monument the sculptor placed a female figure representing Finland, a genius with a bearskin as her cape, an attribute favored by the Svecomen. In her left hand, Finland holds a copper plaque with a couple of verses from the national anthem, *Our Land*.

Runeberg's most important work included "Apollo and Marsyas" (plaster 1872, marble 1874), "Psyche With Lamp and Dagger in Hand" (marble 1878), "The Danaids" (plaster 1893), and "Resurrection" (plaster 1896), which was cast in bronze between 1906 and 1911 and erected in a private patron's garden.

"Apollo and Marsyas" marked an important step forward for the little world of Finnish sculpture, since the Helsinki women who commissioned it wanted it made of marble. And so it was, but the sculpture was not placed as planned in the Student House auditorium designed by Hampus Dahlström. The art historian Juha Ilvas suspects that two nude male figures were too much for the ladies who commissioned the work.

Finland's first marble sculpture ended up where it was protected from the gaze of young students, in the collection of the Finnish Arts Society.

Walter Runeberg became a popular portraitist throughout Scandinavia. J. L. Runeberg's friend, the Norwegian Lorentz Dietrichson, wrote exalted reviews of Walter's work and helped spread his reputation. People began to speak of Runeberg as Finland's Thorvaldsen.

Johannes Takanen, the son of a farm laborer, was good with his hands. He was a skilled whittler, and knew how to make mechanical gadgets. A conscious effort was made in the period to find gifted youths among the common people, and Johannes's abilities attracted the notice of his teachers. Takanen was also popular with the people of Viipuri, who showed his little sculptures to the Russian General Todleben.

The art-loving general is said to have declared as he looked at samples of Takanen's work, "Das ist ein grosses Genie." This is where Takanen's reputation as a genius began. The townspeople of Viipuri sent the youth off to Helsinki to study.

Takanen easily learned the artist's craft, but foreign languages were much more difficult. Takanen studied at the Academy in Copenhagen for quite some time before he was able to carry on even a simple conversation in Danish.

Studies of anatomy amazed the Finnish student. "People here do not sketch after other drawings or printed pictures; they draw from life or plaster models. Yesterday we sketched a flayed body, which had already begun to smell a bit."

Takanen's style showed

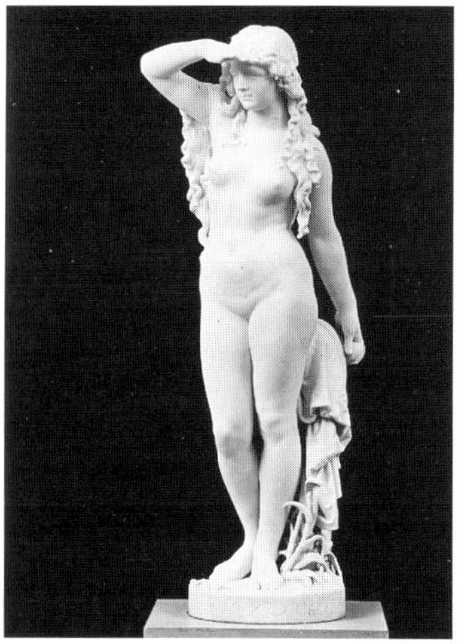

Johannes Takanen:
Aino. 1876,
executed in marble in 1886. 108 cm.
ART MUSEUM OF THE ATENEUM.

quite early that he was not satisfied with the smoothness and generalizations of Classicism. He sculpted softly and flexibly, letting the individual features of his models remain visible. Compared with Runeberg, Takanen's approach was thus more realistic. No decisive difference can be seen in the subject matter chosen by these two rivals, though Takanen did his most famous work on themes from the *Kalevala*.

The figure of Aino, about to drown herself, enthralled the Finnish public. Takanen had been warned against sculpting nude figures, without any attributes or national dress to facilitate interpretation, but the artist did not listen to the guardians of modesty and did what he liked. And to top it all, he used a lush Italian woman as the model for this most Finnish of all Finnish maidens. The hand shading the eyes and the wavy line incised on the base are the only clear references to the sad tale of Aino.

When "Aino" (plaster 1876, executed in marble after the sculptor's death) was brought to Finland from Rome, the reactions were unprecedented. The work was praised and poems were written to it. The first director of the Finnish Arts Society's collection, B.O. Schauman (1821–1895), a crotchety and old-fashioned man, wrote, "When I saw it for the first time, a tear of joy irresistibly fell from my eye because of its loveliness." It was hardly a question just of a love of art and skill. Men found a suitable mixture of idealism and carnal realism in Aino's erotic figure.

The biblical subject of "Rebecca" (plaster 1877, marble 1878) was Takanen's most widely copied work. The sculptor Karl Magnus von Wright (1867–1898) originally purchased the right to copy both Rebecca and Aino. Most of the miniature copies, of uneven quality, were undoubtedly unauthorized, but they spread to Finnish homes over the decades, giving birth to a kind of popular canon of sculpture.

Takanen's best work includes "Andromeda" (plaster 1879, marble 1882). The artist himself was satisfied with the delicately formed figure, which could be viewed from all sides, since in one of his letters he wrote, "I am not ashamed to brag that this same Andromeda has been measured by Danish sculptors for its good lines."

(Male) artists have always understood that the legend of St. George and the tale of Andromeda embodied an idealized sexual theme. The hero saves the young woman from a cruel beast, the evil phallus. Takanen chose a typical moment in the story from antiquity: Andromeda, chained to the rock, glimpses the horrible monster sent by Poseidon rising from the sea.

Takanen's Andromeda shows shyness, not horror, and at most mild disgust. Even the monster is almost hidden in the decorations on the base. Great emotions did not suit Takanen's nature as a sculptor. He concentrated on minimal expressions and gestures, as we can see in his allegory of art, "La Nuova Modella" (1885). The sculpture shows a new model removing her clothes before the artist for the first time. The type can be traced back to the figures of Ve-

Robert Stigell:
The Worker. 1882.
Bronzed plaster, 78 cm.
ARBETETS VÄNNER.

Ville Vallgren:
Boy Playing with a Crayfish. 1884.
Marble, 60 cm.
ART MUSEUM OF THE ATENEUM.

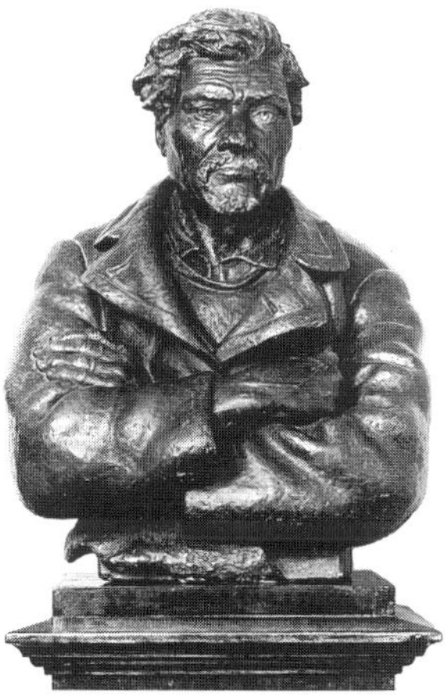

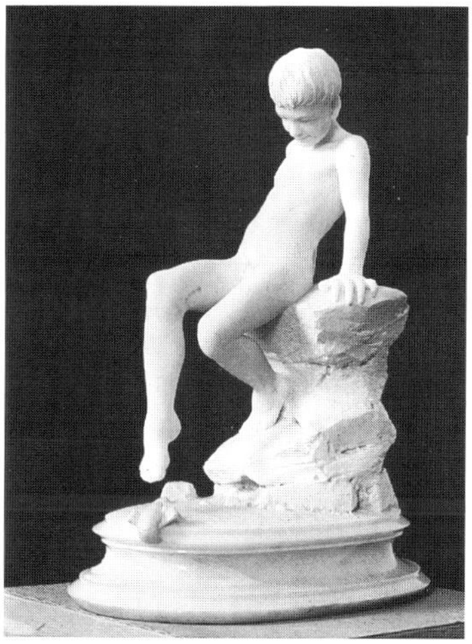

nus from antiquity, the most important adaptation from the 19th century being Antonio Canova's "Venus Italica" (1804–1812).

It would be an exaggeration to speak of trends in Finnish sculpture in the 1870s since there were so few sculptors. A third Finn was working in Rome at the time, however: Robert Stigell. His sculptural ideals were quite different from those of Runeberg and Takanen. Stigell understood the realism found in the sculpture of the Renaissance better than his colleagues, but he especially admired Bernini and the Baroque. It is unclear whether the Italian *verismo* that caused such a stir in the Paris Salon in the end of the 1870s influenced Stigell's approach.

Stigell, who originally intended to be a stone mason, started studying in Rome in 1872 at the four-year art academy of San Lucca. He squeezed himself into the little studio rented by Takanen, one that had been used before by the English sculptor John Flaxman.

In 1877, Stigell went to Paris, to the École des Beaux-Arts, studying under Pierre Jules Cavelier. Stigell thus got an education that differed markedly from that of his Finnish colleagues who had studied in Copenhagen. Walter Runeberg also would have had every opportunity to rethink his style during his stay in Paris, but Realism did not seem to have moved him very much.

Stigell believed that sculpture should interpret powerful emotions and movements. He chose his subjects accordingly, for example "Man with a Slingshot" (1877), "The Archer" (1887), and "Who will Win?" (1901).

The social and individual characterizations of Stigell's portraits can be seen at their most realistic in the bust of a worker, completed in 1882. The artist sculpted the important Finnish art patron and collector Herman Frithiof Antell (1847–1893) at the beginning of the 20th century in the same position, Antell's hands majestically crossed on his chest.

Stigell worked on the plans for "The Shipwrecked" (unveiled in Helsinki in 1898) as early as the 1870s. The dramatic composition of the monument, rising in a spiral, brings to mind the Neo-baroque monuments of the French Second Empire. Stigell certainly knew the dynamic groups created by Jean-Baptiste Carpeaux. The monument has often been compared to Géricault's "The Raft of the 'Medusa'" (1819).

The attraction of Paris decided the career of Ville Vallgren, who was slightly younger than Stigell. The doctor's son from Porvoo was actually to have become an architect, but art and Edelfelt's "beautifully described" metropolis fascinated him more. After reaching Paris for the first time in 1877, Vallgren began to sketch from models at Bonnat's private academy and work in marble in Orsolini's studio. Stigell, however, arranged for Cavelier to instruct his new colleague.

Vallgren remained in Paris for decades. He was fond of the pleasures of life and was a connoisseur of food and drink. The art historian Ludwig Wennervirta describes Vallgren as a thoroughly cultured man to whom "primitive raw power is foreign."

Marble suited Vallgren's goals, and his production in the 1880s in fact largely comprised marble sculptures and plaster models for them. Vallgren found his models in the salon realism of the day. He made not only portrait sculptures, but also two pieces that captured a specific moment "Boy Playing with a Crayfish" (1884) and "Echo" (1888). Their delicate modeling even surpassed Takanen's achievements.

"Echo" is taken from the mythology of antiquity, but the boy with the crayfish continued the naturalistic approach begun with that François Rude's celebrated "Neapolitan Fisherboy" (1831–1833). We should not underestimate the importance of portrayals of children in breaking down conventions. They brought to sculpture the everyday subjects lacking in "beauty" that Neo-classicism had so firmly rejected.

Vincenzo Gemito repeated Rude's trick in 1877. The naturalism of his "Fisherboy" broke the unwritten laws of academy sculpture by depicting an open mouth, for example. Vallgren did not go this far, but instead turned away from Naturalism, towards a more delicate and linearly masterful approach.

In the 1880s, Vallgren made a series of sculptures on themes from the *Kalevala*, such as "Marjatta" and "Aino," but Estlander, who was chairman of the Finnish Arts Society, did not approve of their simple naturalness. He was most critical of Vallgren's relief "Adam and Eve." Estlander considered it a "tasteless whim" that would end up in the Ateneum's attic. Today the piece is in the collection of Vienna's *Kunsthistorisches Museum*.

Salon realism did not fit in with the old-fashioned views of the esthetes who had grown up as Runeberg had. Because of the controversy about Vallgren's art, Estlander in fact relinquished his position as chairman.

Vallgren met with quite different treatment in Paris. He was a success at the Universal Exposition in 1889, was praised by the French foreign minister, Gabriel Hanotaux, and met Auguste Rodin.

Women make a breakthrough

Eveliina Särkelä (1847–1939), the daughter of an Ostrobothnian clockmaker, made a bold decision in the early 1870s when she decided to become a sculptor. She had the support of her teacher, R. W. Ekman, and left for Copenhagen in 1874 to study under A. V. Saabye for a couple of years.

A lack of money drove Särkelä back to Finland, but because of the limited demand for sculptures, it proved difficult to make a living even at home. The artist's sex undoubtedly also caused problems. Only one woman before Särkelä, Aline Forsman (1845–1892), had studied to be a sculptor.

Särkelä won second prize in the Finnish Arts Society's competition for young artists in 1879 for her sculpture "Strawberry

Girl." The first prize was won by Fanny Churberg, and Helene Schjerfbeck came in third. Women were also given a share of the year's seven travel grants. Särkelä and Alma Engblom (1856–1926) were on the list.

The victorious achievements of women have sometimes been considered a "strange coincidence," but statistics show that during the first five years that the prize was awarded to young artists, between 1858 and 1863, only one man received it. Twelve prizes were awarded in all.

Women studied art most often as a cultural hobby or as training for work as a teacher. In 1879, for example, seven women and two men studied in the antiquity class at the Arts Society's art school. This proportion remained unaltered for quite some time. Very few women became professional painters, however. Riitta Konttinen, who has studied art made by Finnish women, has calculated that as late as the 1880s, only 18 of the 249 women who studied at the art school in Helsinki became professional artists. The number is hardly insignificant, however, if we consider Finland's population (under 2.4 million in 1890) and level of development (2/3 of the population employed in agriculture).

Women's social status improved in 1864, when the new guardianship act came into force. An unmarried woman 21 years of age was obliged to submit a notification of her majority to the courts in order to have full right to all her property. At the age of 25, an unmarried woman was considered of age even if she did not submit any notification.

Marriage still bound a woman tightly, since she needed her husband's consent if she wanted to work outside the home. This was one reason why many women artists remained unmarried. The letter of the law naturally contrasted sharply with the spirit of Finland's patriarchal society.

Snellman considered women's education important, but nonetheless felt that the hearth was the right place for them. The opinions of the fathers of national awakening might not have been models of liberal thought, but Cygnaeus, for example, sincerely supported women who intended to become artists. Konttinen finds that even he was guilty of that deadliest of modern sins, sexism.

All art forms were included in the national program of enlightenment, but pictorial art, which promised an uncertain living, did not attract large groups of men. And so women were needed to carry out the program. We could sum up the general attitude by saying that women had to do for lack of something "better."

The success of Finnish artists abroad, the choice of an artist's career by the national poet's son and even by a nobleman like von Becker provided examples that led men to join the ranks. Friction between the sexes started to grow at the end of the 1880s, since increasingly fierce battles had to be waged over the limited resources available to art. There was also a conflict of interests among different groups of women, and the "sisterhood of artists" that had been strengthened by the feminist movement was weakened at times.

The performance of Henrik Ibsen's *A Doll's House* at the Finnish Theater in 1880 sparked off a major discussion, and so did Emma Irene Åström's master's thesis in 1882. Rosina Heikel, a medical doctor, was the only woman to have previously been awarded a university degree.

John Stuart Mill's *The Subjugation of Women* was carefully read in a society that promoted the founding of a secondary school for girls. In 1884, the Finnish Women's Society began to demand women's suffrage. Efforts by the author Minna Canth (1844–1897) spurred the movement for equality between the sexes. She was even bold enough to call herself a "socialist," which at the time was almost an affront.

The unified front of women artists broadened significantly in the 1880s. Riitta Konttinen has emphasized that Finnish Naturalism was developed largely by women. Helene Schjerfbeck and Helena Westermarck (1857–1938) faced the strongest criticism as early as the first half of the 1880s, while their male colleagues enjoyed the fruits of the women's victories. The most heated debate was already over in 1886 when Axel Gallén made his breakthrough with "The Old Woman and the Cat."

The soul and the eye's testimony

The Finnish colony in Paris started to come alive again in autumn 1880. Helena Westermarck returned to the city, evidently after tiring of her vacationing elsewhere in Europe. "Vive la liberté et la travail," she wrote contentedly to her brother.

Helene Schjerfbeck, who had received a Senate grant, arrived in Paris for the first time, as did Ada Thilén (1852–1933) and Sigrid af Forselles (1860–1935), who had specialized in sculpture.

In addition to the established Finnish colony, with Runeberg, Vallgren, Edelfelt, and Uotila, Alma Engblom and Ellen Favorin (1853–1919) also spent the winter there.

Maria Wiik (1853–1928) and Amélie Lundahl (1850–1914) had studied at the Académie Julian for a few years and were now painting independently. Wiik did her best salon work when she made a charming yet vigorous portrait of her sister in 1881, a painting whose fine points were noted even by the newspaper critics. The high point in Wiik's production was nonetheless "Out into the World" (1889), an anecdotal painting built up of tranquil surfaces of color bathed in subdued light. The influence of Puvis de Chavannes has been found in its violet-blue tones.

Amélin Lundahl's most substantial work is linked with the period's fascination with Brittany, the search for authenticity and originality. Lundahl and Uotila painted together in Douarnenez in 1880, but Lundahl's more liberated shore scenes and more profound character studies are from a slightly later date. In spite of the marine light, they often re-

Maria Wiik:
Out into the World. 1889.
Oil, 69 x 61 cm.
ART MUSEUM OF THE ATENEUM.

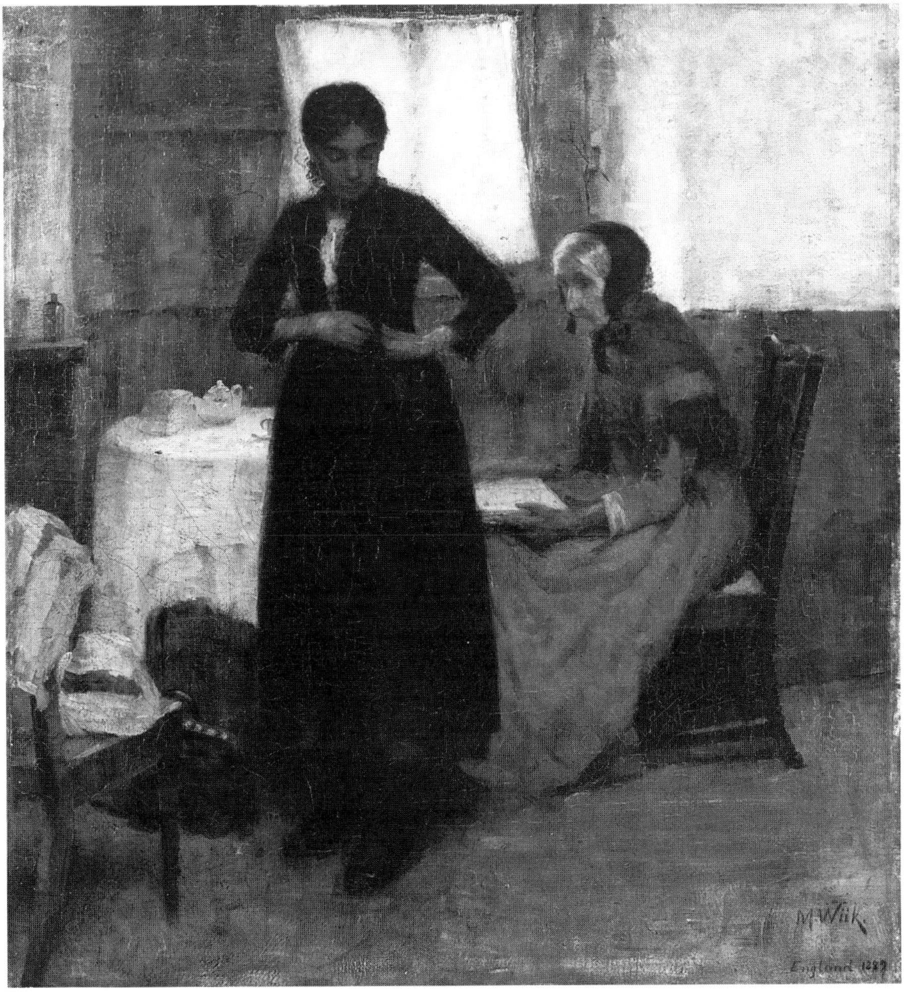

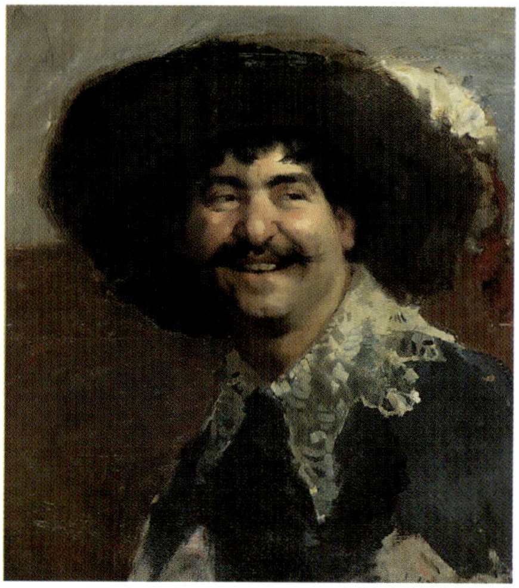

Helene Schjerfbeck: Laughing Colarossi. 1881. Oil, 60 x 50 cm.
PRIVATE COLLECTION.

tained a salon-like atmosphere.

Westermarck, Schjerfbeck, Thilén, Favorin, and Engblom first worked at the Atelier Trélat, whose attractions included teachers such as Bastien-Lepage and Gérôme. When the two cut down their already limited hours, the students remained only because of Bonnat, but left en *masse* the following year (1881) for the Académie Colarossi, after fighting with Mme Trélat, who had behaved like a "demon."

The teachers at the Académie Colarossi included Gérôme's pupil, Gustave Courtois. The school was owned by a former Italian model, who had the rare ability to pose laughing. Schjerfbeck in fact painted a lively portrait of him, "Laughing Colarossi" (1881).

At their new schools, the Finnish women had the first opportunity to make a thorough study of nude models, and Westermarck noted that "the Negro's body is the most beautiful one can see." Schjerfbeck, however, made the best studies.

Brittany was on Schjerfbeck's summer schedule. She traveled to Concarneau in July 1881 together with the Austrian Marianne Preindelsberger, a fellow student. There the two met the English painter Adrian Stokes, and Schjerfbeck painted her first naturalistic genre picture, "Boy Feeding His Little Sister."

Finnish critics considered Schjerfbeck's portrayal of the children ugly and too realistic. The Arts Society nonetheless purchased the painting for its collection, but a few years later, the painting caused a new *succès de scandale* and *Nya Pressen* wrote these immortal words, "The public stops, horrified and abashed before this modern painting … Two half-witted children eating gruel from a clay dish in a rural hut … And nonetheless there is something in this painting that makes one gladly examine it."

Schjerfbeck was understandably hurt by the article and defended her painting, made with broad, sure brush strokes, by remarking that the "subject of the painting is quite simply a bit of everyday life."

And that was the crux of the matter. Everyday life was ugly and reality was unsuitable as art. The period's views about good Realism and bad Naturalism make interesting reading in the history of ideas. Fanny Churberg clearly noted the borderlines of these norms when she criticized Schjerfbeck's painting "The Convalescent" (1888) for depicting a sick child.

Churberg rejected Edelfelt's "Women Outside the Church at Ruokolahti" (1887) because she felt it showed no love of the common people and displayed a "nastiness that is no natural Finnish feature." The belief in peasant idylls remained strong in Churberg's mind even though she, too, was ready to accept the most modern ideas in landscape painting.

"Sea water has always been considered too fresh for it to be presented as it is seen. But as blue as it is, this is how it should be painted, since in nature, truth is the same as beauty."

We could call Churberg's views Darwinism combined with nationalism and a conventional moral code. Accordingly, health and vitality are beautiful. Churberg demanded that even flower paintings have vitality. "Only a single little sprig depicted so that a calf would like to test its nutritional value would be much healthier than this superficial decorativeness that has neither life nor juice."

C. G. Estlander's public and private views had an inestimable influence on the prevailing opinion in Finland. Estlander was fond of studio criticism, and as he wrote with the authority of a philosopher about Naturalism and Impressionism, he was not sparing in his condemnation. For example, Estlander described Manet's paintings as striking, incisive, and magnificent, but brutal and soulless. He wished to clearly separate the testimony of the senses from "the soul."

The opinions of the artists themselves wavered. Helena Westermarck took a positive view of Impressionism's photographic-like technique that aimed at neutrality, but when she wrote about Naturalism and Realism, she inclined towards Realism since it embodied a sympathetic attitude.

Subjects lose ground

Schjerfbeck's production during the 1880s ranged from salon pieces to dazzlingly modern work. She used fewer and fewer subjects, and in passing regenerated the art of the Finnish still-life. Schjerfbeck puzzled at least the Finnish audience by capturing a quick impression in her loosely painted "Drying Clothes" (1883). It is a calculated snap-shot, even though it is not very Impressionistic in its use of color.

"Street in Pont-Aven"(1883) is a geometric composition built up of rectangular surfaces, just like "The Door" (1884), which is even more ascetic in form. Schjerfbeck left it up to the viewer to give shape to the foreground and the cloth draped over the chair in "Toy Rabbits" (1884). Finnish Modernism was being born.

It might seem contradictory that Schjerfbeck, who now had a good grasp of the new approach, simultaneously made a large number of paintings that seem downright affected. She considered them completed works of art according to the taste of the day and made an effort to have them accepted by the Salon. They need not, however, be considered only expressions of a desire for acceptance and buyers.

Schjerfbeck's "Feast of the Tabernacles" (1883) has been considered a mystifying work, and it has been suspected of having links with the Jewish question. Schjerfbeck knew a number of Jews personally, and her sympathies were certainly on their side, but "Feast of the Tabernacles" also has features that are connected with the artist's own life. Or is it a coincidence that the father in the painting is middle-aged, perhaps in his forties, and that the daughter is just reaching puberty? Schjerfbeck's father died at the age of 43, when Helene was 13. Helene's life-long physical disability has traditionally been thought to have affected her art, but a hip injury was not the only tragedy she suffered in her youth.

"Feast of the Tabernacles"

Helene Schjerfbeck:
The Bakery. 1887.
Oil, 61 x 51 cm.
Hedman Collection,
MUSEUM OF OSTROBOTHNIA, VAASA.

Helene Schjerfbeck:
The Door. 1884.
Oil, 41 x 33 cm.
ART MUSEUM OF THE ATENEUM.

Helene Schjerfbeck:
Boys on the Shore at St. Ives. 1887.
Oil on wood, 33 x 42 cm.
PRIVATE COLLECTION.

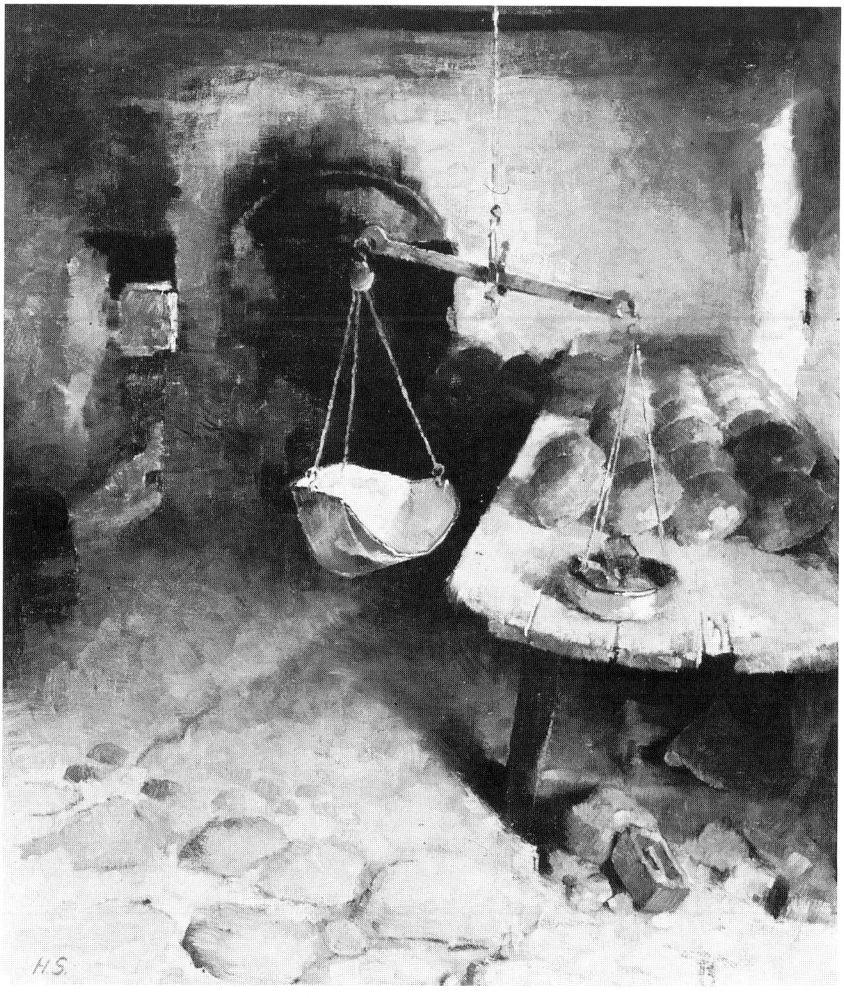

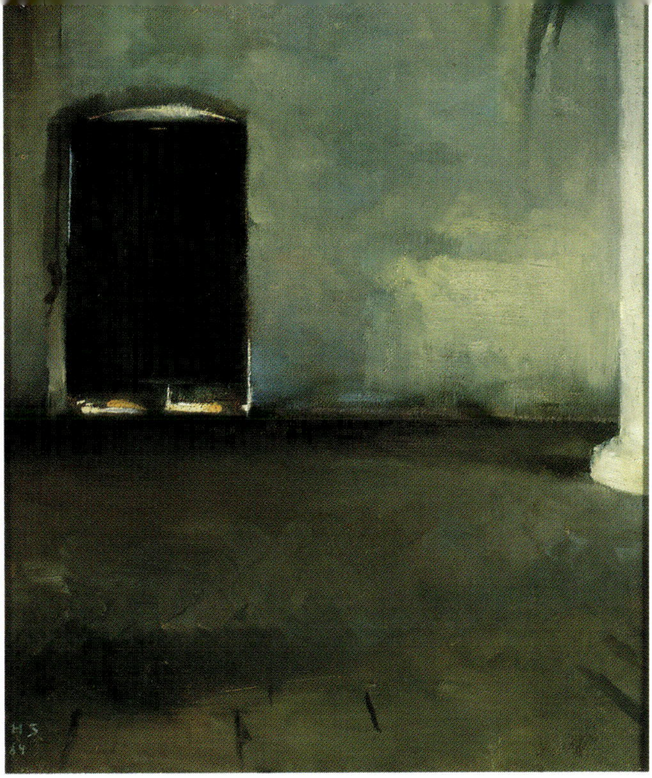

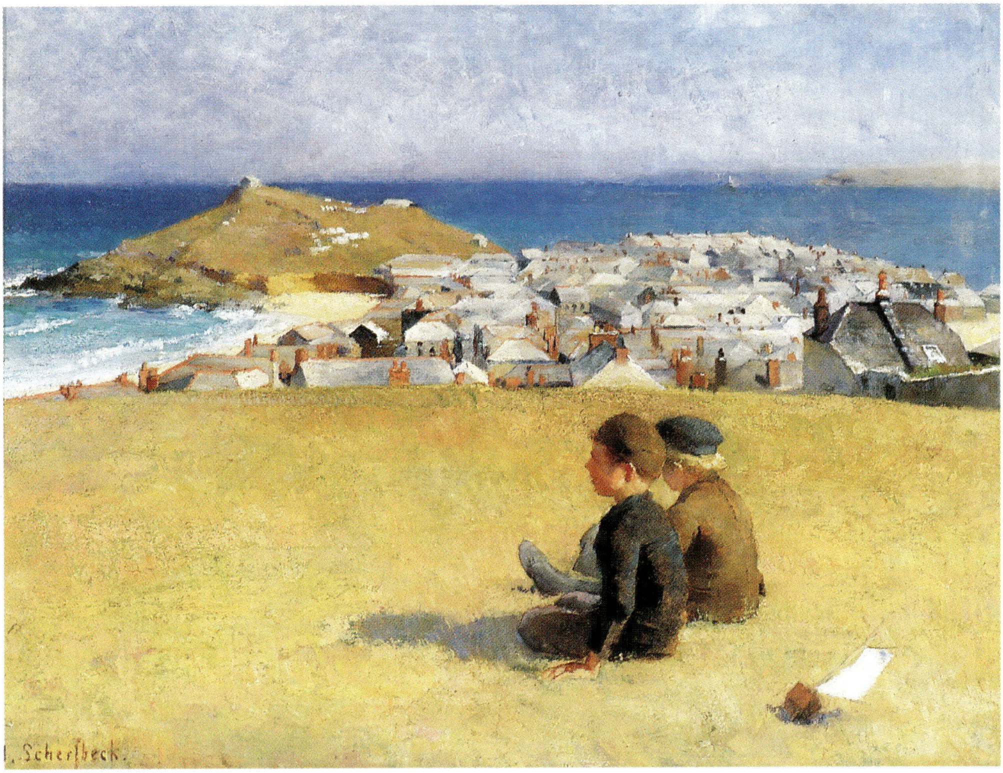
Scherfbeck.

Axel Gallén:
Boy With a Crow. 1884.
Oil, 86.5 x 72.5. Antell Collection,
ART MUSEUM OF THE ATENEUM.

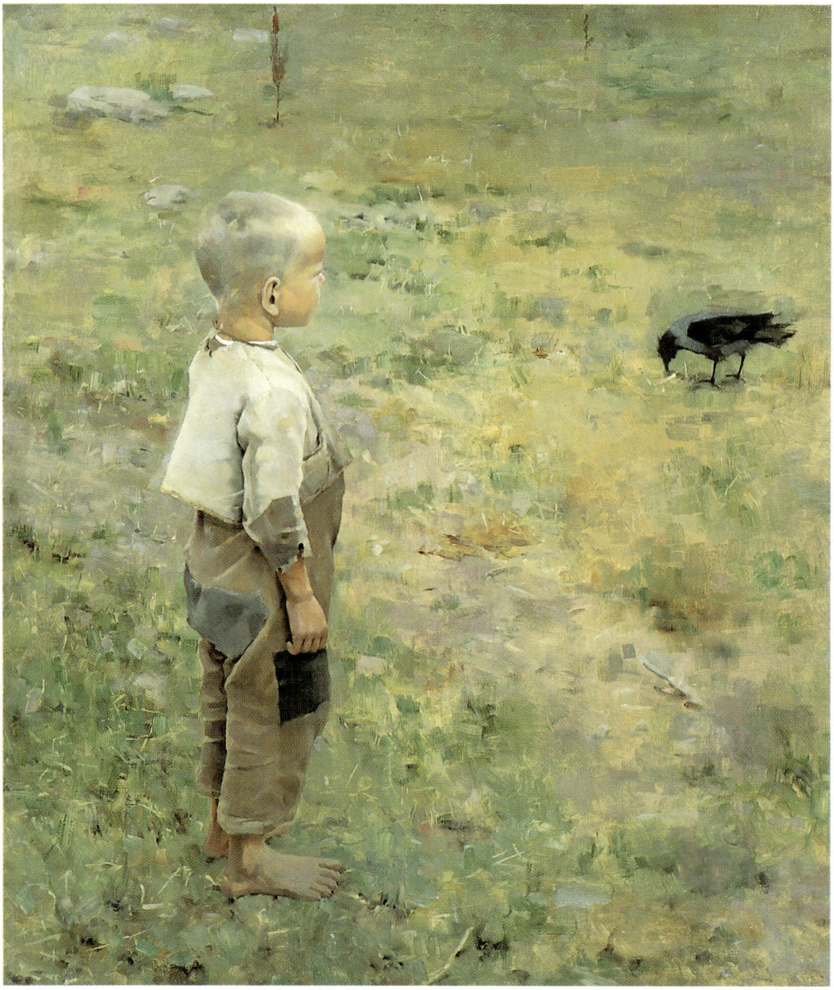

was accepted at the Salon, to Schjerfbeck's great joy, under the title "Fête juive."

Schjerfbeck's finest work done in the latter half of the 1880s included the little painting "Boys on the Shore at St. Ives" (1887). Its light and dizzying perspective bear the mark of the master. "The Bakery" (1887) has an even more exciting treatment of space since it contains a contradictory perspective. The bar of the bread balance creates the impression that the bag intended for bread is turned farther away than the scale. The location of the bag and the scale in relation to the table nonetheless forces the viewer to see it differently: the bag is thrust into the foreground. An illusion makes it seem as if the viewer himself were moving, as he must constantly choose between two different perspectives.

Schjerfbeck returned to the bakery as a motive in the 1900s in what were called "repeats," paintings for which she used her early work as a basis.

Helena Westermarck and Schjerfbeck were good friends, as witnessed by Schjerfbeck's revealing profile of Westermarck (1884). During their years in Paris, their views of art were similar, but Westermarck's development as an artist was combined with increasingly professional literary interests. She did, however, manage to get her share of attacks from Finland's idealistic art critics.

Westermarck's best-known painting, "The Laundresses" (or "An Important Question") from 1884 was criticized, though not unanimously, for being ugly and demagogic. Is it a coincidence or intentional irony that the two girls' discussion about love is witnessed by a print of Jesus hanging in the upper right hand corner of the picture.

"The Laundresses" was awarded an honorable mention at the Universal Exposition in Paris in 1889. Laundresses had been a popular motive for quite some time. They pricked the viewer's social conscience, but also expressed the eroticism that the bourgeoisie projected onto the "lower classes."

The Kullervo of painting

The way in which details were blown up on canvas changed in the 1880s. The esthetic of the terse close-up, incompleteness, and fragmentation finally reached Finland mostly thanks to Schjerfbeck. But the new arrival, Axel Gallén (1865–1931), also showed what the modern technique could do.

Gallén's "Boy with a Crow" (1884) has often been admired for its oblique angle, and its lack of a horizon. The painting concentrates on its subject, the meeting between the ragged boy and the crow. It has none of the saccharine sweetness of genre pictures, and it is completely lacking in didactic content, both factors that usually discomfited its beholders.

The use of space in "Boy with a Crow" was unusual enough for one of Gallén's teachers, William Bougeureau, a skilled proponent of academic kitsch, to shake his head and criticize it for being too "steep." Perhaps he was evaluating the

Axel Gallén:
Demasquée. 1888.
Oil, 65 x 55 cm. Antell Collection,
ART MUSEUM OF THE ATENEUM.

Albert Edelfelt:
Boys Playing on the Shore. 1884.
Oil, 89 x 106.5 cm.
ART MUSEUM OF THE ATENEUM.

painting's perspective from a technical point of view. The steeply rising background is, however, the painting's most important characteristic. The background is not a composed landscape; it is an almost abstract field on which three elements are placed: the boy, the crow, and the sorrel.

Gallén did not manage to get into the École des Beaux-Arts, so he began to study at the Académie Julian. He later moved to the studio of Fernand Cormon, who specialized in prehistorical subjects. Gallén does not seem to have been overly impressed with the teaching of Bouguereau and Tony Robert-Fleury.

Gallén's work was marked by an unpolished and macabre touch from the very beginning. He painted "The Dead Calf" (1883) as neutrally as if he had been studying a coat lying on the ground. When he painted "Decaying Fish" (1884), on the other hand, he spoke of the "divine beauty" of the dead fish and painted it with passionate, rapid brush strokes. He captured lone boats pulled up on the beach just as enthusiastically. They do not point directly to the theme of death, but later boats were to glide over the mythical waters of Gallén's creations, in the battlegrounds of the *Kalevala*, on the river of the Finnish Hades, Tuonela, or symbolize the artist's solitude.

Delacroix wrote in 1857 as he pondered over Géricault's painting "Severed Limbs," "The painting does not always need a motive." Delacroix's prophesy did not come completely true even on the easels of the Realists and Naturalists, since the more clearly artists distanced themselves from customary thematic patterns, the closer they came to individual symbolism. As he painted "The Trout" (1871) struggling on a line, Courbet did not believe that his message had been understood, so he wrote at the bottom of the painting, "G. Courbet. In vinculis faciebat." (Courbet painted it, in Ornans, after he had served a sentence for taking part in the Paris Commune.)

Gallén felt no compulsion to explain his choice of motive, but a romantic undertone began to appear in his art as early as the end of the 1880s. Depictions of the people that strove for truth were put to good use in the new kinds of illustrations for the *Kalevala*, and the threat of physical death was soon replaced by a spiritistic and Symbolist worship of death.

The art historian Salme Sarajas-Korte noted that in his first years in Paris, Gallén's art was influenced not only by Bastien-Lepage, but at least equally much by the supporters of atheism and natural science, by Gallén's Norwegian roommate Adam Dörnberger, and above all by the writer August Strindberg. At the time he worshipped man's free natural state, as extolled by Rousseau.

Gallén explained that he began painting "The Old Woman and the Cat" (1885) as he was trying to capture the windy atmosphere in the open land in southwestern Finland. His gaze fell on an old woman, who seemed to suit the landscape, and he intended to use the figure as staffage for his painting. The old woman in fact became the actual subject of the work.

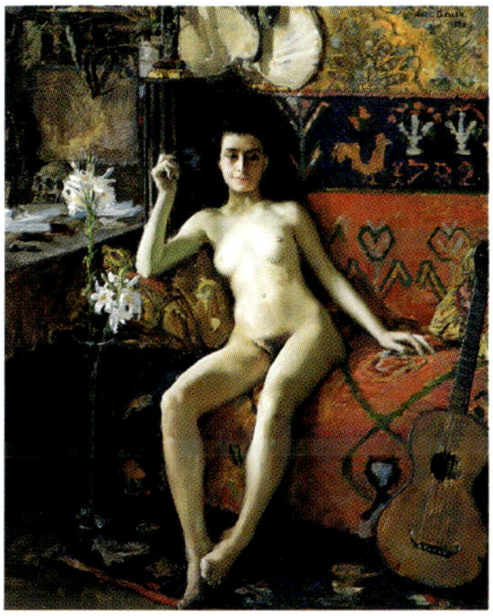

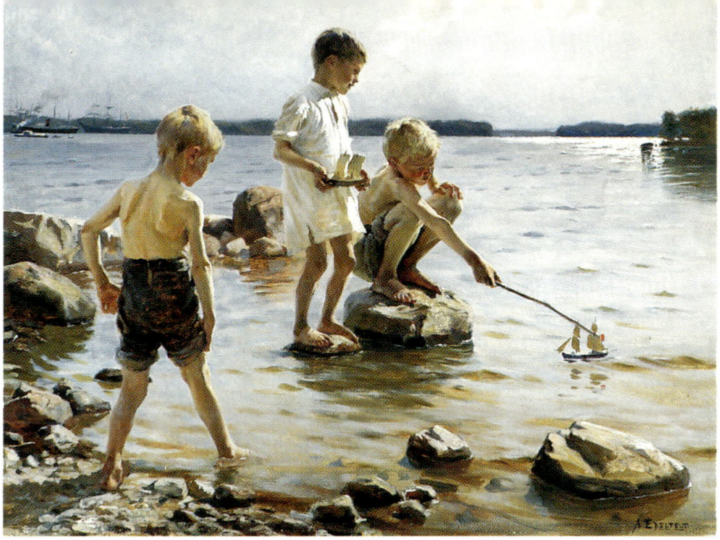

"I have tried to paint the way I feel and see, without any reminiscences," Gallén wrote to Edelfelt, adding that he had not used the same affected style here as in "Boy with a Crow."

Gallén painted the old woman in a sketch-like and straightforward style, but the painting was given a fairly good reception in Finland. Churberg called Gallén a natural talent, as fierce as little Kullervo breaking out of his swaddling clothes. Edelfelt was so enthusiastic about Gallén's painting that he wanted to go off with his young colleague on a painting trip to Kainuu, in the north. But an invitation took Gallén to Mänttä to paint G. A. Serlachius, the pioneer of Finland's paper industry, and to Korpilahti to look for Finnish prototypes. He found Finnish "racial features" that he no longer depicted as sharply as he had in "The Old Woman and the Cat."

Gallén had briskly rejected Impressionism in his youthful self-assurance, but at the end of the 1880s, he painted a number of worldly, Impressionistic Parisian views. The most delectable is "After the Masked Ball" (1888).

Gallén had to eat his words when it came to Symbolism, too. The Dane Georg Brandes's lectures spread the ideology of Nietzsche throughout Scandinavia at the end of the 1880s, and it quickly reached artist circles. Many had recognized themselves in the bohemians of the Norwegian Hans Jæger's novel about Oslo, but now their self-portraits had to be given the features of a superman. Gallén was one of them.

Gallén's road to Symbolism did not just travel along literary paths. It also required a great deal of work, "Démasquée" (1888), an epitome of bohemian life, and especially Gallén's major endeavor, the "Aino Myth" triptych on a theme from the *Kalevala*.

Gallén painted "Démasquée," a nude model smoking a cigaret during a break, in Paris. The work had been commissioned by H. F. Antell, but it became a kind of preliminary exercise in Symbolism. The painting is filled with metaphorical props: the white lilies of innocence; the skull reminiscent of death; and the guitar, a metaphor for the nude body. Gallén's biographer, Onni Okkonen, saw a characterization of the times in "Démasquée": "...a being that carries the fashionable stamp of a culture, a body like the flow of an electric current, the tiredly playful, nervously radiant *fin de siècle* gaze."

The search for atmosphere

Finnish artists often confused Impressionism with *plein-air* painting, but as they made more trips to Paris and more of their own personal observations, Impressionism gained a fairly strong foothold in Finnish art in the latter half of the 1880s.

The opponents of Impressionism did not always represent Düsseldorf ideals. An enraged Gallén declared in 1884 after he had seen Impressionist paintings that "each of them is a bloody, dastardly deed." Edelfelt, in contrast, was more open to every innovation. From the

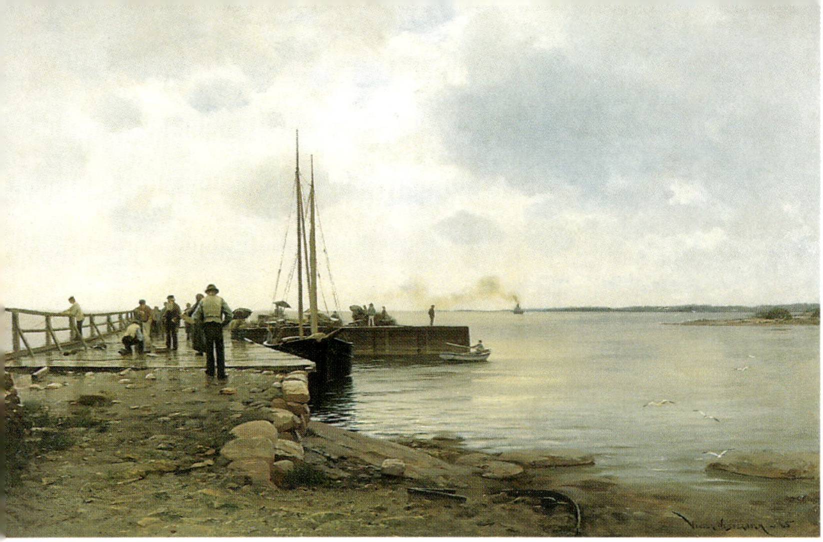

Victor Westerholm: Mail Jetty at Eckerö. 1885, oil, 99.5 x 145.5 cm.
HÄMEENLINNA ART MUSEUM.

Victor Westerholm: Paris Seen from Mont Valerien. 1890. Oil, 32.5 x 40.5 cm.
HELSINGIN KAUPUNGIN TAIDEMUSEO (HELSINKI CITY ART MUSEUM).

Elin Danielson-Gambogi: Mother. 1893. Oil, 95 x 57 cm.
ART MUSEUM OF THE ATENEUM.

beginning he took part in the exhibitions of the Galérie Georges Petit, and in 1887, he was on the Salon's jury together with Monet.

One of the most magnificent achievements of Edelfelt's *plein-air* Realism is "Boys Playing on the Shore," completed in 1884, but at the end of the decade, he partly gave up his attachment to values and painted a number of sun-drenched, Impressionistic landscapes in both Paris and Helsinki.

Victor Westerholm (1860–1919), who depicted the Åland archipelago, gradually progressed towards a rapid, sketch-like brush technique and a fresh use of color. After liberating himself from Realism's demands for a smoothly finished surface, he continued his Impressionistic approach far into the 1890s in the midst of new trends that had risen to counter "Positivism." Westerholm did not have an easy time of it, since he was one of the last Finns to study in Düsseldorf, along with Torsten Wasastjerna (1863–1924).

The key work of Westerholm's German period, "Cows in a Birch Forest" (188), is reminiscent of *plein-air* Realism, but only reminiscent: the sketches had been made in Finland, and the painting itself was made in the old way in a studio, improving the composition and refining details.

"Cows in a Birch Forest" followed generally accepted norms, but it precipitated a crisis for its creator. Westerholm felt that he had to tear himself away from what he had learned in Düsseldorf and become a true *plein-air* painter. Westerholm believed it would be easier to implement the decision if he could gather together a group of artists. And so in 1886, he suggested to his friends Frederik (1839–1901) and Nina (1855–1929) Ahlstedt, and through them to a few other artists, that they spend the summer in Åland, in the village of Önningeby, where the Westerholm family owned a summer place around which the artists could establish their colony.

In addition to the Ahlstedts, Westerholm's invitation was accepted by Hanna Rönnberg (1862–1946), Elin Danielson-Gambogi (1861–1919), and Alexander Federley (1864–1932). During the summer, the colony received an unexpected reinforcement with the arrival of the Swedish painter Axel Andersson, "J. A. G. Acke."

The Önningeby colony resembled the one founded in the 1870s by Danish artists at Skagen, but its model was taken from France.

Danielson and the Westerholms spent both the summer and the winter in Åland. Information about the painters' work spread far and wide since newspapers followed events in the colony with interest. The following summer, the colony was joined by Eva Topelius (1855–1929), daughter of Zachris Topelius, and the Swedish painter Edvard Westman.

We might imagine that Westerholm's first Impressionist paintings were born in the glitter of Åland's marine light, but the beauty of the archipelago was not enough: he needed experiences from Paris. Westerholm used them to execute his large painting "The Birch Grove"

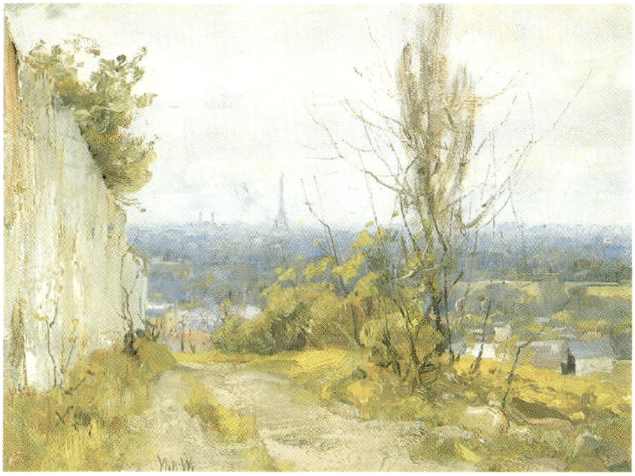

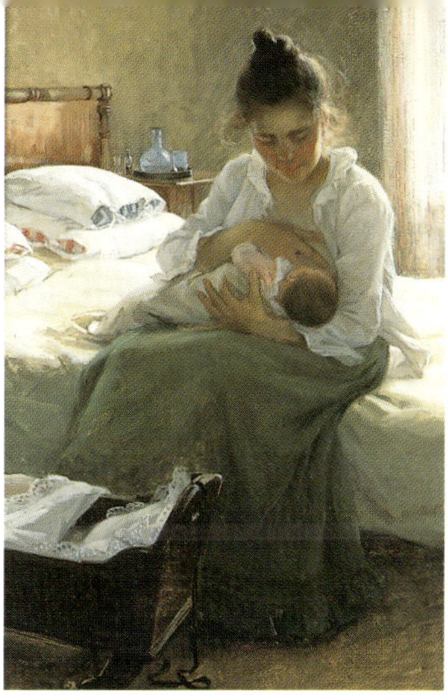

(1888) and the Monet-like "The Seine, Paris" (1888). In the ensuing years, he used liberated brush strokes to paint Parisian views, especially outside the city, in Suresnes. The artist's Impressionist period culminated with the winter scenes painted in Hanko in 1893.

Elin Danielson's style approached Impressionism but soon returned to Realism. "Digging Potatoes" (1893) was painted with firm brush strokes, showing her characteristic style, while "Mother," painted the same year, shows the delicate and plastically successful side of the artist's idiom.

Danielson was considered to have great promise, but her work is not known well enough for us to confirm or reject the comparison to Gallén that was made at the time.

The end of the Arts Society's power

Young artists had criticized the Arts Society's autocratic behavior for quite some time. The Society's exhibition policy did not satisfy the Realists, whose work constantly suffered from being hung in out-of-the-way places.

The Arts Society's power began to diminish rapidly after artists arranged their own exhibition for the first time in 1891. The Society's authority had already suffered a blow in 1880 with the implementation of copyright legislation. Artists refused to sell their work to the Society unless it relinquished its right to copy them. The artists took their direct model for their strike from the Norwegian artists' protest against the purchasing policy of their own arts society.

The Artists' Association of Finland originally gathered together the representatives of all the arts, including architects, writers, and actors. The Association was founded in 1864, and its liberal outlook was shown by its acceptance of women as members beginning in 1866.

The artists' own first exhibition raised spirits to a new high. O. E. Tudeer wrote in the magazine *Valvoja* that "artists have broken down the old, confined system represented here by the Arts Society, as it is elsewhere by academies of fine art."

The Arts Society still operated over a broad spectrum even though it no longer held exhibitions. The Society took care of its collection and school, and its importance as a purchaser of art did not decrease significantly.

The strife between the two associations was in essence due to profoundly different concepts of art and not organizational policy. The veteran of the Arts Society, C. G. Estlander, gave vent to his feelings: "Since the Impressionists now want to thrust our greatly esteemed artists behind the scenes, then the Impressionists also deserve for the goddess of revenge to send from Paris tomorrow a flock of Symbolists who in turn will show them and their work the door!"

His wish very nearly came true.

The dream of a Renaissance in the north

Axel Gallén:
The Aino Myth. 1891.
Oil, center panel 153 x 153 cm,
wings 153 x 77 cm.
ART MUSEUM OF THE ATENEUM.

Myths and their bards

At the end of the 1870s, Edelfelt had dreamed of painting the *Kalevala* myth of Aino. But it proved only a dream, one whose fulfillment remained uncertain even when Gallén tackled the subject.

The Student Union for Savokarelia tried to arouse interest in *Kalevala* subjects by arranging a competition to illustrate the epic. The results were hopeless, but the entries for the new competition in 1890 were anticipated with greater optimism. Even the newspapers wrote that Gallén had gone off with his young bride on their honeymoon to the land of the *Kalevala* in the north. The Swedish painter Count Louis Sparre went along – perhaps a bit *de trop*. They were to find the authentic lands and people of the Finnish epic.

The writer and critic Kasimir Leino explained in a newspaper article that nothing attracts so much attention in Paris as a work of art that presents new regions, new faces, new people, and new atmosphere. To back up his words, Leino quoted a French painter as saying that regeneration in art will come from the north. "And why?" Leino asked himself, and answered, "Because this is where there is a freshness of new subjects, this is where we find the humus without which all farming remains artificial and growth withers."

Gallén had been dissatisfied with his "Aino Myth," painted in Paris in 1889, and with the triptych's heavy decorative frame. The professional models made the painting seem un-Finnish and Salon-like. In the spirit of the day, the artist's mother contributed to the discussion by writing from Finland that her medium prophesied great success for the painting if only Aino were made into the Juno of Finnish art.

The Senate commissioned a replica of the triptych, but sparing no efforts, Gallén began to develop it into a completely new painting, more believable, more intense. The problems posed by the painting were gradually resolved in the midst of the wilderness.

In Lentiira, at a forest cottage, Gallén met an old farmer, Uljaska, who was perfectly suited to the figure of Väinämöinen. The daughter of the group's guide served as the model for Aino. Gallén's wife Mary also began to pose patiently as a model for the maiden. The Finnish landscape and national prototypes finally began to take shape.

The results of the illustration competition were published before the new version of the Aino triptych had been completed. Gallén won the competition with drawings, something that hardly satisfied the old-fashioned decision-makers, such as T. Rein, rector of Helsinki University. He had demanded that the illustrators of the epic bring out the "dreamily magical shamanistic feature" of the *Kalevala*. The younger generation took a different view. The writer Juhani Aho wanted the *Kalevala* illustrations to be authentic, reaching back to its deepest roots.

It has often been felt that Gallén was interested in the myth of Aino for personal rea-

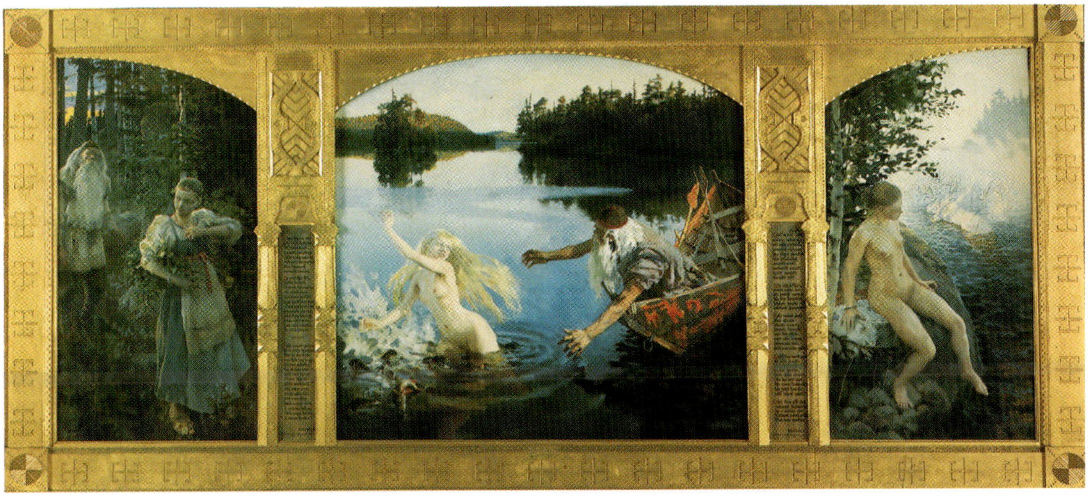

sons. Perhaps he saw his own rivals in old Väinämöinen trying to win young Aino. At least the young man's imagination had been constantly preoccupied with Mary Slöör before her father consented to her making what he considered an uncertain marriage.

The Finns experienced the Aino triptych as a revelation, but when Gallén presented the large canvas in Paris in 1892, even the young Finnish artists examined it with admiration, but little real interest. They had gotten a taste for Symbolism, and old-fashioned Realism bored them. Gallén gave vent to his disappointment in a characteristic way. He wrote off Symbolism and all French art in one fell swoop: "The fruit will never ripen; it rotted green."

Kalevala fever climaxed that same year. Louis Sparre and the sculptor Emil Wikström (1864–1942) left for Russian Karelia in the summer and met Gallén, who was painting in Paanajärvi. Juhani Aho and the painter Eero Järnefelt (1863–1937) also traveled to find the roots of the *Kalevala*. Jean Sibelius left with his bride Aino, née Järnefelt, for northern Karelia, and the young painter Pekka Halonen (1865–1933) went off to the shores of Lake Ladoga.

This romantic search for the *Kalevala* fulfilled the universal dream of the 19th century to find the original way of life to replace what they considered a degenerate culture. Finland was no Tahiti, but it was possible to view Karelia as a kind of parallel to Brittany. On the other hand, Karelianism (the term was coined by the cultural historian Yrjö Hirn in the 1930s) was linked with Finland's domestic and international situation.

The radical wing of the Fennomen, the Young Finns, considered it more important to be moderate when it came to the question of language than it did in bowing to decisions that weakened Finland's autonomy. The Young Finns founded their official newspaper, *Päivälehti*, in 1889 and established a formal party in 1894. Their program also included improving the position of tenant farmers and the proletariat, and expanding suffrage.

People began to speak more openly about a Finnish state, even though this meant embodying Finland's special rights in a constitution and not complete independence. Finland's historical background was studied in greater depth and art, on a parallel with science, was considered a weapon for fighting oppression.

Russia's Slavophiles had long demanded that the country be incorporated into the empire and that Finland's privileges, such as customs barriers, be revoked, but Alexander III did not take concrete steps until 1890, issuing the "Postal Manifesto" that placed the Finnish post office under the supervision of Russian authorities.

This administrative change did not mean much in practice, but Finland's ruling circles and intelligensia openly opposed a symbolic gesture that presaged worse to come. Karelianism's political motivation was consequently strong, and Gallén in particular consciously incorporated tendentiousness into his work. According to Reitala, the magnificent hilly landscape of

Gallén's "The Great Black Woodpecker" (1893) became one of the symbols of the Fin nish nationalist movement.

One of the romantic phenomena of Karelianism was the construction of impressive wilderness studios. Gallén actually competed with Wikström to achieve the truest wilderness spirit. Wikström's studio "castle" in Visavuori was completed in 1894, but Gallén wanted to go farther into the backwoods, and his studio, Kalela, in Ruovesi was ready the following summer. The style of these "castles" influenced the National Romantic Art Nouveau architecture of the turn of the century.

Another major project of the day was the book compiled at the instigation of Leo Mechelin, *Suomi 19:lla vuosisadalla* (Finland in the 19th Century). The country's best artists illustrated this magnificent volume, completed in 1893.

The search for a national identity

Edelfelt met the Swedish painter Anders Zorn in the latter half of the 1880s. Edelfelt's open admiration for Zorn's skill as a painter certainly strengthened their mutual attraction. Edelfelt was amazed by his friend's ability to capture the force of the moment, and claimed that no one in the world had ever painted water better than Zorn.

Depicting water especially fascinated Edelfelt. The still surface of a lake reflects the sun's nuances of color in what was perhaps his best landscape painting, "Kaukola Ridge at Sunset" (1889). The ever-changing play of the water's surface was a central focal point in numerous harbor scenes painted by Edelfelt. They culminated in a painting commissioned by Alexander III, "At the Copenhagen Roadstead" (1890). Edelfelt made a second version of the painting as well.

Water was given a seemingly unnoticed role to play in one of Edelfelt's most significant achievements, "Christ and the Magdalen" (1890). Haikko bay, with its spring birches, formed a Finnish background for the figures in the foreground. Edelfelt had chosen the subject for the painting from the *Kanteletar* epic.

Mataleena (also the Finnish name for Mary Magdalene), the daughter of a rich farmer, meets her father's shepherd as she goes to fetch water. She haughtily refuses to give the shepherd water, but the roles are reversed when the lowly man tells Mataleena her most innermost secrets. "You must be the Lord Jesus himself, when you can reveal my evil deeds," Mataleena exclaims.

Edelfelt knew of Fritz von Uhde's efforts to modernize the visualization of the New Testament and depict "everyday religion." Edelfelt, however, wanted to find something both more universal and national from among the themes of the Bible.

Rune-singing was very common in Karelia in the 19th

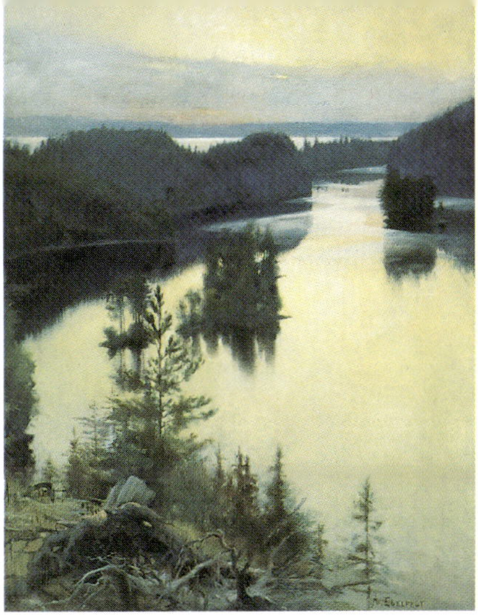

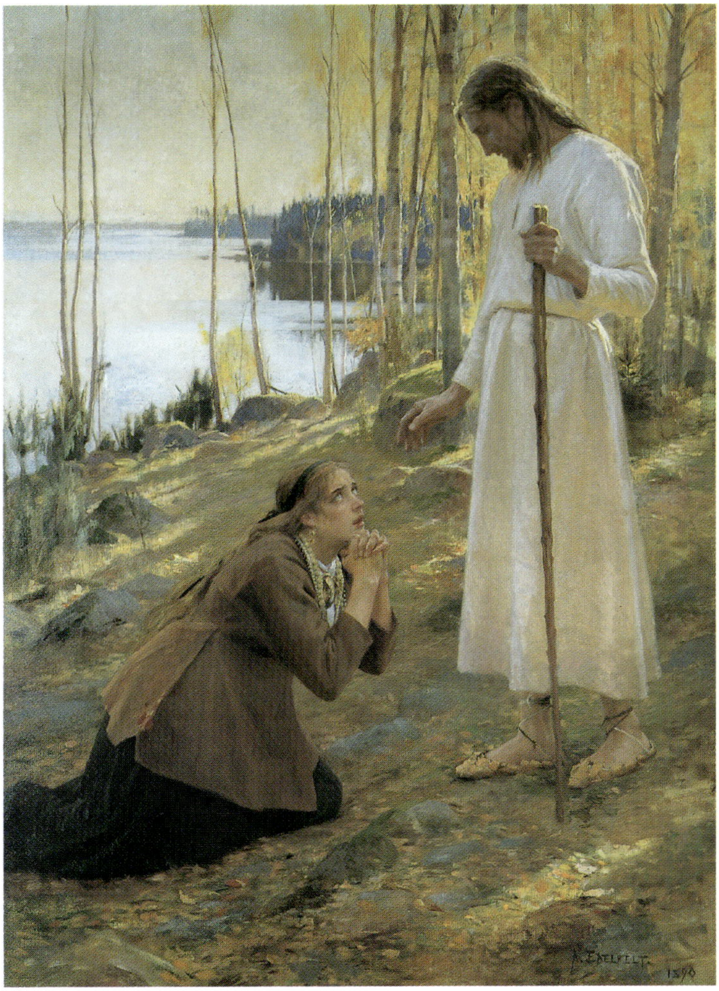

Albert Edelfelt:
Kaukola Ridge at Sunset. 1889–1890.
Oil, 116 x 83 cm.
ART MUSEUM OF THE ATENEUM.

Albert Edelfelt:
Christ and the Magdalen. 1890.
Oil, 221 x 154 cm.
ART MUSEUM OF THE ATENEUM.

Eero Järnefelt:
Burning the Forest Clearing
(The Wage Slaves). 1893.
Oil, 131 x 167.5 cm.
ART MUSEUM OF THE ATENEUM.

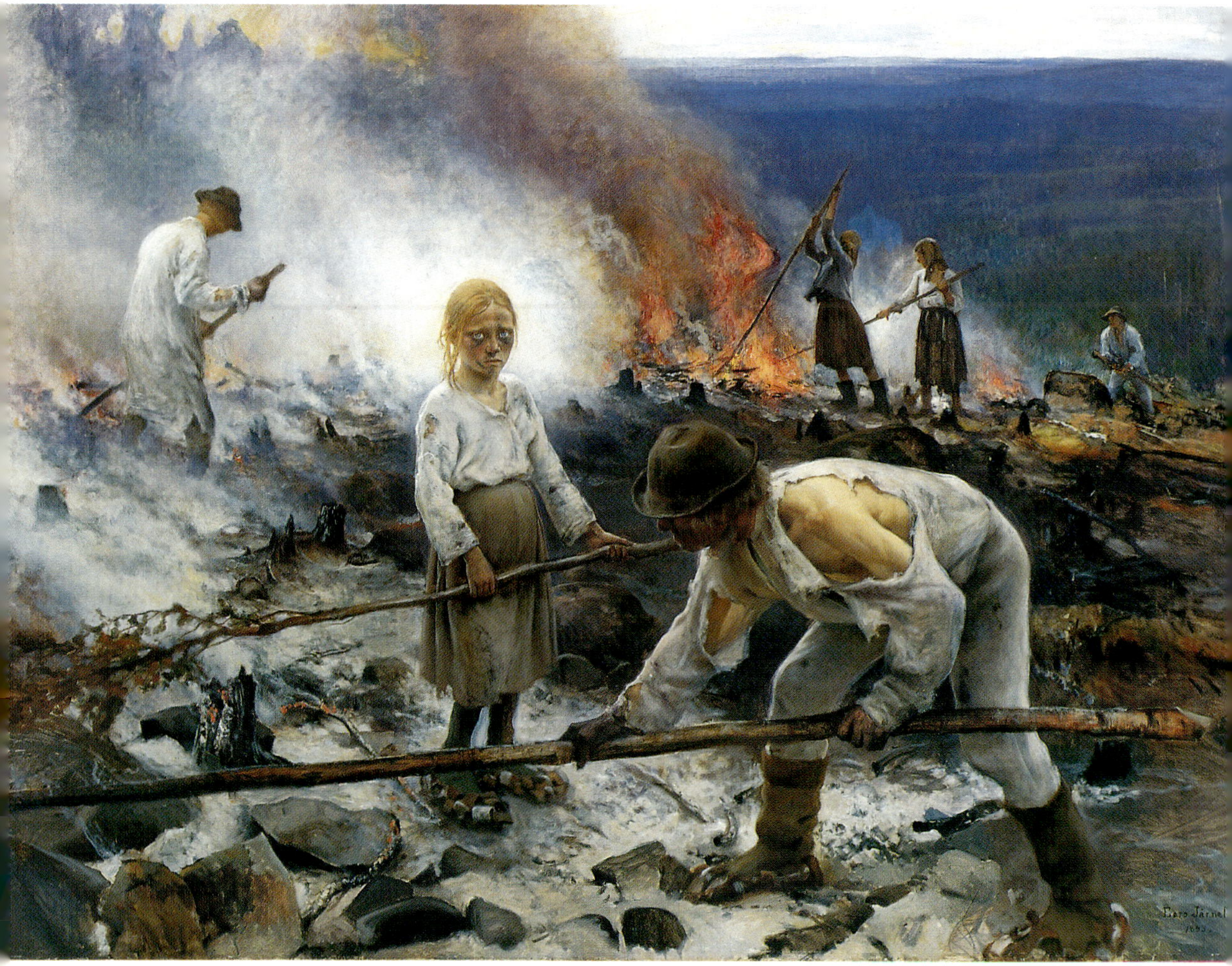

century, and the most skillful singers, such as Larin Paraske, were enticed to perform their songs for both folklorists and the public at large. Edelfelt met Paraske and painted not one but three portraits of her. Paraske is said to have fallen in love with the genteel artist.

After the the proclamation of the "Postal Manifesto," Edelfelt and innumerable other Finns felt less inclined to be loyal to their grand duke, the czar. Since Edelfelt had painted several portraits of the imperial family, demonstrably patriotic paintings such as "Finnish Soldiers in the War of 1808–1809" (1892) showed that he had made a clear emotional break with the highest authorities.

Slaves or the masters of their own destiny

Eero Järnefelt attended the art academy in St. Petersburg between 1883 and 1886, but no noticeable traces of Russian Realism can be found in his work. They were eradicated at the Académie Julian and especially under the influence of Bastien-Lepage.

In the early 1890s, Järnefelt developed into a noteworthy landscape painter and depictor of the people. His first major success was "Day in July" (1891).

Järnefelt wanted to portray life as it really was, declaring that he was unable to love anything "made up." The artist's description of himself and his work was accurate enough, but the impression it creates must be filled out a bit.

In his little paintings, Järnefelt isolated details from nature and treated the background in such a way that details grew into a monumental element. Adapting reality played an even greater role in his painting "Burning the Forest Clearing" (1893), Järnefelt's most famous depiction of the people.

The painting's original name was "The Wage Slaves," but its social connotations were too radical for the public at large, and a more neutral title was chosen. Järnefelt immortalized the slash and burn process at a time when the benefits and drawbacks of this outdated agricultural method were being debated publicly. In addition, the poor harvests of 1892–1893 made the painting disconsolately current. But instead of creating a social battle hymn to the "slaves," Järnefelt painted an idealized picture of a hardworking nation.

Järnefelt was well versed in Tolstoy's theories, thanks to his brother Arvid, a writer.

No wonder "Burning the Forest Clearing" has often been interpreted as a Tolstoyan expression of sympathy for the common people. The artist's own views, however, provide quite a different picture of the painting's ideological content.

The aristocratic Järnefelt did not try to understand the common people on their own level. He respected the drudgery of the peasant as he respected nature. It had the same status as an animal or a landscape. It could be sanctified if the beauty of the sight were great enough.

Pekka Halonen:
The Harvesters. 1891.
Oil, 91 x 64 cm.
PRIVATE COLLECTION.

Magnus Enckell:
The Awakening. 1894.
Oil, 113 x 86 cm.
Antell Collection,
ART MUSEUM OF THE ATENEUM.

Magnus Enckell:
Boy Reclining. 1892.
Charcoal and watercolor,
54 x 57 cm.
ART MUSEUM OF THE ATENEUM.

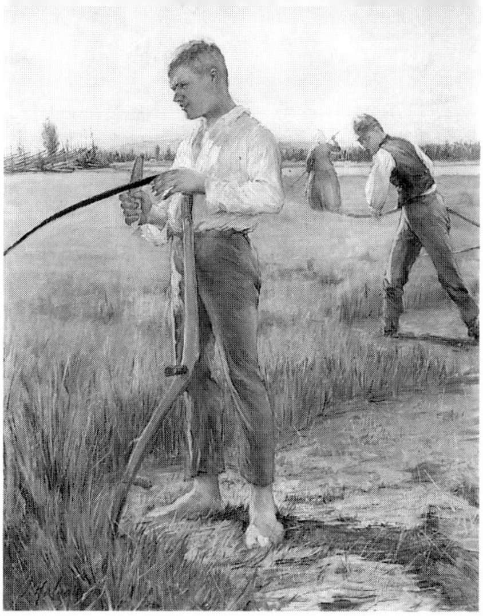

Järnefelt considered one of Realism's greatest achievements its efforts to capture man's "animality," man's insignificance, and the poverty of his emotional life.

Järnefelt followed the course of the work, making sketches. He also took photographs, with the one of the girl holding the trunk of a young birch facilitating the composition of the final painting. The artist distinguished the girl from the other figures by posing her, as he would in a photograph, having her looking straight at the beholder, and by painting a halo of smoke around the girl's head. Holy poverty, holy drudgery: Darwinism and Romanticism intertwined.

The little girl, smudged with soot, is a new kind of version of the century's innumerable portrayals of children that appealed to the public sympathy. The picture's paternalistic goals become clear if we imagine a determined adult looking out at us instead of the child.

Järnefelt painted a satirical gouache in 1893, "The Master and the Farmhands." Its simplified and boldly outlined approach presaged the artist's move towards a more synthetic style. His trip to Italy in 1894 solidified the change. The early Renaissance and "Puvinism" became Järnefelt's ideals. A few of Järnefelt's pieces from his Italian period, such as "Children Playing" (1895), bear witness to a furtive interest in Symbolism.

During his years in Paris, Järnefelt painted a little atmospheric gouache of his fellow student Pekka Halonen playing the kantele (1891). The painting is appropriately enough called "Homesick." Pekka Halonen, who sincerely missed Finland, made his debut by showing his most important work done during his student years: "Harvesters" (1891). It depicted farmers working energetically in the fields, not "wage slaves" but independent, self-respecting farmers. The change in emphasis is socially significant. The people were no longer treated as objects to be examined; they were social subjects, the masters of their own destiny. Halonen came from the countryside himself and knew what he was painting.

Puvis de Chavannes won Halonen's admiration, even though he otherwise criticized the state of French art in no uncertain terms. After coming back to Paris in 1893, Halonen and Väinö Blomstedt (1871–1947) became students of Gauguin, who had returned from Tahiti. The experience meant everything to Blomstedt, and Halonen made no effort to conceal his satisfaction, either. He considered Gauguin a good teacher and felt that his broadmindedness was an advantage: "He knows about conditions everywhere. Is not one-sided as other Frenchmen usually are."

Gauguin's teaching strengthened Halonen's compositional skills and his desire for simplicity. Otherwise Gauguin's influence remained minimal.

Symbolism

Edelfelt used the handsome young art student Magnus Enckell (1870–1925) as the model for Christ in his painting "Christ and the Magdalen." The painting diverted the flow of Realism

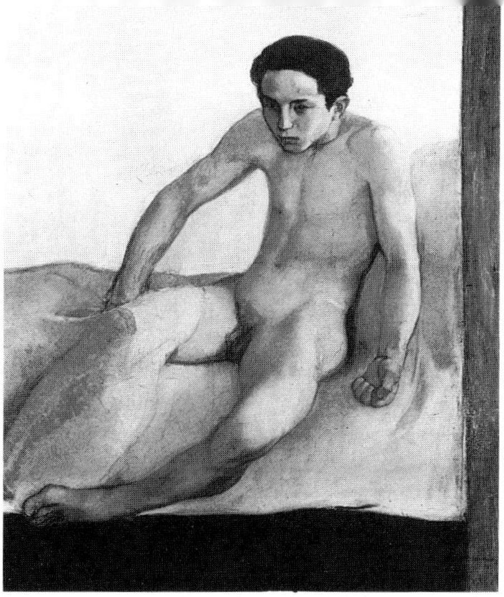

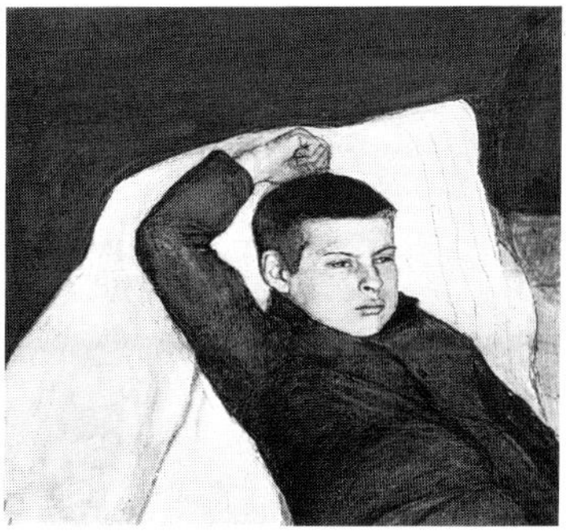

in a more Romantic direction, but its model, Enckell, made an even greater turnabout by adopting Symbolism.

Enckell received his basic training in the French style under Gunnar Berndtson. After arriving in Paris in 1891, Enckell registered at the Académie Julian, as did Ellen Thesleff (1869–1954) and Beda Stjernschantz (1867–1910). The old-fashioned teaching did not especially inspire Enckell, but the academy's students proved all the more important to the whole Finnish trio.

The assistant at the academy was Paul Sérusier, who helped open the new arrivals' eyes to new trends. The Synthetist colorism of the Nabis, the Rosicrucian mysticism of Joséphin Péladan, and Platonism were hot topics of debate.

By the following autumn, Enckell had matured into a Symbolist. He did his first work in the new style in charcoal and watercolors. The influence of Carrière was evident. Väinö Blomstedt noted that Enckell had told him back in 1891, "Nature has no colors."

In Finland, Enckell's drawings were thought to be sketches, and it took quite some time before they were recognized as major creations of Finnish Symbolism. They portrayed nude boys and youths in anonymous, simplified surroundings. There were hardly any explanatory attributes. One of the boys is shown playing with a skull, but *Vanitas* motives never became an actual theme in Enckell's work.

The myth of the androgyne lurking in the background of these pictures was one of the most popular themes in the "decadent" period at the end of the 19th century. According to Plato, the androgyne represented man's perfect ideal. Péladan believed that the model for the "third sex" could be found in boys approaching puberty. Artists sought an age at which the male and female characteristics were in balance and neutralized one another.

To Enckell, androgyny did not just mean a dream of perfection and discovering an esthetic philosophy of life; it also had homoerotic undertones. The artist wrote a poem about Antinous, the pet of the Emperor Hadrian, who committed suicide in order to give the old ruler his vitality. Enckell addressed his words to Antinous:

"I, too, am your kin
and I swear you my oath:
By your memory -
mystical, mysterious, eternal,
exalted, despised, holy -
by all that you dreamed of,
of beauty, of life,
of unity,
of love, of sacrifice, of perfection…"

The synthesis of Enckell's portrayals of boys is "The Awakening" (1893). A great deal of symbolic significance has been read into the figure of this boy at puberty, but it can be seen in the light of both idealism and psychology. The youth is awakening to a knowledge of the mystical truths of beauty and love, but at the same time he experiences the melancholy of puberty, the anguish brought by awakening sexuality.

The esthetic of Symbolism emphasized the search for reality hidden behind external

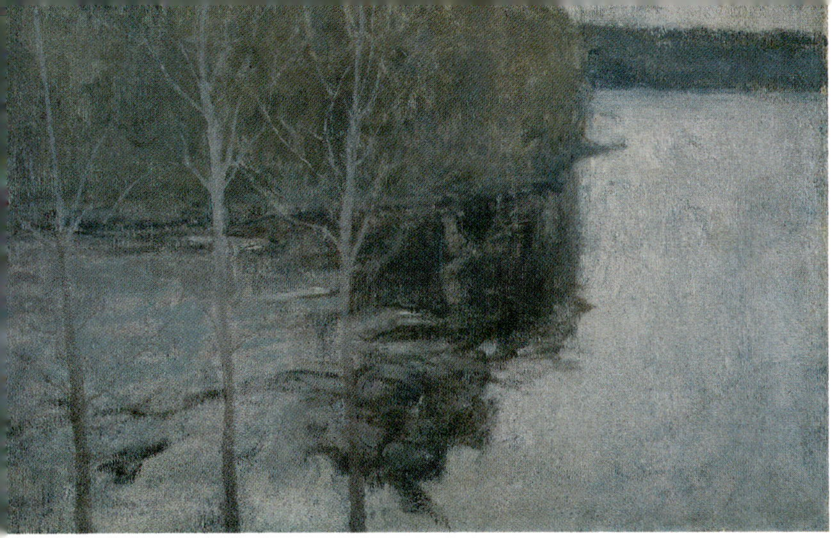

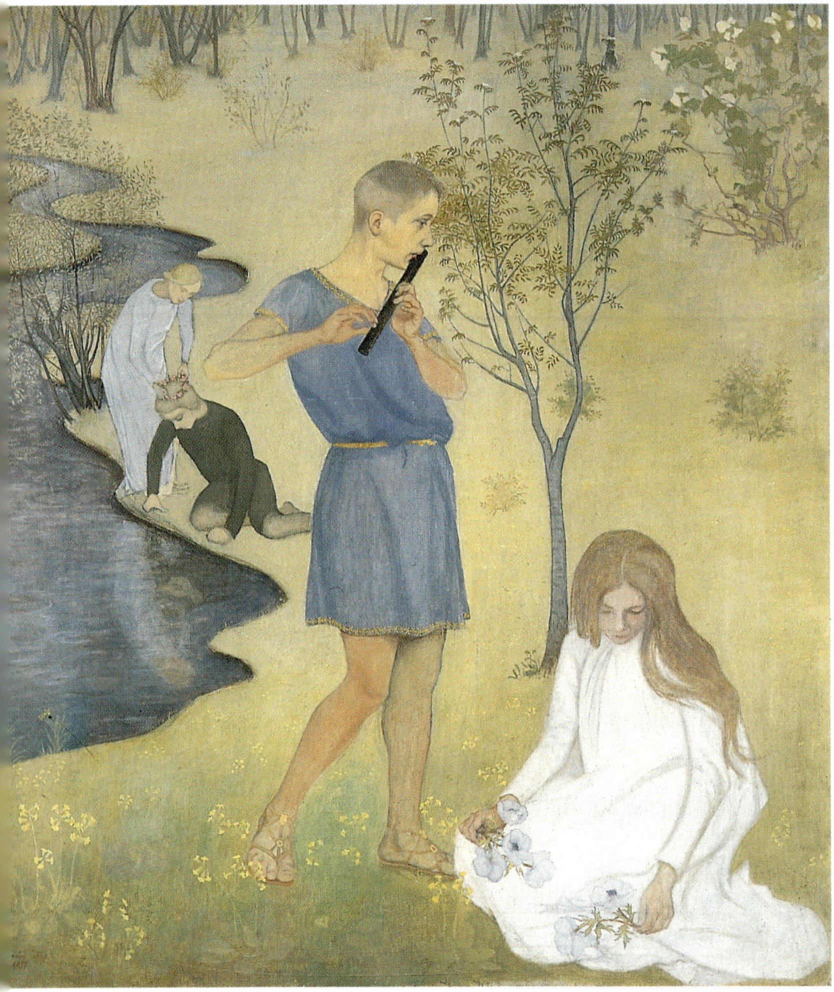

Magnus Enckell:
Fantasy. 1895.
Watercolor, 47 x 44 cm.
ART MUSEUM OF THE ATENEUM.

Ellen Thesleff:
Thyra Elisabeth. 1892.
Oil, 42 x 24 cm.
Bäcksbacka Collection.
Helsingin Kaupungin Taidemuseo
(HELSINKI CITY ART MUSEUM).

Ellen Thesleff:
Landscape, Spring Night. 1894.
Oil, 38 x 46.5 cm.
ART MUSEUM OF THE ATENEUM.

Beda Stjernschantz:
Pastoral (Primavera). 1897.
Oil, 83 x 101 cm.
K.H. RENLUND ART MUSEUM, KOKKOLA.

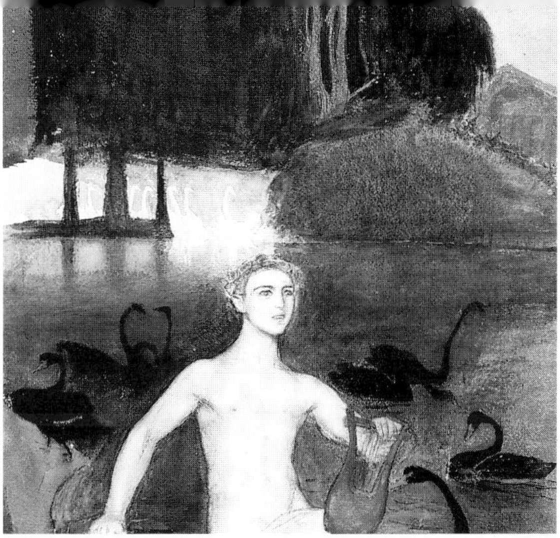

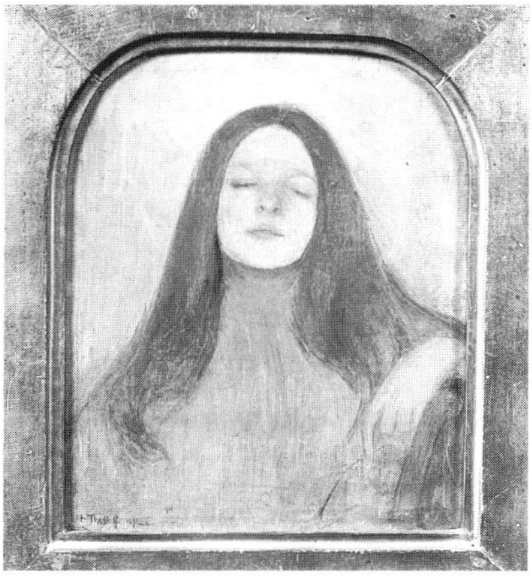

manifestations. Enckell's goal was to find the most sublime concept, God. The artist described his goal as a journey to the farthest room whose walls collapse, letting "our eyes see everything."

Enckell sought a glimpse of the eternal as he painted "Making Nets" (1894). The model for its stiff figure was one of the pearls of the Louvre's Egyptian collection, the sculpture of the "the bureaucrat of eternity," "Seated Scribe" from Sakkara. The moment of enlightenment is probably also depicted in "Fantasies" (1895), painted in Italy. In the version in the collection of the Art Museum of the Ateneum, the youth holding Apollo's golden lyre gazes into the distance. Behind him swim black and white swans, and in the background rises the tympanum of a Greek temple.

The swans were part of the myth of Apollo from his very birth, when they circumvented the island of Delos seven times. Enckell was probably not trying to illustrate any particular story from antiquity, but instead used the swans to express the contrast between life and death, between darkness and light. The legend of Orpheus might also have been brought into the painting. Enckell repeatedly compared art to music.

In a few years, the swan became the favorite bird of all the arts, a symbol of death, but also of Finland's distinctiveness as a nation.

Finns who had discovered literary Symbolism were initially not sure what symbol meant. They easily confused it with allegory, ignoring the intuitiveness of symbols and the concept of correspondence as clarified by Swedenborg: "...in the world of nature and its three rings there is not the smallest object that does not represent something in the world of the spirit and does not have its correspondence in it."

The Finnish critics, schooled in Realism, were often puzzled as they inspected Symbolist art. Kasimir Leino was also afraid of the Symbolist's "artistry": "He studies theosophy and loves artificial flowers more than nature's own."

Ellen Thesleff's portrait of her sister, "Thyra Elisabeth" (1892), was considered a Symbolist painting even in Finland, but its significance escaped the audience. Later it has been compared to Puvis de Chavannes' "L'Abondance" and to the work of the Pre-Raphaelites, especially Dante Gabriel Rosetti's "Beata Beatrix."

Thesleff had adopted the same "colorless" approach as Enckell, but there are considerable differences between the two though they had studied together. While Enckell concentrated on figures highlighted by outlines, Thesleff developed misty surfaces of color which suited depictions of the long, dusky Finnish summer evenings. "Landscape, Spring Night" (1894) was among Thesleff's finest pieces.

One of Beda Stjernschantz's best Symbolist paintings was made *en face*, like Thesleff's, the portrait "Irma (Head of a Girl)" (1895–1896). It was completed in Estonia, on the island of Vorms, where she also painted the somewhat mysterious "Everywhere a Voice Invites Us" (1895). The title of the painting is a quotation from the beginning of a song by Emil von Qvanten, perhaps indicating a Svecoman ideology behind Stjernschantz's painting. Vorms was inhabited by the descendants of the Swedes who came to the island as conquerors.

Stjernschantz's most famous painting is "Pastoral (Primavera)" from 1897. A possible source of inspiration for the painting is the Swedish writer Viktor Rydberg's poem about Antinous which the artist had copied in her sketch book.

The style of "Pastoral" is largely indebted to Puvis de Chavannes' new visions of Arcadia. Besides, allegories of the seasons had once again become modern. Take Maurice Denis' "April" (1892), which could also have provided inspiration for Stjernschantz's "Pastoral."

The preachers of a new Renaissance

After recovering from his initial shock, Gallén "toyed" with Symbolism, but soon became involved in earnest. Edelfelt was interested (though his interest was tinged with disgust) in Gallén first important Symbolist painting "Symposion" (or "Symposium"), also called "The Problem" (1894).

Edelfelt explained in a letter that Gallén was working on a very curious painting, Symbolist of course. "Kajanus, drunk, is preaching to Merikanto, Sibelius, and Gallén. Matter, in the guise of a flayed sphinx, is sitting on the table among the bottles of punch, as an astral body is shown as a silhouette against the planet Jupiter." Edelfelt was astonished that all the people portrayed in the painting were enchanted with it.

Gallén painted the second version of "Symposion" in 1894, toning it down and making it more serious, evidently because of Edelfelt's criticism. In the new painting, the wings of Osiris are spread out above the men, sunk deep in thought. The flayed sphinx had disappeared. It popped up again in "Conceptio Artis" (1894) as the symbol of the elusive secret of art. The painting is based on a dream that the writer Adolf Paul had related to Gallén.

The participants in the symposium did not just spend their time drinking. Their discussions also touched on the renaissance of Finnish intellectual life, one that would come from the north this time. Gallén wrote that new strength, a rebirth would be needed to take the place of wretched, melancholy decadence. "Ad Astra" (1894), painted soon after "Symposion," can be seen as a crystallization of Gallén's dreams. He said that the painting depicted a resurrection and noted that the figure of the woman, her arms spread, took "the position of the savior of the world on the cross."

Gallén hoped that he would be able to settle down in the silence of the wilderness, but left for Berlin, which Nordic writers and artists considered the center of their world. Munch, Vigeland, and many others were living in this rapidly growing German metropolis.

Gallén was introduced to German thinking mostly by the "Zum Schwarzen Ferkel." It emphasized the masculine phi-

Axel Gallén:
Symposion (The Problem), sketch. 1894.
Oil, 58.5 x 56.5 cm.
GÖSTA SERLACHIUS FINE ARTS FOUNDATION, MÄNTTÄ.
Matter in the guise of a flayed sphinx, beside bottles on the left, with an astral body shown as a silhouette against the planet Jupiter on the upper left. Only part of the sphinx can be seen, since Gallén cut part of the canvas off on Edelfelt's advice.

Axel Gallén: Ad Astra. 1907.
Oil, 76.5 x 85 cm.
SIGNE AND ANE GYLLENBERG FOUNDATION.

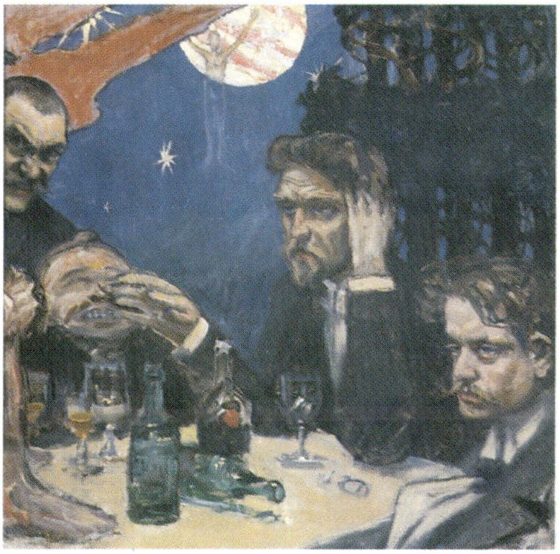

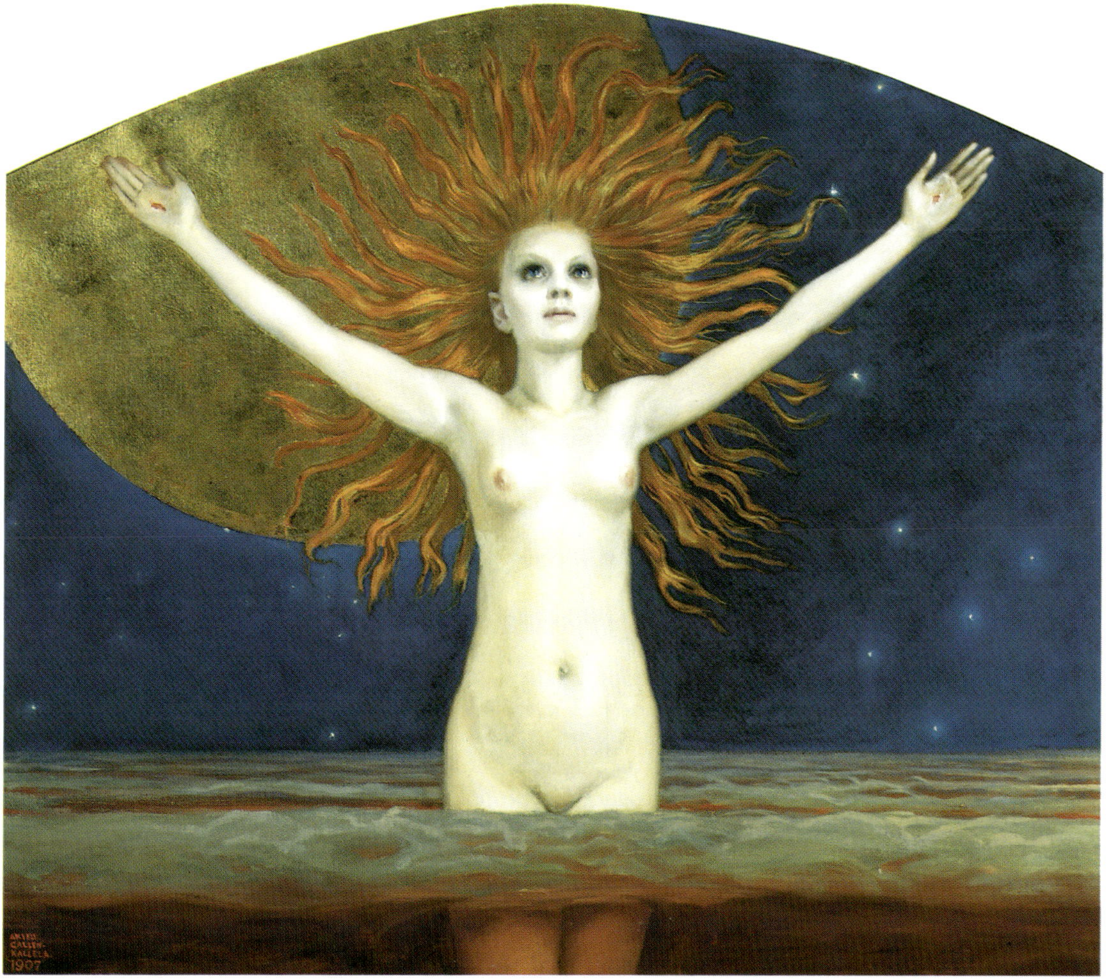

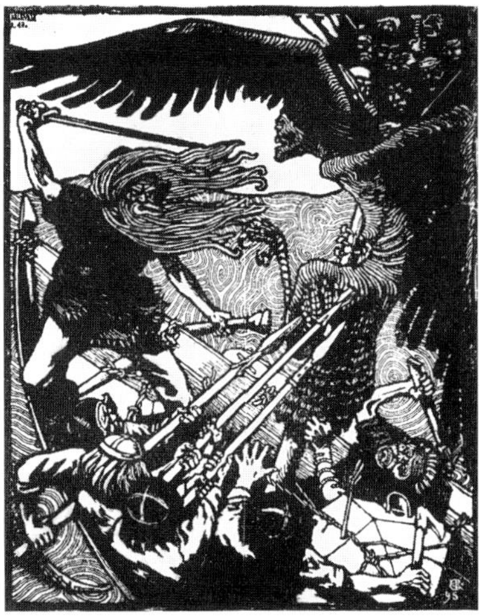

Axel Gallén:
The Defense of the Sampo. 1895.
Woodcut, 22.5 x 18 cm.
GALLEN-KALLELA MUSEUM, TARVASPÄÄ.

Axel Gallén:
Lemminkäinen's Mother. 1897.
Tempera, 85 x 118 cm. Antell Collection,
ART MUSEUM OF THE ATENEUM.

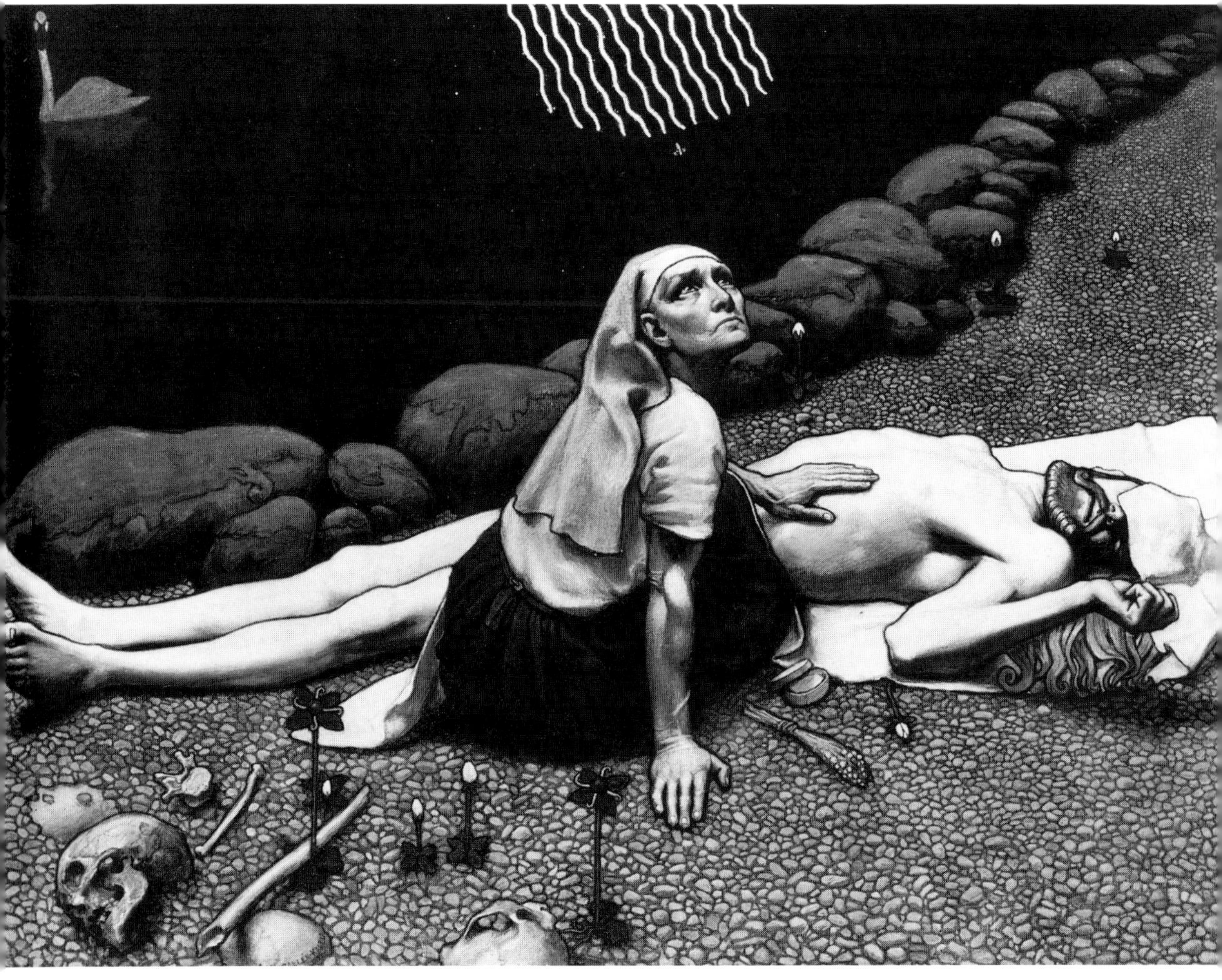

losophy of Eros rather than androgyny. Its influence had already been seen in "Symposion" thanks to Adolf Paul; female matter is counterbalanced by the spirituality of the masculine creative instinct.

Gallén exhibited together with Munch, but he got his most important experience illustrating *Pan* and studying graphics under Josef Sattler. His stay abroad was suddenly cut short by news of the death of his little daughter, Marjatta.

The romance of the Kalevala

Gallén began to shape the renaissance of the north in his wilderness studio in Ruovesi. He had a great many irons in the fire between 1895 and 1900. He created a new romantic style for themes from the *Kalevala* dominated by dense, Synthetist surfaces of color, powerful, simple outlines, a Japanese cropping technique, and almost aggressive composition.

In addition to his other work, Gallén raised Finnish graphic art to a level that was not reached until Ellen Thesleff began work with the medium in the 20th century. Gallén also became increasingly interested in decorative art.

In the midst of the wilderness, Gallén transformed the wings of Orisis into the eagle wings of the hag Louhi in "The Defense of the Sampo" (1896), and a Nietzschean superman took the guise of the tragic heroes of the *Kalevala*: Kullervo cursing his fate, Lemminkäinen going off to war, Joukahainen thirsting for revenge.

The *Kalevala* itself seemed to have been transformed into a mystical source of knowledge for Gallén. It was no longer just an ancient epic: it was a book of revelations to be studied from a theosopher's point of view.

Gallén's independent attitude towards the *Kalevala* can, however, be seen in his comment that he did not use the subject as his point of departure (as liberties and errors show), but rather his own soul and concepts as an artist.

While Gallén was in Ruovesi planning a painting of the final scene in Lemminkäinen's journey to the realm of death, Tuonela, Helsinki witnessed the premiere of Sibelius's *Lemminkäinen Suite*. The discussions of the "symposium" group began to take tangible shape in different ways. The music historian Erik Tawaststjerna believes that it was Gallén who got Sibelius interested in the subject of Lemminkäinen.

Gallén's subject was the happy ending of Lemminkäinen's gruesome journey. The hero's mother has begged the bee to bring salve from God with which to heal her son's wounds. Lemminkäinen lies on the stony shore like the dead Christ in Holbein's predella: flowers of death grow amidst skulls and bones. The shore is lined with bloody stones, and the Swan of Tuonela, gliding on the black water, mocks the hero.

Gallén asked his mother Mathilda to pose for the painting. The artist in fact said that it is actually an ode of gratitude to his mother. From a psychological point of view, it is an effective picture of depression

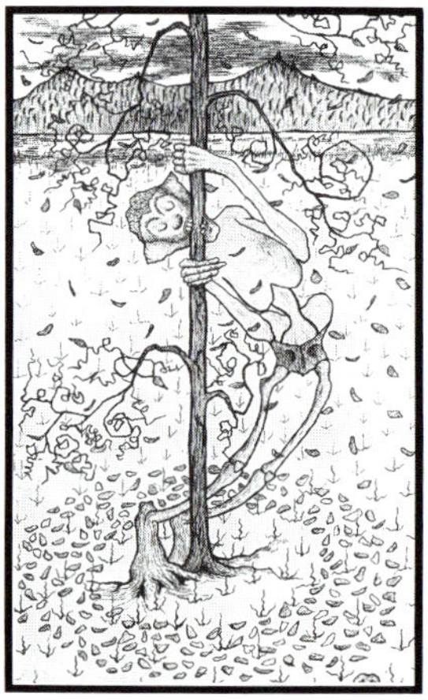

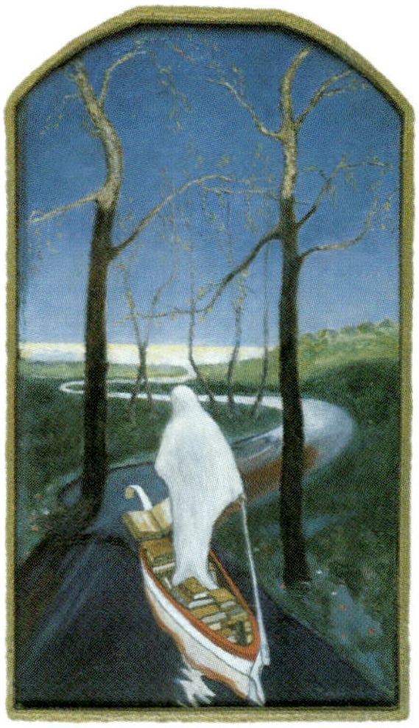

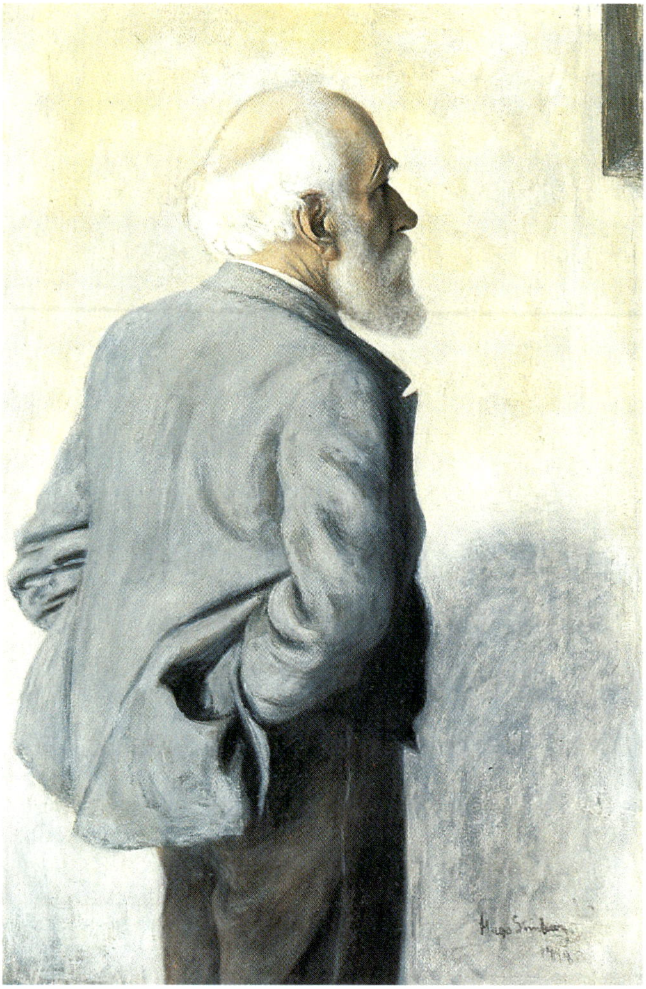

Hugo Simberg:
Autumn. 1896.
India ink, 24 x 14.5 cm.
PRIVATE COLLECTION.

Hugo Simberg:
On the River of Life. 1896.
Oil on wood. 32 x 12 cm.
PRIVATE COLLECTION.

Hugo Simberg:
Portrait of the Artist's Father. 1898.
Oil, 103 x 64 cm.
PRIVATE COLLECTION.

Hugo Simberg:
The Wind is Rising. 1897.
Gouache, 23 x 37 cm.
ART MUSEUM OF THE ATENEUM.

Hugo Simberg:
The Devil is Dead. 1907.
Watercolor, 18 x 26.5 cm.
PRIVATE COLLECTION.

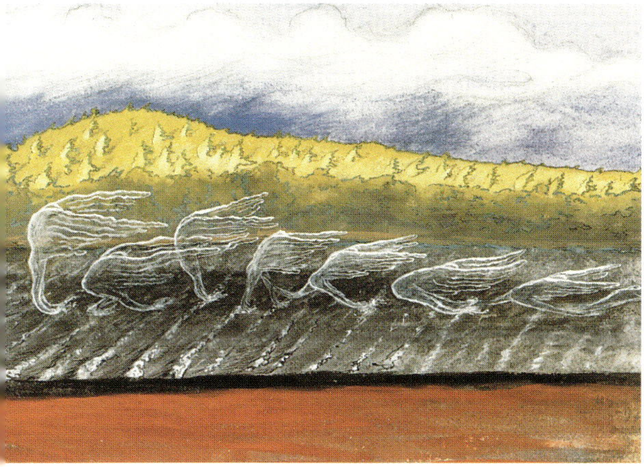

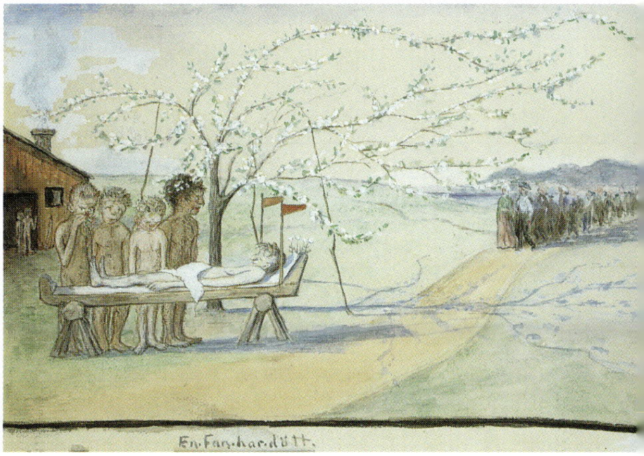

and how it can be overcome through the power of a mother's and son's symbiosis.

Ludwig Wennervirta pointed out in the 1920s that Gallén's "Joukahainen's Revenge," "The Fratricide," and "Lemminkäinen's Mother" form a unique trilogy in Finnish art, a eulogy to maternal love. All three paintings were made the same year, in 1897.

The tamer of frost and death

Gallén did not isolate himself in Ruovesi even though it lay quite a distance from the capital, considering travel speeds at the time. Trips abroad interrupted his periods of work, and students, which Gallén seems to have more than tolerated, brought a change of pace.

Eric O. W. Ehrström (1881–1934) mostly received training in decorative art from Gallén, while Hugo Simberg (1873–1917) was instructed in graphic art and tempera painting. Simberg had studied at an art school in Viipuri and at the Helsinki Arts Society's school, where one of his teachers was Helene Schjerfbeck.

Simberg had not fitted in with the normal pattern of art training, and wanted to receive additional tutoring from Gallén, whom he admired. Simberg wrote to the master from Ruovesi in summer 1895 and received a positive reply to his request. In a letter to Louis Sparre, Gallén told about the amazing talent of his new pupil, "quite in the style of the old masters of the 14th and 15th centuries. And it is real (and not acquired) naivety. His work looks like prophecies that everyone should listen to and bear in mind."

Gallén's understanding guidance brought rapid results. That same year, Simberg painted a series of incomparable watercolors. Versions of "Frost" and "Autumn" have become emblems of Finnish Symbolism. They combined international trends with national motives in an exceptionally distinctive way.

Simberg was undoubtedly interested in Gallén's endeavors to personify nature. In "Waterfall at Mäntykoski" (1892), Gallén had intended to make a parallel to Ernst Josephson's "The Water Sprite," but in fact painted over the original male figure. Gallén did not return the figure to the edge of the water until he made his etching "Listening to the Rapids" in 1896. Gallén's illustrations for *Pan* and his other work done in Germany certainly also provided important inspiration for Simberg.

Folk tales interested the young artist, and he had an empathy for peasants, who even in Ruovesi lived in constant fear of frost and famine.

Arnold Böcklin's influence on Simberg has not been clarified in detail. Simberg did say, "Böcklin is an artist by God's grace; everyone must bow before him." He did not mean that the Swiss master was to be copied. Perhaps the robust humor of Böcklin's work liberated Simberg's imagination. *Götterkomik* was given a Finnish guise in his hands.

Simberg traveled to London, Paris, and Berlin in 1896, and

went to Italy the following year. He saw with his own eyes everything that he had previously seen only in reproductions: the British Museum's Egyptian art, miniatures, and Japanese woodcuts. Simberg's interest also extended to the frescoes of the early Renaissance and to the work of the Renaissance masters of the north, such as Dürer and Holbein.

In spite of his new experiences, Simberg remained true to his own approach. He concentrated on the devils, trolls, and grim reaper of folk tales, taming them into touching, melancholically comic figures. They walked among men burdened with many cares, sometimes even plagued by hunger.

In Simberg's work, the demonic evil of Symbolism was transformed into a detente between good and evil. The art historian Riikka Stewen has drawn attention to an early etching by Simberg that shows a midnight meeting between the artist and the grim reaper. The meeting is not fatal, since death has only come to ask for a decoration for his scythe. Simberg's "Faustian" pact can be seen in the easygoing fashion with which he depicts both "The Garden of Death" (1896) and events in "The Entrance to Hades" (1898).

Gallén treated the subject of death more somberly than Simberg, but even his work with the theme has anecdotal features, as in the India ink wash "Finis" (1893). It seems likely that these little pieces exerted some influence on Simberg.

Simberg's work is a challenge to those who wish to interpret it today, but his contemporaries did not take much note of his fairy tale-like watercolors and gouaches. They were considered too childish. Matters did not improve until Simberg exhibited his fine portrait, "The Artist's Aunt" (1898); Simberg was recognized as a masterful painter. "The Artist's Aunt" was also given a fine reception in Vienna, Paris, and Copenhagen.

Upheavals in society and art

Artists and the first period of Russification

Nicholas II (ruled between 1894 and 1917) appointed Nicholas Ivanovitch Bobrikov Governor General of Finland in 1898. The appointment was partly linked with the international situation. The continental alliance and England and Turkey were trying to isolate Russia at the same time as Japan's increasing might was causing unrest in the empire. The northwest corner of the empire had to be safeguarded with forceful measures aimed at Russification.

After arriving in Helsinki, Bobrikov explained to the leading bureaucrats and the press that Finland's internal affairs would remain unchanged only if they were not in conflict with the interests and dignity of Russia. The principles of Russification were laid down in the "February Manifesto" issued by the czar on February 15, 1900. This was the beginning of the first period of Russification, which lasted until 1905.

The February Manifesto aroused public indignation and led to many kinds of symbolic protests. In a conspicuous demonstration, flowers were laid at Alexander II's statue on March 13, 1899. Stigell's "Shipwrecked" found its way onto post cards, expressing Finland's appeal for help from the west. Albert Edelfelt illustrated *The Tales of Ensign Ståhl* under the eyes of the censors, and when this major artistic achievement was published in 1900, a patriotic celebration was held. Edelfelt dressed up in the uniform of the Pori Regiment, and with drawn sword sang its official marching song.

Gallén's militant *Kalevala* creations were projected right into the present. In a burst of patriotism, Pekka Halonen painted Finland's stalwart pine forests in "Wilderness" (1899). Its blackened trunks conveyed the message that not even a wounded nation would surrender. The artist was satisfied with the results of public protests: "That is what is so damned encouraging

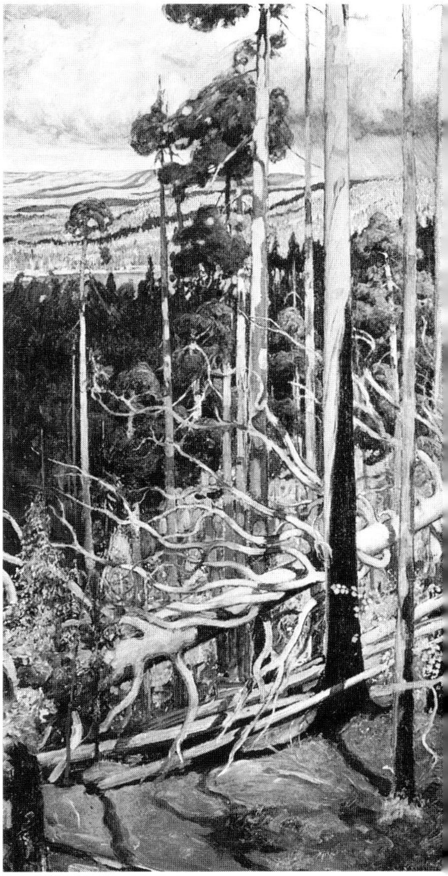

Pekka Halonen: Wilderness. 1899. Oil, 110 x 55.5 cm.
TURKU ART MUSEUM.

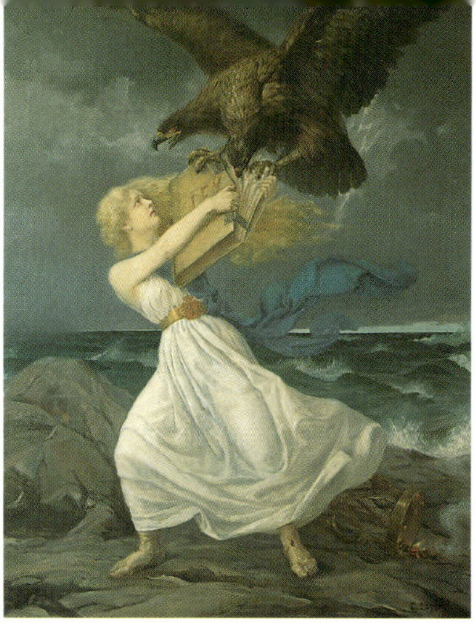

Edvard Isto:
The Attack. 1899.
Oil, 200 x 140 cm.
NATIONAL MUSEUM OF FINLAND.
A two-headed eagle tries to wrench a law book from the hands of the Maid of Finland.

about it all! The land and the people are alive!" he wrote in a letter to Emil Wikström.

Wikström had gone through some exciting moments as he completed the large group for the tympanum of the House of Estates entitled "The development of the Finnish people through toil and strife to the first Diet of 1809." Just when all the bronze parts of the group had been brought to Finland and the work of installing them had begun, Governor General Bobrikov asked to see the designs for the project. It was only a false alarm, however, and the work was completed in 1903.

Even lesser-quality work reached all strata of society in the form of post cards and heliogravures. This is what happened to "The Attack," painted by Edvard Isto (1865–1905). It shows a two-headed eagle wrenching a law book from the hands of the Maid of Finland. Gallén designed a black mourning stamp, and in 1903, Wikström exhibited a little wooden sculpture which he entitled "Deliver Us From Evil."

Creating a synthesis

The Finnish pavilion at the 1900 Universal Exposition in Paris provided a thorough review of art, industry, and architecture. Finland considered having a pavilion of its own an important expression of independence. From the czar's point of view, Finland was allowed to take part on its own for the same reason as Siberia, for its geographic and ethnic distinctiveness and not because it enjoyed national autonomy.

The Dreyfus scandal aroused a feeling of revulsion towards France, and the Finns' participation in the Exposition was in danger of being cancelled. But national interests weighed more heavily, and the competition proposal for the pavilion submitted by the architects Gesellius, Lindgren, and Saarinen (1898) was implemented. Gallén painted frescoes with themes from the *Kalevala*, one of them showing Ilmari tilling a field with adders. One of the cartoons for the fresco shows that the artist painted an imperial crown on the head of one of the snakes.

The presentation of Finnish art grew very broad indeed: Symbolists, from Enckell to Simberg; depictors of nature, from Westerholm to Halonen; portrayers of the people, from Venny Soldan (1863–1945) to Juho Rissanen (1873–1950); sculptors, from Emil Wikström and Ville Vallgren to Eemil Halonen (1875–1950).

A diplomatic battle of bribes was carried on with the Russian pavilion. Once again the Russians offered Edelfelt, who was commissioner of the Finnish pavilion, a professorship at the academy of fine arts in St. Petersburg. He was also asked to be commissioner of the whole Russian pavilion. Edelfelt declined.

The Finnish pavilion attracted a great deal of attention. The artists were hailed, partly for political reasons: Vallgren was given a Grand Prix, and Gallén, Järnefelt, and Stigell were awarded gold medals. All this built up Finland's national and artistic self-confidence. The consequences proved very practical

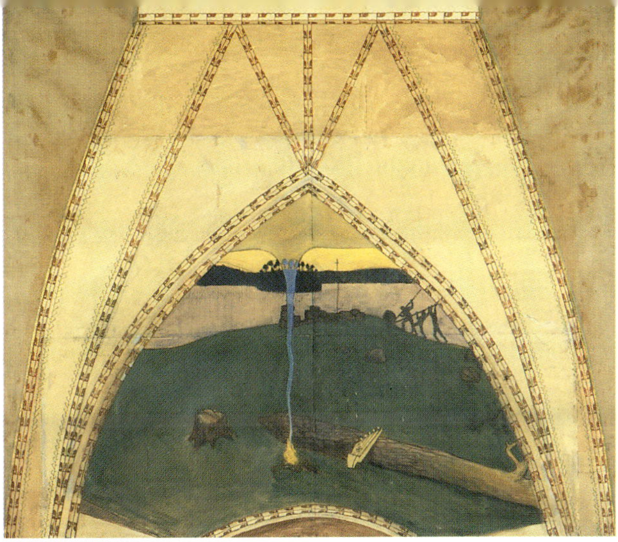

The Finnish pavilion at the Universal Exposition in Paris in 1900.
Axel Gallén:
Paganism and Christianity. 1900.
Sketch for a fresco.
ART MUSEUM OF THE ATENEUM.

indeed when it came to architecture. The trend towards a National Romantic Art Nouveau style became stronger.

In 1899, in the midst of the work on the pavilion in Paris, Gallén received a tempting commission from the architect Josef Stenbäck. The flamboyant businessman F. A. Jusélius had decided to build a mausoleum for his daughter, who had died at the age of 11. It was to be decorated with frescoes whose motive was to be "death's victory over matter."

Gallén accepted the commission despite his doubts. He seems to have felt uncomfortable with Stenbäck's Neo-Gothic architecture. Their work together progressed harmoniously enough, however, and the architect discussed designs for the interior with Gallén. The ornamentation required for the work fascinated the artist, since like William Morris, he had developed ornamentation based on motives from nature, during his stays in Ruovesi. Gallén was in deadly earnest. "The dreadful mystery of life stares at us from even the simplest ornament."

In the octagonal Jusélius monument, Gallén was able to apply the fresco technique that he had learned in Italy, this time in a building that was to remain standing, unlike the pavilion. On the highest walls of the interior the artist painted "Cosmos," where the organ of the universe plays the music of the spheres, and "Paradise," where a temple of ideals stands uppermost.

The star-studded vault was decorated with foliate ornaments, in the fashion of medieval church frescoes, and the panels under the six opposing windows of the sides contained the following frescoes (seen counterclockwise): "Spring," Building," "On the River of Tuonela," "Destruction (Armageddon)," "Autumn," and "Winter."

The styles of the frescoes range from simplified Realism to a synthetic approach, creating a synthesis of a decade of development work by Gallén.

Damp and chemical changes soon destroyed some of the frescoes, and the artist's son, Jorma, repainted them in the 1930s.

St. John's Church in Tampere (1903–1907, now Tampere Cathedral), designed by Lars Sonck, is one of the most grandiose buildings in National Romantic style. It implemented the ideals of the unity of the arts and an organic esthetic that dictated the use of genuine, "honest" materials. The granite-clad church was given a freer form, and the lower parts of the towers thickened like tree trunks.

At Edelfelt's recommendation, Magnus Enckell and Hugo Simberg were commissioned to create the decorations for the church. The artists agreed that Enckell would work on the choir and altar fresco while Simberg would be responsible for the general decorations of the body of the church. Simberg started the work. Enckell did not paint the altar fresco ("The Resurrection") until 1907.

Simberg went off to Florence and Padua in 1904 to study fresco painting. That same year, he was given a state art prize for his painting "The Wounded Angel," an award which helped boost the artist's self-confidence.

Simberg used wing patterns

Victor Westerholm:
From the Kymijoki River Valley. 1901.
Oil, 58 x 108 cm.
TURKU ART MUSEUM.

Hugo Simberg:
The Wounded Angel. 1903.
Oil, 127 x 154 cm.
NATIONAL GALLERY OF FINLAND.
Simberg painted a second version as a fresco for St. John's Church (today Tampere Cathedral).

for the decorations on the vaults and on the cupola-like main vault he painted a red winged serpent of Paradise, holding an apple in its mouth. The serpent sparked off a considerable protest, and as late as 1946, the bishop of Tampere Diocese proposed that it be removed.

Along the edge of the gallery, Simberg painted a continuous fresco, "The Garland Bearers," the boys in the fresco representing Jesus's twelve disciples carrying the vine of life.

Under the northern gallery, near the pulpit, Simberg painted "The Garden of Death" and in the south gallery "The Wounded Angel." Simberg also designed the church's stained-glass windows.

Valter Jung (1879–1946), who worked at Lars Sonck's office, created the church's numerous reliefs and furnishings. Eric O. W. Ehrström designed the church's communion plate.

Monumentalism and national melancholy

Monumentalism in painting had a natural place in architectural projects, but at the turn of the century, the ideal of size spread quickly to independent works of art. Monumentalism was nurtured by Synthetism, the frescoes of Italy, and subject matter that emphasized Finland's national distinctiveness.

The rejuvenation of ceramics at the Iris Factory in Porvoo bears witness to the influence of William Morris's ideas. Artists embarked on a search for a uniform style based on natural ornamentation.

Finland's National Romantic Art Nouveau architecture was combined with the wooden architecture of Karelia and that of medieval granite churches, supplemented with international elements. The English and American trends mediated by *The Studio* were initially of key importance, followed by German and Austrian influences. Art Nouveau architecture, which emphasized individuality, gave rise to a need for a new kind of decorative sculpture. Finnish stone, such as granite and soapstone, was used for sculptural elements.

On close inspection, art's national features often fade into nothingness. The concept of the distinctive art of a northern "race" was one of the fictions cherished in the period, but international comments still show that sobriety and melancholy were customarily associated with Finnish art at the turn of the century. At the Universal Exposition in Paris, Gustave Geffroy presented the rhetorical exhortation: "Rissanen, painter of the peasants, remain in the world that you depict so soberly and that you so greatly love, and never come to Paris to learn art." It took eight years before Juho Rissanen visited Paris for the first time.

The melancholy of the north was found in the other arts as well. After hearing Sibelius's "Swan of Tuonela," the French critic Gaston Carraud wrote that "its indefinable melody in the English horn, strangely veiled in

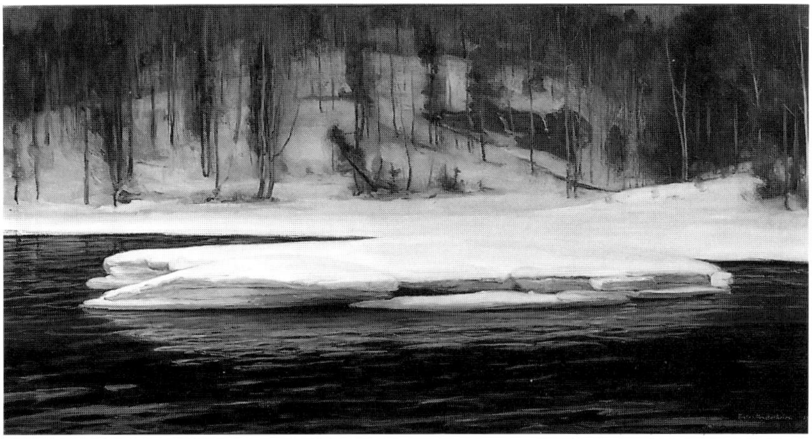

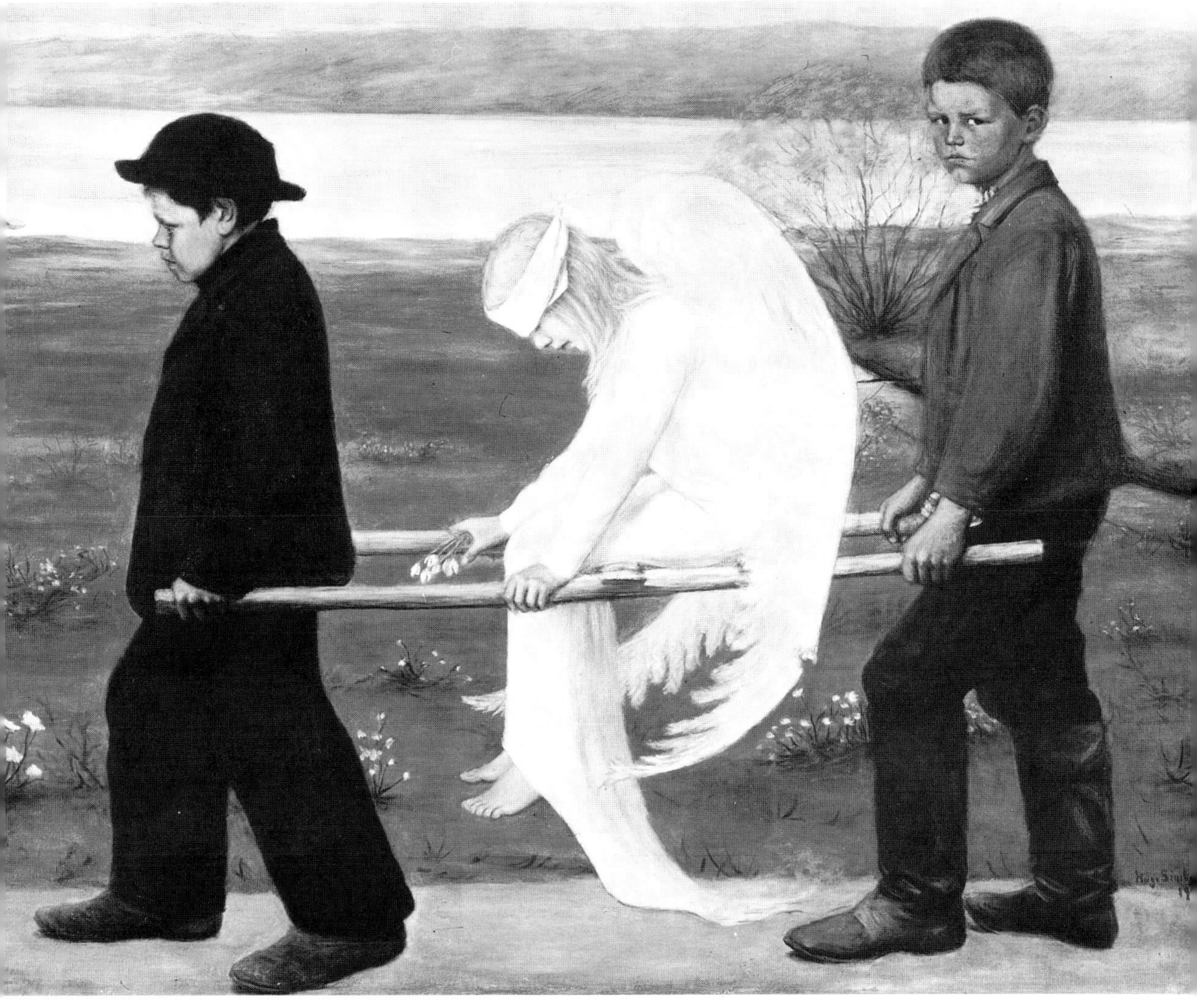

Juho Rissanen:
Head of a Girl, Selma Savolainen. 1897.
Watercolor, 35 x 23 cm.
ART MUSEUM OF THE ATENEUM.

Pekka Halonen:
Leaving Work. 1907.
Oil, 165 x 175 cm. Hedman Collection.
MUSEUM OF OSTROBOTHNIA, VAASA.

Juho Rissanen:
The Fortune-teller. 1899. Watercolor, 100 x 112 cm.
Art Museum of the Ateneum.

Juho Rissanen:
At the Pillory. 1900.
Watercolor, 113 x 64.5 cm
ART MUSEUM OF THE ATENEUM.

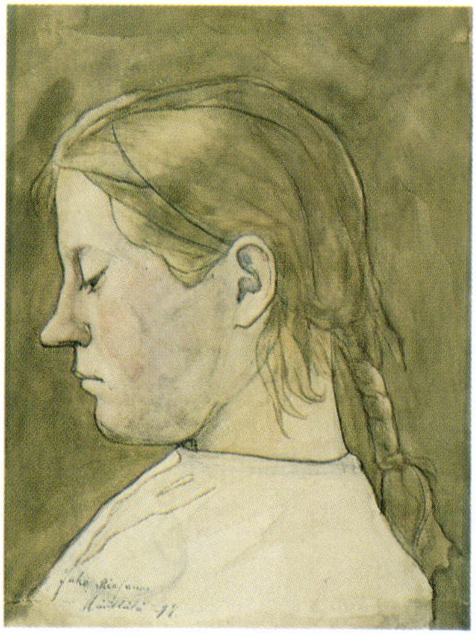

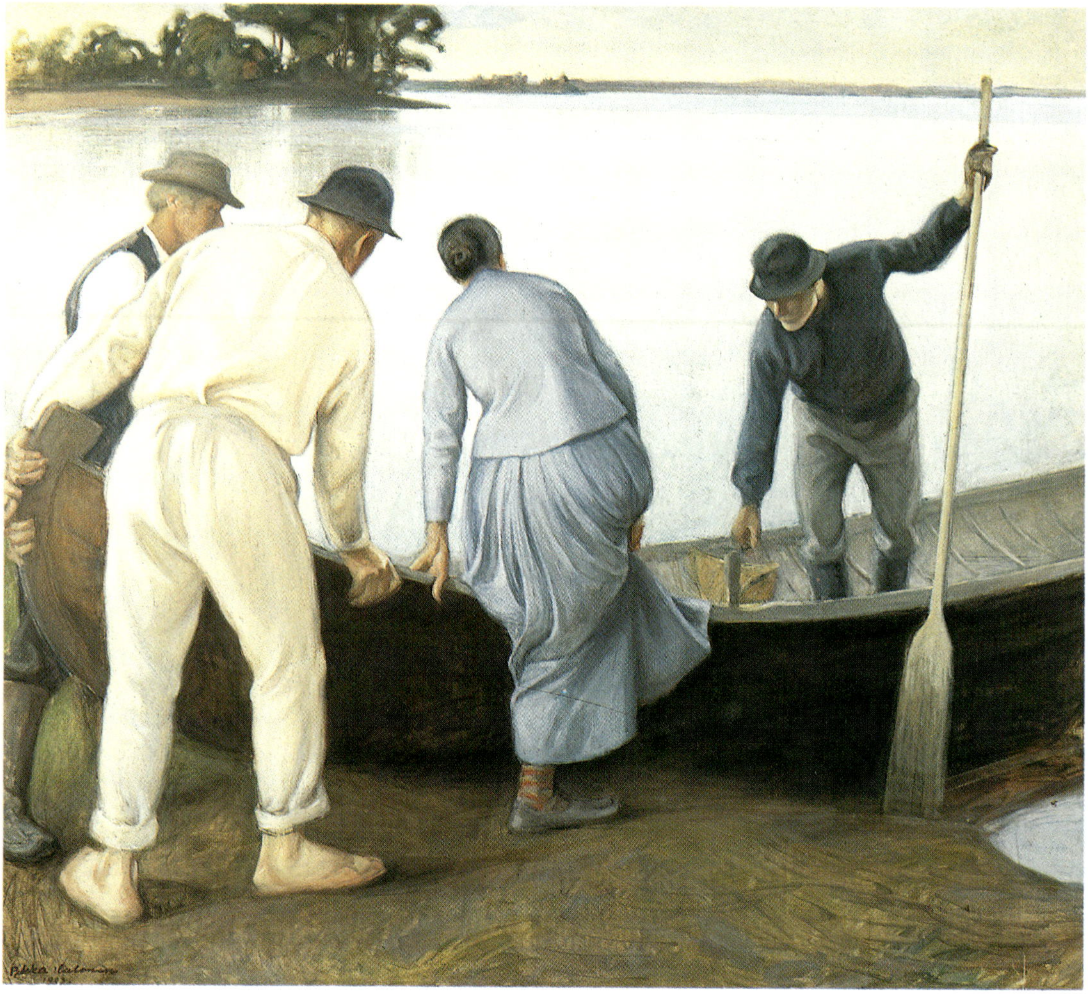

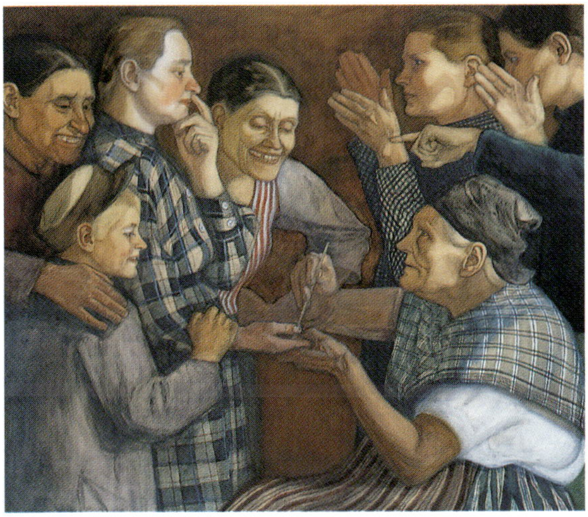

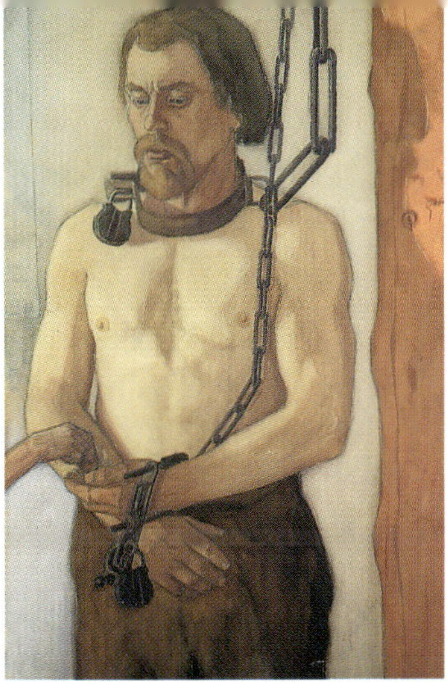

melancholy strains, [is] the vision of a true and great poet."

Dark strains found their way into every field. Even that master of light and atmosphere, Victor Westerholm, gave up his delicate palette and evolved a luxuriant style based on the biomorphic creations of Art Nouveau in his landscapes of the Kymijoki River.

The wood-processing industry had already harnessed the great watercourses, but Westerholm's winter rivers flowed on, like irresistible natural forces. The decorative forms of white ice floes created a powerful contrast to the violet-black of the water in such paintings as "The Rapids" (1902) and "The Kymijoki River" (1902). The concept of the River of Tuonela, the Finnish Styx, is not far removed, but Reitala believes that the painter strove to portray an ideal river landscape.

Westerholm began work on his monumental painting "Åland" in 1899. He intended it as his *chef d'oeuvre* and matured his ideas for a decade. The synthesis of the rocky archipelago, the sea, and the (setting) sun was the artist's declaration of love to the Åland Islands. The perspective in this large canvas is breathtaking, but the effect can only be properly experienced in front of the painting itself.

Pekka Halonen also tackled monumentalism. He softened the color scale of his fresh landscapes ("Winter Sunset," 1899) and used a simple fresco-like style in his delicate, melancholy painting "Washing on the Ice" (1900) and in his tribute to physical labor, "Pioneers in Karelia" (1900). The influence of Puvis de Chavannes has been found in both.

Juho Rissanen, the gifted depictor of the common man, did some of his best work at the end of he 1890s: "The Old Woman" (1897, playfully called the Mona Lisa of Savolax), "The Cupper" (1899), "The Blind Woman" (1899), and the anecdotal "The Fortune-Teller" (1899). The pictorial concept behind "The Fortune-teller" is Ilja Repin's "Zaporozhian Cossacks Writing a Reply to the Turkish Sultan." Rissanen was familiar with Russian art since he had studied in St. Petersburg. The different versions of "At the Pillory" are among Rissanen's most impressive work, variations on the theme *Ecce homo*.

Rissanen generally used water colors, and developed a bold use of Art Nouveau-style outlines under the influence of his teacher Albert Gebhard (1869–1937) and the work of his admired colleague Axel Gallén. Rissanen was actually considered a fighter against social injustice, but in fact he was not at all interested in tendentiousness. What his work does show is sympathy for the less fortunate, and plenty of humor. Rissanen's gallery of characters grew into a sociological cross-section of rural eastern Finland.

Humor played a minor role as Rissanen began to plan a triptych depicting his father's death. In the course of a long process of development, this experience from his childhood gave birth to a series of impressive, Primitivist sketches. The work remained Rissanen's "unfinished symphony."

Only the center section of the watercolor "A Memory of Childhood (1900–1903) was fin-

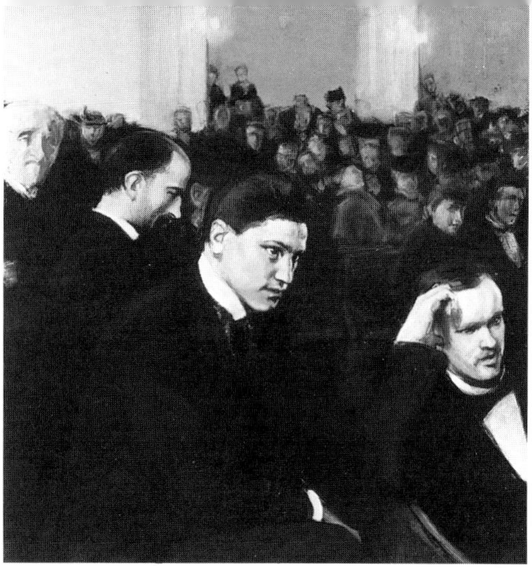

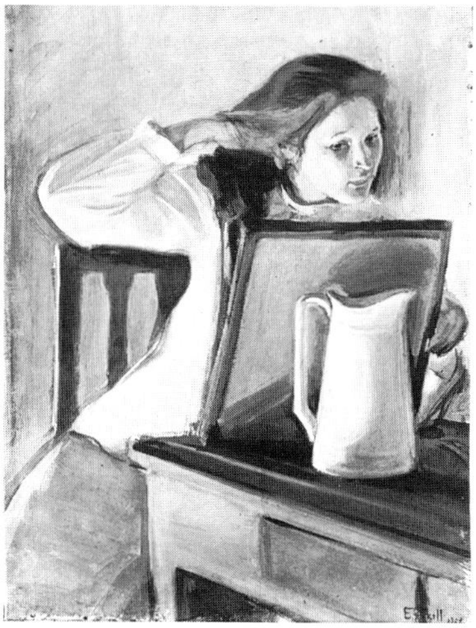

ished, showing his father's body being borne away. One of the wings showed the artist's father lying frozen on the ice of the lake, a liquor bottle in his hand; the pale dawn can be seen spreading across the sky. Rissanen neither shied away from nor idealized death. As depicted by him, it is a horrible and everyday event, uncomplicated by any passionate *fin de siècle* Thanatos and Eros mystique.

Rissanen traveled to Italy in autumn 1900, studied in Florence in the studio of Filadelfio Sim, and viewed the great classics, the art of Giotto, Fra Angelico, Masaccio, and Ghirlandaio. Rissanen nonetheless considered seeing Francesco Traini's "The Triumph of Death" at Pisa's Campo Santo one of his most memorable experiences. It certainly encouraged him to continue his plans for the triptych, and led him to work with frescoes. The earliest, "Returning from Work" (1904), was painted for Helsinki's municipal library.

Rissanen returned to the theme of death in "Washing the Body" (1908). The body in this ponderous anecdotal painting brings to mind Mantegna's "Dead Christ," though seen from the head. One of the rhythmic patterns of the composition is based on a carefully calculated alternation between profile and *en face* depictions.

Manet's influence on the use of black by Finnish artists increased as more of them studied the classics of Spanish art on their own, especially the work of Velazquez.

Enckell had painted "Boy Reclining" (1892), adapting the position of the upper body in Manet's "Olympia," and as he painted "The Concert" in an abundance of black tones, Manet's influence could be seen again, but now enriched by Enckell's experiences from Spain.

Inspired by the frescoes of Italy and Gallén's example, Enckell began to plan two lunettes for the Helsinki University library. He wanted to cover up Severin Falkman's "unsuccessful" pictures, but only one of the two oil paintings he planned was completed (1904), and even it required help from Verner Thomé (1874–1953). The painting was originally to have depicted Adam, Eve, and the tree of knowledge, but the final title, the Arcadian "The Golden Age", refers to antiquity's division into ages of metal, with the golden age being the best and most perfect.

The critics spoke of Enckell's new symphony of color, but the values of "The Golden Age" have nothing to do with Impressionism or Neo-impressionism either. In smaller paintings, the importance of colorism grew stronger, however. "Girl Combing her Hair" (1902) and "Boy in a Boat" (1902) are examples.

"The golden age" was later used as the romanticizing term for the national renaissance of Finnish national art (from about 1890 to about 1906).

Schjerfbeck had seen work by Cézanne and van Gogh back in the 1880s, but Manet remained her permanent source of inspiration. After leaving her slightly faltering and partly Realism-dominated quest in the 1890s, she created the first synthesis in her art in a series of stark but delicate portraits of

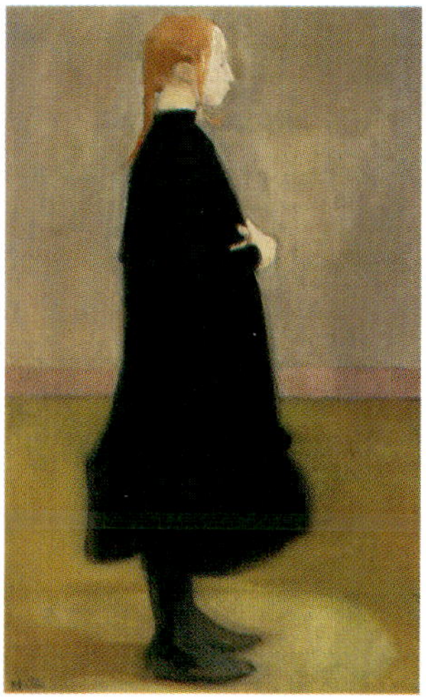

Magnus Enckell:
The Concert. 1898.
Oil, 90 x 76 cm.
ART MUSEUM OF THE ATENEUM.

Magnus Enckell:
Girl Combing her Hair. 1902.
Tempera, 69 x 50.5 cm.
ART MUSEUM OF THE ATENEUM.

Helene Schjerfbeck:
The School Girl. 1908.
Oil, 70.5 x 40.5 cm.
ART MUSEUM OF THE ATENEUM.

Helene Schjerfbeck:
The Seamstress. 1903.
Oil, 95.5 x 84.5 cm.
ART MUSEUM OF THE ATENEUM.

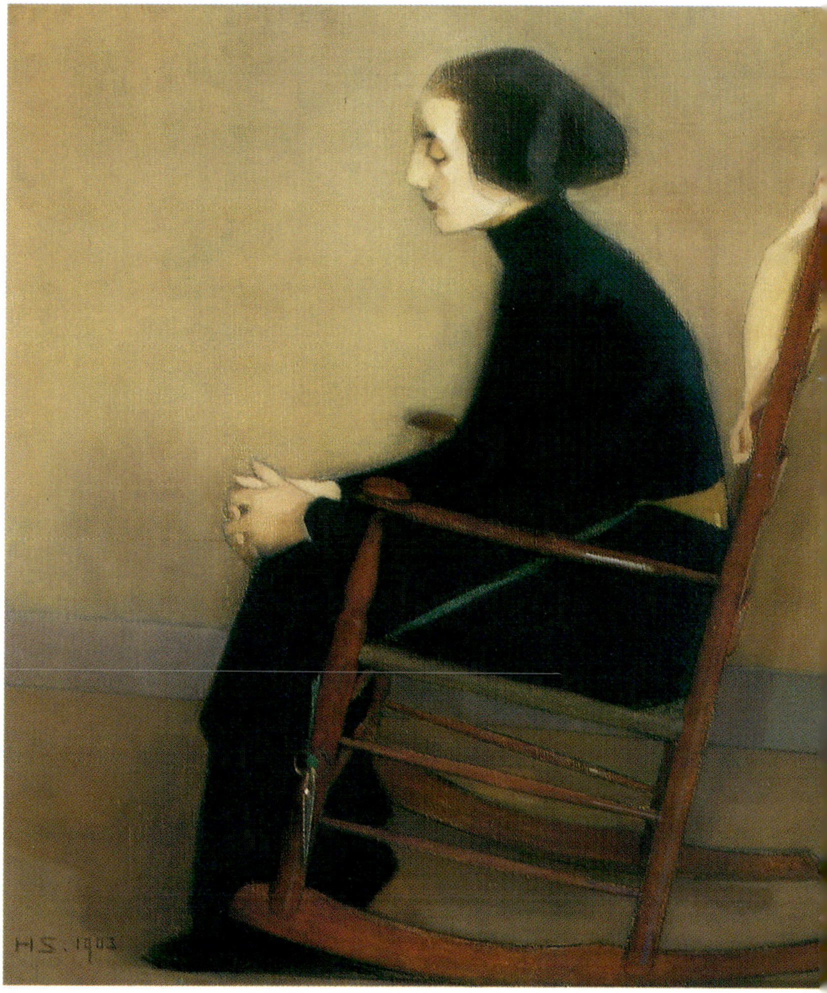

Ville Vallgren:
Havis Amanda. 1908.
Bronze, fountain granite, 5 m.
Helsinki Market Square.

women: "The Artist's Mother" (1902), "At Home" (1903), "The Seamstress" (1905), "Girl Reading"(1907). Behind the paintings' expansive black surfaces and glowing gray tones is an unfaltering geometrically oriented feeling for outline.

Schjerfbeck and Rissanen after her reached the same kind of final result from different points of departure: an abstract division and grouping of the surface displaced a plastic approach and weakened the position of outlines.

Schjerfbeck knew of the work of James Whistler from the pages of *The Studio* and other art journals, but denied that they influenced her own art. Believe it if you like, and note Schjerfbeck's designs for tapestries. Their simplicity and treatment of the surface paralleled the approach used in her paintings. Schjerfbeck respected Fanny Churberg and tried to implement her ideology of bringing a new renaissance to handicrafts.

A maid rising from the Baltic

Sculptors were given a great deal of work decorating the granite Art Nouveau buildings at the turn of the century, but there were relatively few major individual sculptural monuments. The national approach was continued especially in the work of Wikström. He sculptured the rather old-fashioned monument to Elias Lönnrot (1899–1902) and a fountain sculpture of the Aino myth commissioned by the businessman Uno Staudinger.

The fountain elicited a negative reaction before long since "it breaks the rule that the different arts, just as little as any form of art, may not be combined with nature." Wikström had only followed the principle of illusionism derived from the garden planning of the Renaissance. He sculpted the main group for the fountain on top of natural stones, and placed one figure of a maiden in the water. Six pike perches and perches, spouting water, linked the maid with the main group. The asymmetrical basin became an integral part of the garden.

The Finns like to subject their public monuments to thorough criticism, but Ville Vallgren's "Havis Amanda" (1908) drove the debaters almost out of their minds. A shapely, nude maiden at the end of Esplanade Park turned out to be not Aino from the *Kalevala* but the Maid of Helsinki, the personification of the city, rising like Aphrodite from the Baltic.

The sea lions – the Finnish answer to dolphins – spouting water on the edge of the basin were considered as foreign as the sculpture's whole supple Art Nouveau design. The feminist movement was especially indignant about the maid's nudity, and there was even argument about whether it was proper that the figure was shown taking a step forward, spreading her legs a bit.

The art historian J. J. Tikkanen satirized the discussion, but explained that it was partly due to convention. "The legs spread slightly apart express greater self-esteem, something which art

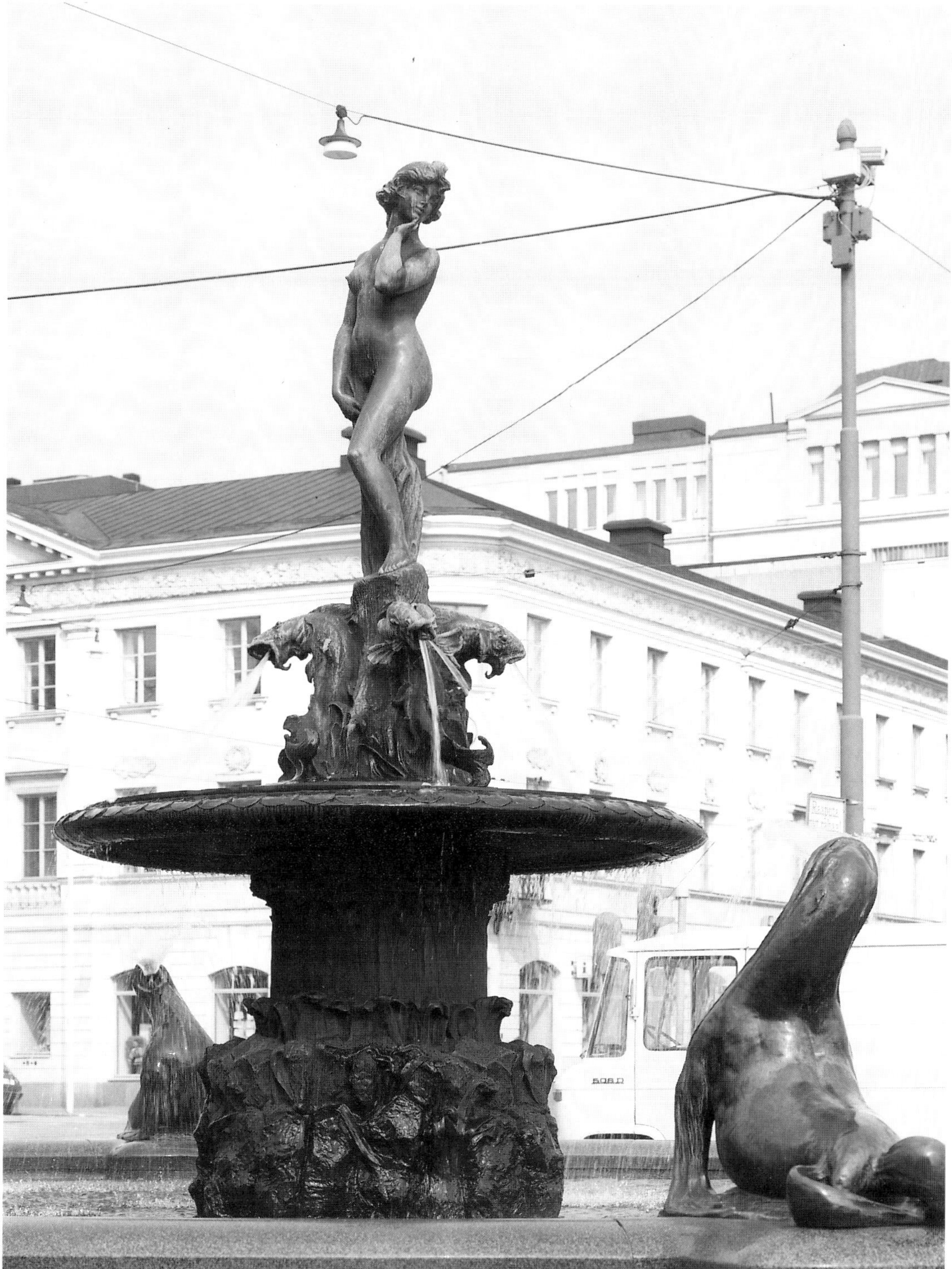

Axel Gallén.
Portrait of Maxim Gorky. 1906.
Oil, 70 x 89 cm.
ART MUSEUM OF THE ATENEUM.

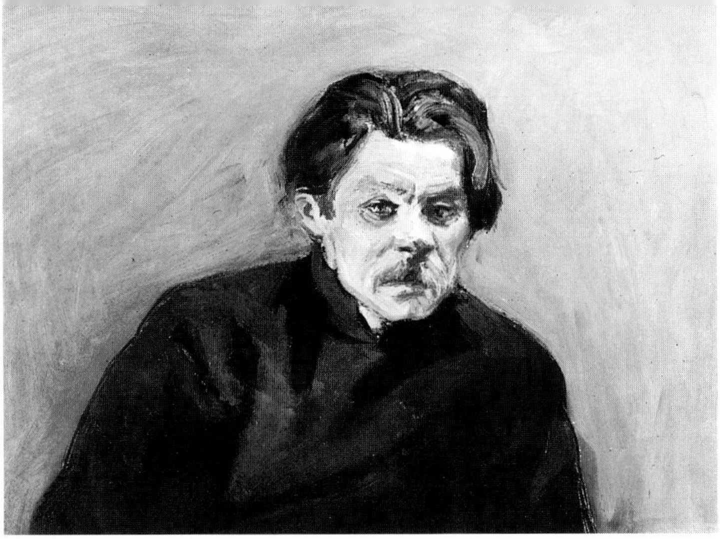

in general has not considered suitable for a woman since it easily seems shameless or comic. Knees pressed together, in contrast, bear witness to a lack of self-confidence which arouses pity instead of causing laughter."

Vallgren and Edelfelt were the most cosmopolitan Finnish artists at the turn of the century. Paris's public and buyers at times meant more to each of them than Finland's little art world, so narrow-minded in its idealism. Vallgren's friends and supporters included Rodin, whose forms that "emerged from inside the stone" had taught him a great deal. Vallgren skillfully adapted his mentor's methods, but tried to create a more graceful and more subtle form of expression than Rodin, whose creations burst with power and passion. Vallgren in fact developed into the most enchanting Art Nouveau artist, one who was able in his miniature sculptures and decorative art to combine the age's decorative ideals with organic sculpturalness.

Rodin's innovative circle was joined by Emil Wikström, Viktor Malmberg (1867–1936), Emil Cedercreutz (1879–1949), and Hilda Flodin (1877–1918), but all applied the plastic expressiveness of the French master more discretely than Vallgren.

Sigrid af Forselles (1860–1935) knew Rodin and his art best of all. She worked as his pupil and then his assistant in making "The Burghers of Calais." Rodin had hoped that they would continue working together on "Gates of Hell," but the artist was concentrating on her own cycle of allegoric reliefs on the development of mankind through conflict to reconciliation. The cycle was never completed.

Turbulent society, benumbed art

Monumentalism in art did not only have positive effects. The art world wrapped itself up in its achievements, and during Governor General Bobrikov's time, Finland considered national interests the only valid, justifiable ones. People were not sure that the newest trends were justified.

Exhibitions of foreign art showed that the little country had reached a dead end. An exhibition of French art was held in Helsinki in 1901, but an unfriendly reception was given to the work of such artists as Signac and Seurat. The effects on Finnish art remained minimal even after the exhibition of French and Belgian artists in 1904.

Society, in contrast, was in a state of turmoil. Passive resistance was joined by the hard line taken by activists. In 1904, the painter Sigrid Schauman's brother, Eugen, shot Governor General Bobrikov, the man who was seen as the subject of Sibelius's solo song composed in 1898, "The Spider" ("... spider as big and as black as the night ...").

The first period of Russification ended with the General Strike of 1905. A Constitutional reform was carried out in its aftermath under the leadership of Leo Mechelin; the reform was signed by Nicholas II in spring 1906. Soon Helsinki witnessed the first scuffle between the

Alfred William Finch:
Night in August. 1898.
Oil, 35 x 45 cm.
ART MUSEUM OF THE ATENEUM.
Finch's first work painted in Finland was an experiment with new lighting conditions.

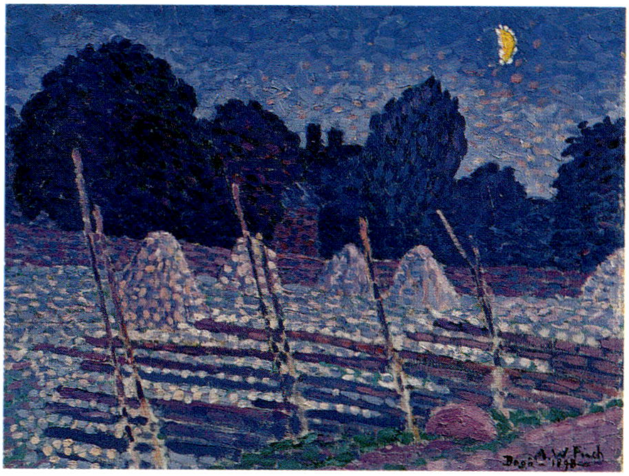

socialist "red guards" and the bourgeois "white" civil guards. It started with the Bolsheviks' revolt at the Russian garrison on Suomenlinna fortress; both external and internal upheavals shook society's power structures.

The artists in different parts of the empire were united for a time in their opposition to the czar's rule. Gallén helped Maxim Gorky and Maria Andreyevna get abroad safely from the gendarmes by arranging a way-station at Hvitträsk, the studio and home of the architects Eliel Saarinen, Armas Lindgren, and Herman Gesellius.

The first parliamentary election with universal suffrage was held in 1907 and upset the parties' own predictions: the Social Democrats received 80 out of 200 seats. The increasing dichotomy in society was quickly reflected in the field of art. The bourgeoisie repeatedly believed that modern art trends were Bolshevik in origin. The young "bohemian artists" were associated with the proletariat, and not even their carryings on were looked on with favor.

Theory and the liberation of color

The first shots were fired at the bastion of Finnish National Romanticism in 1904. The architect Sigurd Frosterus (1876–1956) went to battle together with his friend and colleague Gustaf Strengell (1878–1937) on behalf of the modern "iron and brain style" in a pamphlet entitled *Arkitektur, en stridsskrift tillägnad våra motståndare* (Architecture, a polemical pamphlet dedicated to our opponents).

Frosterus's Rationalist plans for the main railway stations in Helsinki and Viipuri had been ignored, while Eliel Saarinen's winning proposal for the station in Helsinki was praised for having its "own enchanting charm and powerful, individualistic feeling."

Frosterus opposed emotional architecture. He had worked with Henry van de Velde in Weimar in 1903 and had adopted the new principles of planning based on reason and function. Frosterus in fact noted that architects have more to learn from the structures of machines, cars, warships, and railroad bridges than they do from historical styles.

In 1905, Frosterus outlined the new turning point in art in his lecture on the art of the future. He predicted that national art would be followed by a cosmopolitan class art, which would appeal to a small audience.

Frosterus considered Neo-impressionism to be the cornerstone of this reform. He laid great emphasis on Seurat's Divisionism and in his articles discussed the Divisionist painting of Alfred William Finch (1854–1930) a Belgian-English painter and ceramist who had worked in Finland since 1897.

Finch, a member of "Les Vingts," had been enticed to Finland to head ceramics production at the Iris Factory in Porvoo. After the factory closed because its production costs were too high, Finch moved to Helsinki in 1902, started to paint once more, and inaugurated instruction in graphic art at the Arts Society's school.

Frosterus hoped that the Finns would be inspired by

Finch's example to start working with "scientific luminist painting." In evaluating the significance for art of Young-Helmholtz's hypothesis of color, Frosterus took an uncompromising stand: "The technique of color division is not only scientifically justified, it is also the only way of depicting nature's colors during daylight" (*Finsk Tidskrift* I/1909).

Divisionism did not spread the way Frosterus hoped it would, but a complete turn to Colorism could already be seen in Enckell's exhibition in 1909. The critics were nonetheless delighted that the turn had not been too sharp: "They are light and colorful pictures that one views with unequivocal admiration since the artist avoids the extremes of the Neo-impressionists and other 'luminist painters,' Pointillism, etc.," wrote Ludvig Wennervirta.

Like their colleagues elsewhere in Scandinavia, Finnish artists reacted slowly to the avant-garde trends of the beginning of the century: Fauvism, Expressionism, and Cubism. The earliest reformer was neither Enckell, who visited Paris so often, nor the restless Gallén, who was asked to be a member of the Expressionist "Die Brücke" group in 1907, but in fact Ellen Thesleff, who had worked in Italy. She had gone over to an Expressivist idiom in Italy back in 1904–1905.

Thesleff worked in Finland again in summer 1906 near Ruovesi. This is where she painted her lively "Girls in a Meadow," considered Finland's first Expressionist work of art. It has been difficult to explain its history. Frosterus linked Thesleff's "radiant visions" with Kandinsky, but the link does not seem so obvious even in the light of later research.

The frankness of Thesleff's palette knife technique had never before been seen in Finnish art. It gave her paintings a dynamism and abstraction that it took her Finnish colleagues years to attain. Unfortunately, Thesleff's influence remained negligible.

Gordon Craig, the English stage designer and producer, claimed that he taught Thesleff the basics of woodcut in Florence in 1906. Be that as it may, Thesleff contributed woodcuts to Craig's journal *The Mask*. The results of these experiments with graphics proved far-reaching; Thesleff's colored woodcuts took a major step beyond Gallén's achievements at the turn of the century.

The lesson of the Autumn Salon

Magnus Enckell and his friend the Russian ballet impresario Sergei Diaghilev convinced the president of Paris's *Salon d'Automne*, André Saglio, to give the Finns the opportunity to have a separate showing in 1908. The exhibition's reception delivered the final blow to the national "golden age."

Action Française noted that one could not doubt the existence of a Finnish school, "when one passes by the miserable things [pauvretes] gathered there." The most polite opinions considered the Finns' work to be mournful and soulful even

Ellen Thesleff:
Girls in a Meadow. 1906.
Oil, 38 x 46 cm.
Bäcksbacka Collection,
HELSINGIN KAUPUNGIN TAIDEMUSEO
(HELSINKI CITY ART MUSEUM).

Verner Thomé:
Borély Park. 1909.
Oil, 110 x 140 cm.
ART MUSEUM OF THE ATENEUM.

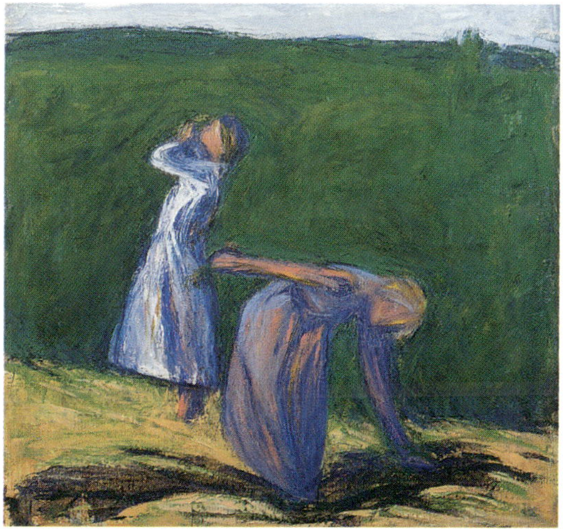

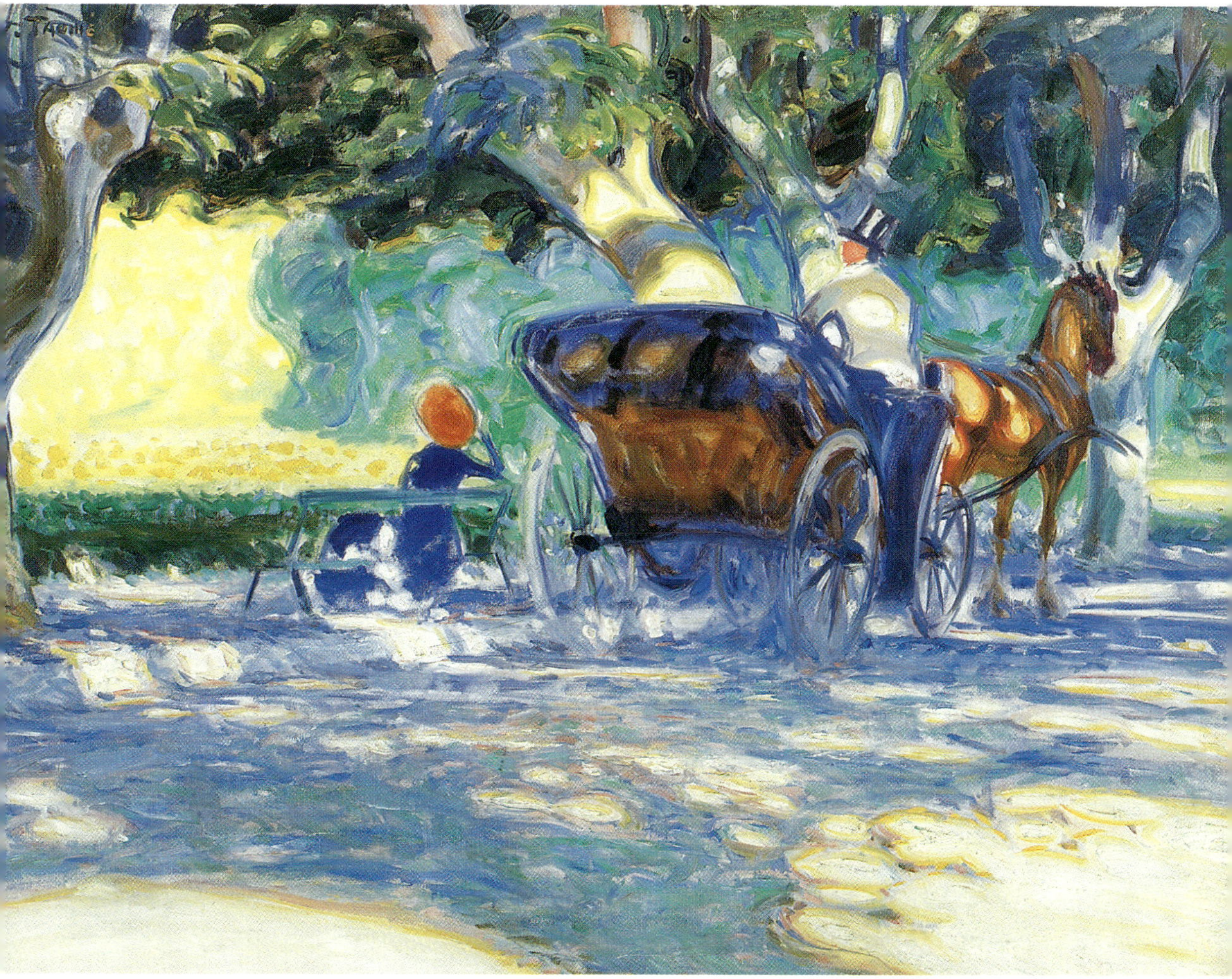

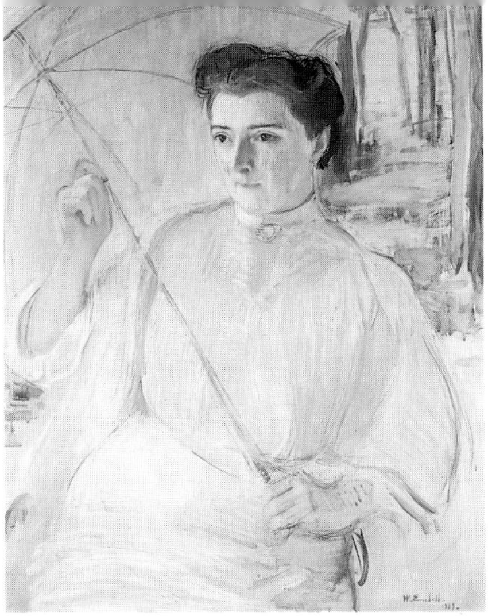

Magnus Enckell:
Portrait of Emmy Frosterus. 1909.
Oil, 95 x 70 cm.
PRIVATE COLLECTION.

Marcus Collin:
The Carousel. 1910. Oil, 90 x 100.
PRIVATE COLLECTION.

Wilho Sjöström:
March Sun. 1910.
Oil, 54 x 68 cm.
TURKU ART MUSEUM.

Juho Mäkelä:
Sunset. 1910. Oil, 42 x 35 cm.
Hedman Collection.
MUSEUM OF OSTROBOTHNIA, VAASA.

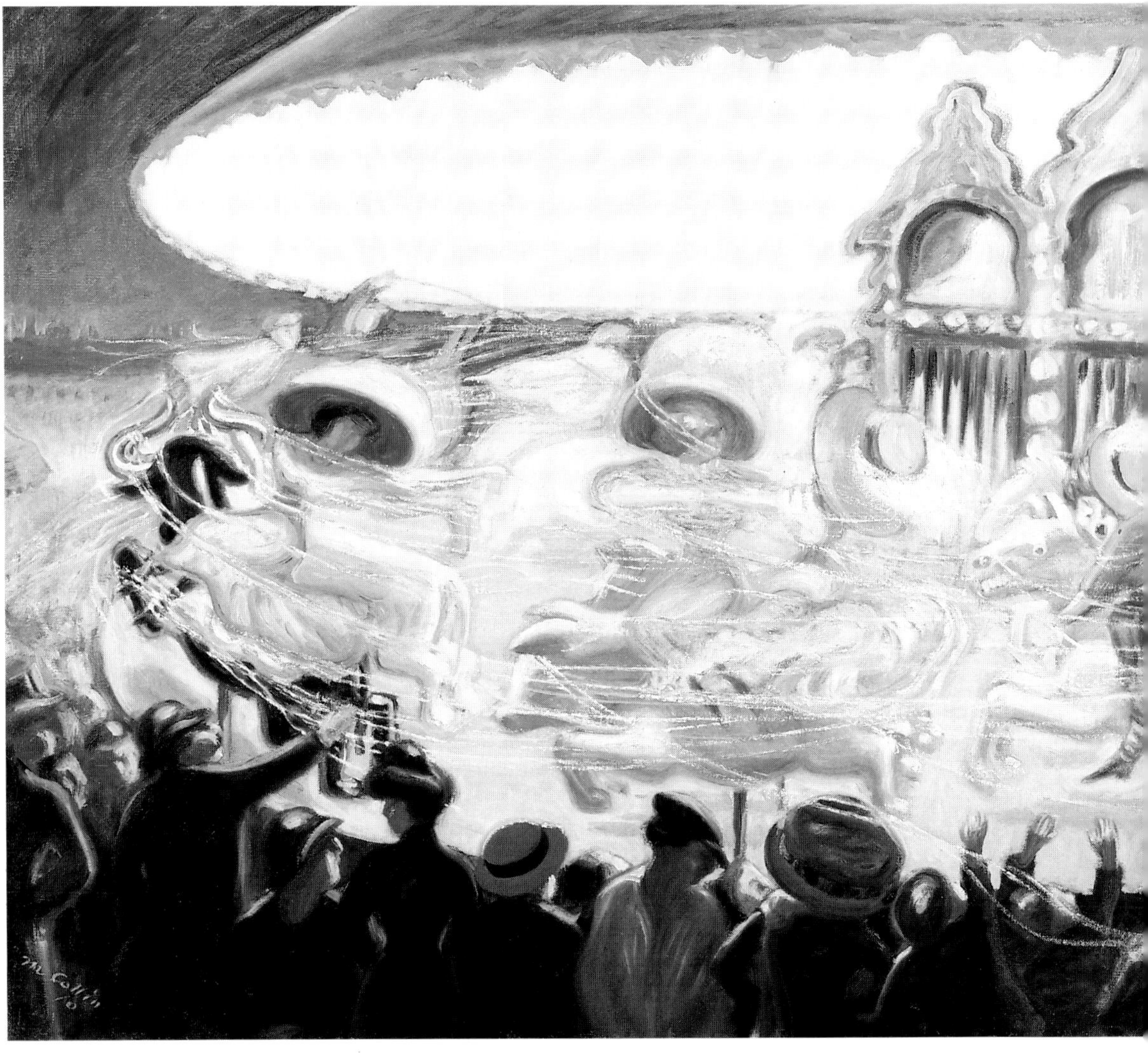

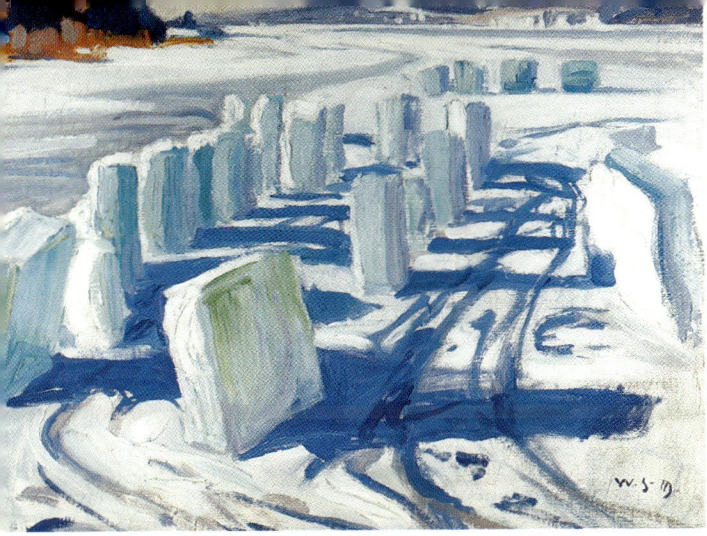

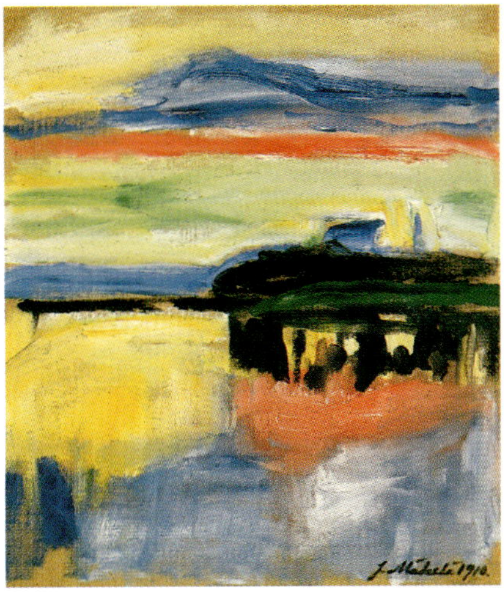

though it was impossible to find anything that was pleasing to the eye.

In Finland, Frosterus lectured his fellow countrymen and felt that the criticism that had been voiced for years would now take effect. And it did; the reform of color was carried out by 1910.

Finch's regular exhibitions between 1906 and 1910 had made Neo-impressionism familiar to critics and the enlightened public. And so when Verner Thomé exhibited his work at the Art Museum of the Ateneum in 1909, inspired by Fauvism, the reception was reservedly positive. Strengell, in contrast, left all his reservations at home: "Let me immediately shout out loud and clear, so that everyone may hear, that this is an event in our art life" – and here Strengell told a truth about artists that was highly unpopular on the other side of the language gap – "in which the nature of Finland's Swedish-speaking nation has achieved its finest flowering, all the while, in favoring light in the clarity of their art, approaching the French."

Swedish-speaking circles gave birth to Modernism not only in pictorial art, but also in literature. The short-lived journal *Euterpe*, founded in 1902, provided an important forum for discussion, one where Frosterus, too, spoke out in favor of Neo-impressionism for the first time.

The supporters of the "pure palette" made a breakthrough on a broad front at the 20th exhibition of Finnish artists in 1910. The young painters Yrjö Ollila (1887–1932), Alvar Cawén (1886–1935), Jalmari Ruokokoski (1886–1936), Oskari Paatela (1888–1952), and Yrjö Ramstedt (1880–1931) received varying degrees of publicity for their work, which ranged from Pointillist to Fauvist. Thesleff's style still irritated the critics, and Wennervirta asked, "Is this any longer healthy art?" since nature was stylized so much that it almost disappeared into nothingness.

Art during this period of upheaval did not coalesce into clear trends; Neo-impressionism was mixed with Expressionist and Synthetic elements. Magnus Enckell's key painting "Portrait of Emmy Frosterus" (1909) combined bright colors and form into an elegant entity, while Verner Thomé tried Pointillism in the style of Signac in his painting "Boys Bathing" (1910). Juho Rissanen made a careful study of Maurice Denis's style and adapted the decorative approach of the French master for his mural "In the Harbor" (1909), commissioned by the Viipuri company Häkli & Lallukka. Marcus Collin (1882–1966) did not give up his Synthetic form and line, but made full use of a bright range of colors in his Paris pictures, for example "Carousel" (1910): Daumier with electric light!

Alvar Cawén did some work with the Pointillist technique even though he did not make use of actual color division. Wilho Sjöström (1897–1944) favored a union of synthetic form and primary colors, as can be seen in his winter picture "March Sun" (1910).

Juho Mäkelä (1885–1943) was among the Finnish painters who admiringly took in Edvard Munch's exhibition at the Art Museum of the Ateneum in

Jalmari Ruokokoski:
Portrait of T. K. Sallinen. 1921.
Oil, 47 x 38.5 cm.
ART MUSEUM OF THE ATENEUM.

Tyko Sallinen:
The Washerwomen. 1911.
Oil, 154 x 136 cm.
ART MUSEUM OF THE ATENEUM.

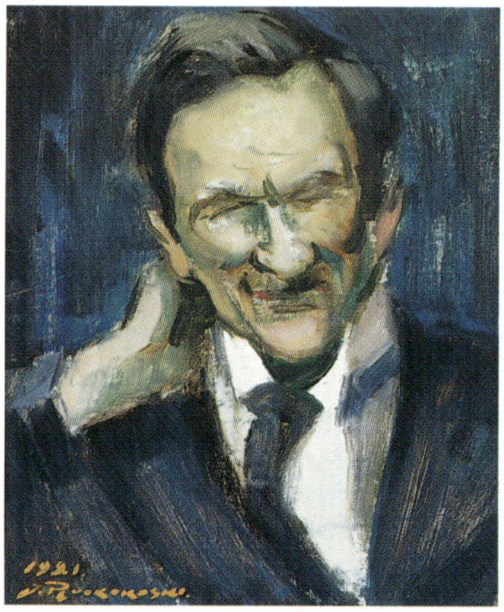

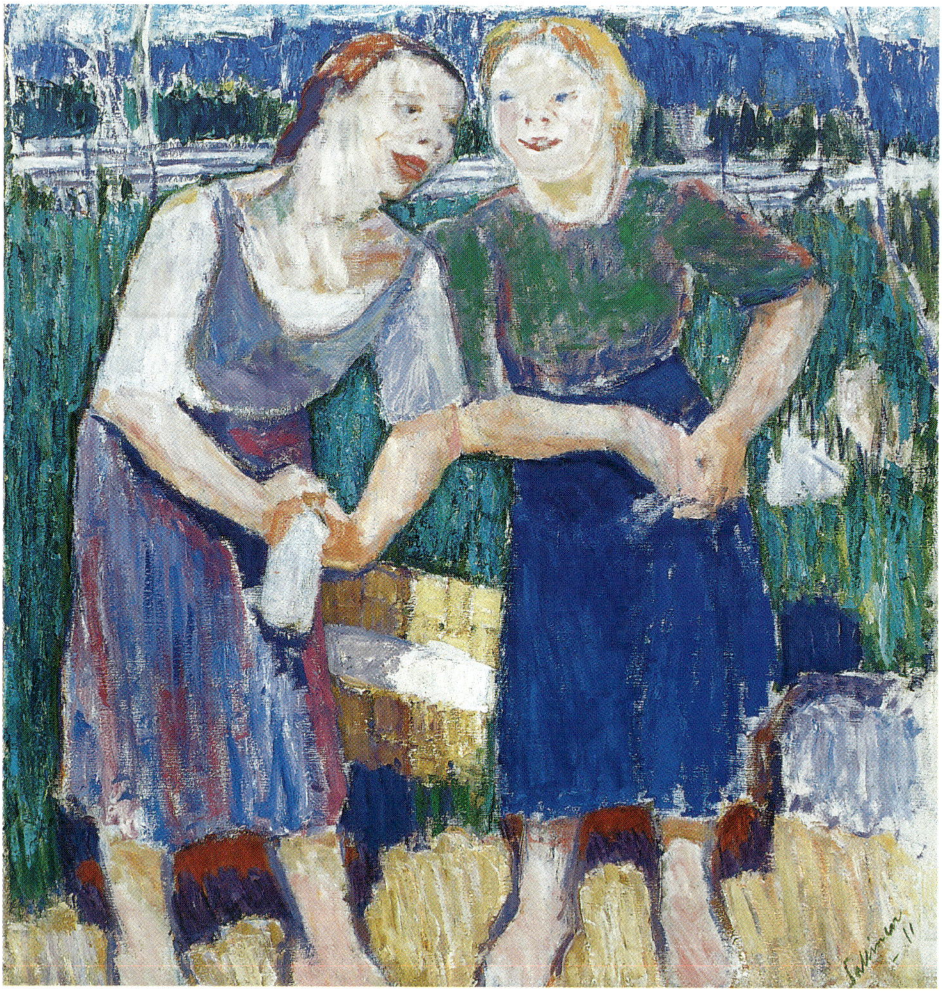

Mikko Oinonen: *Back of a Woman.* 1912. Aquatint and soft-ground engraving. 31 x 23 cm.
ART MUSEUM OF THE ATENEUM.

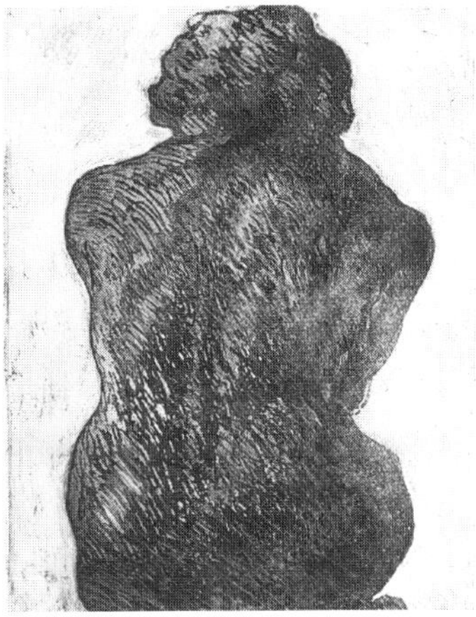

1908. Mäkelä inspected the paintings' contrast technique, obtaining material for his "Self-Portrait" (1910), made with magnificent thick brush strokes. Mäkelä's independence, in contrast, was seen in such frankly abstract paintings as "At Sunset" (1910). Its free, separate surfaces of color are indebted to their subject only for their point of departure.

The young journalist Gösta Stenman (1888–1947) met Juho Mäkelä at around this time, became interested in his art, and bought a few pictures. They formed the germ of an extensive collection and finally led Stenman to embark on a career as an art dealer. In 1912, Stenman founded a salon, and actively began supporting the Finnish Modernism of the day. He brought Helene Schjerfbeck to the attention of Scandinavia as a whole, and financed the work of the highly controversial Expressionist Tyko Sallinen (1879–1945).

The battles over Sallinen

The "first battle over Sallinen" was started in 1912 at the joint exhibition of four artists at the Art Museum of the Ateneum. Not much was written about the work of Sigrid Schauman (1877–1979), Einar Ilmoni (1880–1946), and Heikki Tandefelt (1882–1943), though the critics did mention Tandefelt's work painted in the Cubist fashion.

Sallinen, in contrast, was given a thorough going over. Or what should we say about what the pseudonym Publius (A. M. Tollet) wrote in *Hufvudstadsbladet*? "Of all the excesses of which the school of so-called Expressionists (if this is what Mr. S. represents) have been guilty, the ones documented here by Mr. Sallinen are the worst."

"Mr. Sallinen" and his paintings became a easy target for the satirical magazines. The cartoonist Erik Vasström did not even think it necessary to make a caricature of the most important painting in the exhibition, "The Washerwomen" (1911): he only had to sketch its outlines.

More serious critics recognized Sallinen's gifts and the forcefulness of his temperament. Stenman considered Sallinen's group an incomparable triumph. He said that "The Washerwomen" was a "fierce and sonorous chord before which all dissonance will fall silent." It was youthful wishful thinking.

The stylistic background for "The Washerwomen" can be found in the painting of Kees van Dongen, but slightly earlier work by Sallinen also revealed the influence of Matisse's Fauvism.

Sallinen was no longer a member of the youngest generation of artists when he made his breakthrough. He had been born in northern Karelia, but when his father joined a revivalist movement, he took his family to Haparanda, Sweden. The elder Sallinen, a tailor, was a strict man, and Tyko did not have the patience to stay meekly in his father's shop. During his colorful life, Sallinen worked in

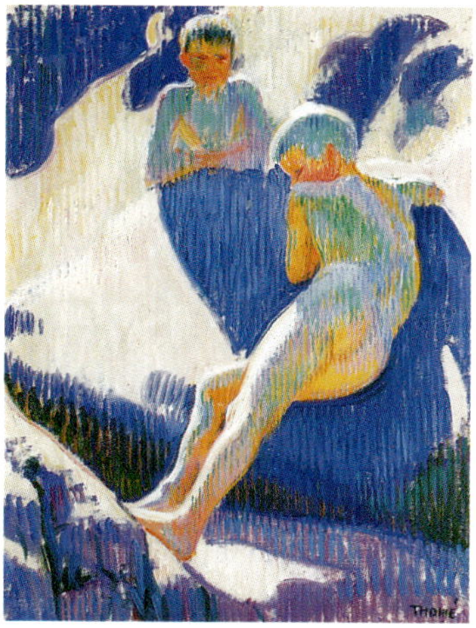

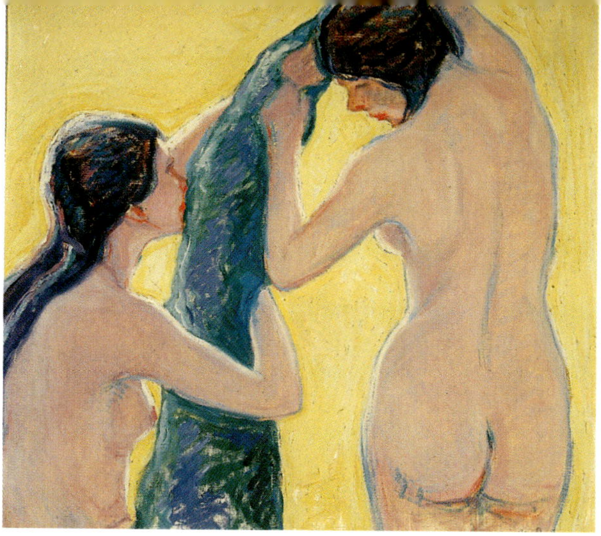

Copenhagen, and then in Elsinore with the master tailor N. P. Rydeng.

Rydeng was interested in art, and gathered around him a great many Expressionist painters. In addition to Sallinen and Mäkelä, Jalmari Ruokokoski often came to paint at "Rydeng's colony." At different times it received visits by William Lönnberg (1887–1949), Jonas Petterson (1887–1952), and Ragnar Ekelund (1892–1960).

Matisse's words at the beginning of the manifesto *Notes d'un peintre* (1908) began to be implemented in Finnish art: "ce que je poursuis par-dessus tout, c'est l'expression."

Septem and the November Group

The great movements in art began to take shape as Enckell arranged a Finnish exhibition to be shown in St. Petersburg in 1911. Its participants were to be Enckell, Finch, Oinonen, Thomé, Rissanen, Thesleff, and Ollila. The plans were never carried out, but the following spring, the same artists appeared as a group at the Art Museum of the Ateneum.

The group was not a permanent one, but beginning in 1914, it began to exhibit under the name of Septem. In order to emphasize its links with the subdued Post-impressionism of the Nabis, the Finns invited Pierre Bonnard, Charles Guerin, and Ker-Xavier Roussell to exhibit their work in 1913. The change in emphasis was seen in such things as the decorative use of line in Yrjö Ollila's pastoral idylls and Enckell's periodical return to Symbolist and classical motives.

Septem tried to come to an understanding with the Expressionists, and invited Tyko Sallinen, Ragnar Ekelund, Valle Rosenberg (1891–1915), Alvar Cawén, and Werner Åström (1885–1979) to their exhibition in 1914. The artists' appearances together had no practical significance since they had already gone their own ways when it came to their concept of art.

Sallinen's return to Finland further strengthened the Expressionist front. The autumn meeting of the Artists' Association of Finland headed by Akseli Gallen-Kallela (Axel Gallén had Finnicized his name, as did many cultural figures at around this time) had thrown Sallinen out in 1912 for abusive behavior. The artist, who otherwise tolerated the treatment he received, left for the United States for a year, where he earned a living drawing cartoons and ads for *Amerikan työmies*, the Finnish-American newspaper in Hancock, Michigan.

"The second battle over Sallinen" was waged in 1915 when he exhibited a painting entitled "The Dwarf" (1915). The architect Werner von Essen wrote, "A brutish human being intentionally pours the contents of a sauce boat over a table cloth." Sallinen's straightforward portrayal touched a sensitive spot. Ugliness pricked the Finns' conscience. What was truly interesting about "The Dwarf," however, was its style. It reveals a brisk adaptation of Cézanne's geometric approach and Sallinen's increasing interest in the

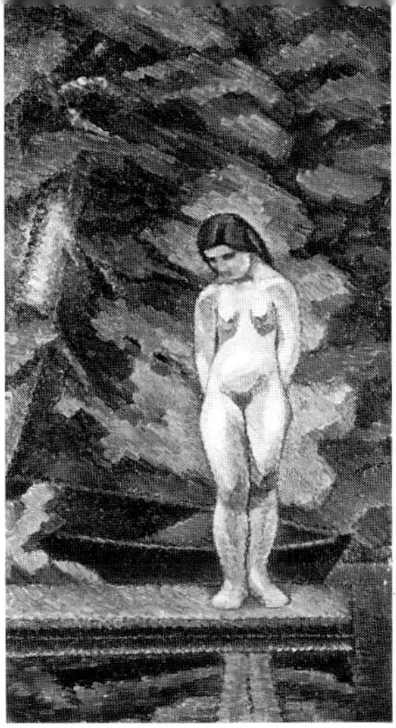

Verner Thomé:
Boys on the Shore. 1910.
Oil, 60 x 45.5 cm.
EMIL CEDERCREUTZ MUSEUM, HARJAVALTA.

Alvar Cawén: Two Girls. 1912.
Oil, 72 x 72 cm.
PRIVATE COLLECTION.

Uno Alanco:
Girl on the Shore (Aino). 1917.
Oil. 144 x 70 cm.
PRIVATE COLLECTION.

faceted structures of Cubism.

Sallinen had become the natural spiritual leader of the Expressionists, and his "group" was the topic of much discussion. It gathered together its first exhibition in 1916. There were only five participants, but there were already fourteen the following year. The artists formed the November Group, whose founding meeting was attended by Sallinen; Ilmari Aalto (1891–1934); the group's only sculptor, Wäinö Aaltonen (1894–1966); Mikko Carlstedt (1892–1964); Alvar Cawén; Marcus Collin; Ragnar Ekelund; Viljo Kojo (1891–1966); Anton Lindfors (1890–1943); Alex Matson (1888–1972); Eero Nelimarkka (1891–1977); Juho Rissanen; and Antti Vanninen (1890–1985).

Under the influence of Cubism, the Expressionism of the November Group became preponderantly geometrical and relied on earth colors.

The intermezzo of cubism

"The world is no longer round; this is the new invention of 'cube-artists.' It is faceted," wrote Rusticus, alias the author Joel Lehtonen of the Paris *Salon d'Automne* in 1911. He actually pitied poor Cubism for seemingly not being appreciated by anyone.

From a Finnish point of view, Cubism remained a curiosity for quite some time. The situation changed when Uno Alanco (nom de plume, 1878–1964, who started to use his real name, Uuno Alanko, in 1925) almost accidentally – perhaps thanks to Sweden's John Sten – in early December 1912 ended up at the Cubists' academy, "La palette." where Le Fauconnier was largely responsible for his training. Alanco also took part in the *Salon des Indépendents* in 1913, showing his slightly Cubist painting "La Résignation."

Alanco did not try to break down forms or paint simultaneous perspective, but instead developed the angular plasticity of early Cubism, the style of Cézanne, and the sculpture of Egypt that he so much admired into his own restrained approach. Instead of being primitively heavy, his nude figures were in fact almost as graceful as the sculptures of Art Nouveau.

When he had his first Cubist exhibition in Helsinki in October-November 1913, Alanco brought out the concept of a new art in the foreword to the exhibition catalogue. Alanco hoped that the different branches of art would unite into an intimate entity instead of isolating themselves. He believed that the lack of ideals and faith gave birth to spiritually impoverished art. Alanco did not, however, feel that reflecting scientific progress in the technique of art would prevent the artist from expressing his personality and nationality.

Alanco's belief in the possibility of reconciling Cubism with Finnishness was given tangible form: a Cubist "Aino" took shape on his canvas in 1914.

A Cubist exhibition was opened in Viipuri, too, even

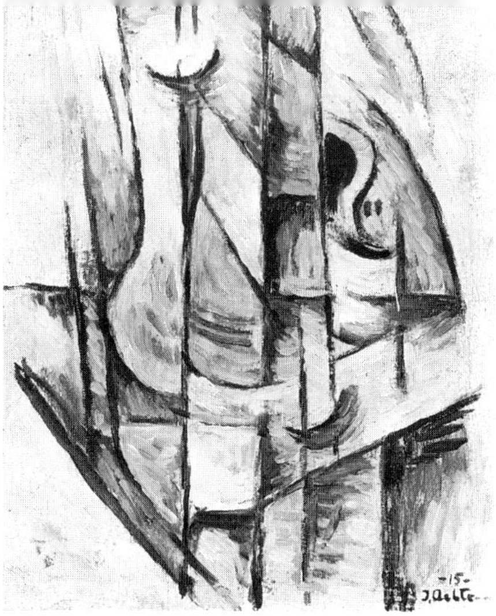

Ilmari Aalto:
Cubist Still-life. 1915.
Oil, 38 x 47 cm.
ART MUSEUM OF THE ATENEUM.

earlier than Alanco's. Kalle Kuutola, who had studied in Paris between 1911 and 1913, exhibited work together with Bruno Tuukkanen that the critics considered Cubist-Futurist.

The Futurist element was probably imaginary, since the Finnish artists' contacts with both Italian Futurism and Russian Cubo-futurism were almost non-existent. Plans were made, but never carried out, to bring the "Donkey's Tail" exhibition from St. Petersburg to Finland in 1912.

The lack of current information bothered the Finns, and not even the Norwegian Jens Thiis's lecture "From Neo-impressionism to Cubism" delivered at Helsinki University in 1913 helped, though it was received "like the word of God." The Finns' mystification was obvious when the Salon Strindberg in Helsinki arranged an exhibition featuring "Der Blaue Reiter" in February 1914. It was an important event, since this was the first time a Finnish audience had the opportunity to see work by such artists as Aleksi von Jawlensky, Wassily Kandinsky, Paul Klee, Franz Marck, Gabriele Münter, and Heinrich Campendonck, but also by Natalie Goncharova and the Burljuk brothers. Many of the reviews of the exhibition called Kandinsky's abstract, "radical" work Futurist.

Ilmari Aalto progressed farthest on the road of Cubism. His "Cubist Still-life" from 1916 is one of the few Finnish examples of analytic Cubism. Aalto evidently found the models for his painting from the art journalists subscribed to by Stenman's salon.

The Bohemian Aalto never managed to go into Cubism in depth, and drifted on to a more Expressionist style.

Reflections of the civil war

The rise of the Bolsheviks to power in Russia in October 1917 created a favorable opportunity to sever ties between Finland and Russia. Parliament, which had a bourgeois majority, proclaimed Finland's independence on December 6, 1917. It is one of the paradoxes of history that the government headed by Lenin recognized its new neighboring state in January 1918.

The Socialists' program, "We Demand," had suffered a defeat in Finland's Parliament. It had not even been possible to promote its goals through a general strike, but no effort was made to stop the stir it had caused. The shortage of food in winter brought unrest, and the Russian soldiers that were still stationed in Finland reinforced the belief that a "red coup" would be successful. The order

Alvar Cawén:
The Russian Fleet in Helsinki Harbor. 1918.
Oil on paper, 54 x 74 cm.
PRIVATE COLLECTION.
Finch made several paintings on the same theme, depicting the scene at night.

Eero Nelimarkka:
The Announcement. 1917.
Oil, 55 x 76.5 cm.
PRIVATE COLLECTION.
The inhabitants of a northern village read the proclamation of Finnish independence.

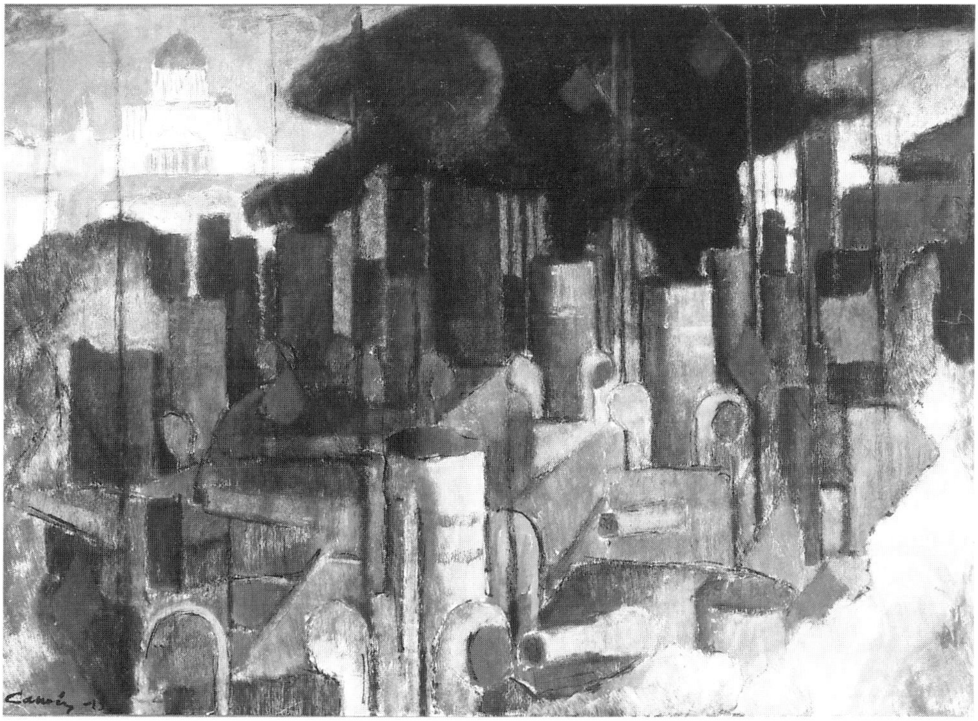

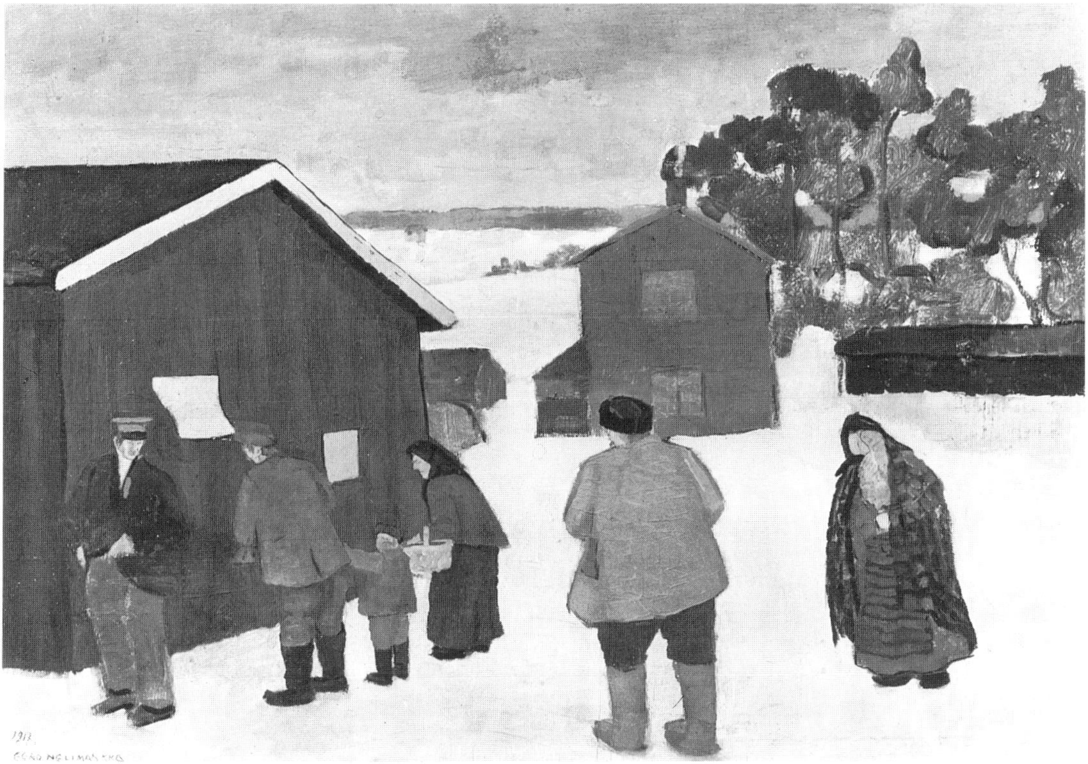

Tyko Sallinen:
Holy Jumpers. 1918.
Oil, 168 x 185 cm.
ART MUSEUM OF THE ATENEUM.

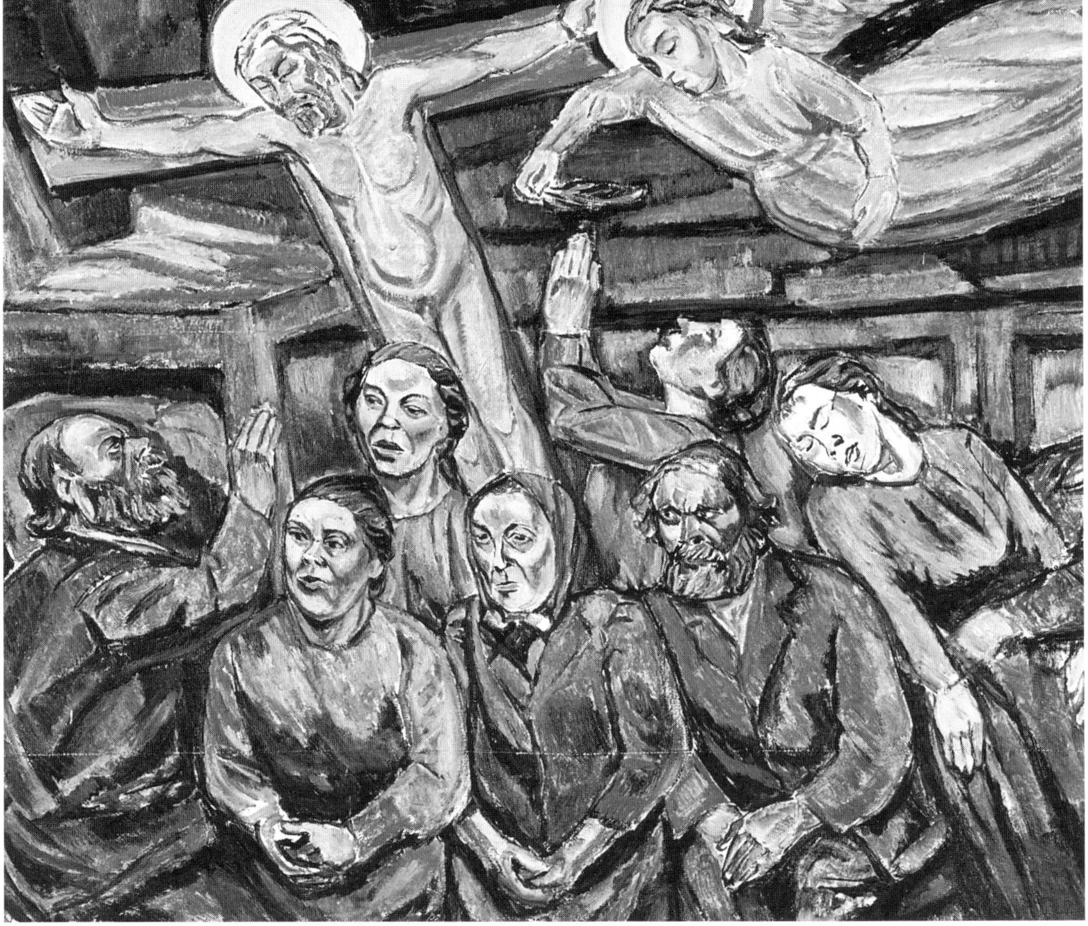

to start the revolution was given in Helsinki on January 26, 1918, in the name of the Social Democratic Party's committee and the Red Guards. The "white" government met in Vaasa and started to seek Germany's help.

The civil war was a bitter conflict. The "red terror" was avenged after the war with "white terror" executions and by letting reds die in the inhuman conditions of the prison camps. Over half a century was needed to heal the wounds left by the war. The last reflections of the civil war were seen in the historical proletarian subjects of committed art in the 1970s.

Unrest is not conducive to art, but a small cross-section of the work done in 1917 and 1918 shows the depth of the split in society.

Alvar Cawén painted his last Cubist work in Helsinki, which was ruled by the reds. He was able to see from his window how the vessels of the Russian revolutionary fleet anchored at Katajanokka dock to bring help to the Red Guards. Cawén depicted the somber cluster of smokestacks as black Léger-like cylinders, and in the upper left-hand corner, he painted a radiant Helsinki Cathedral, the symbol of "white" Finland.

The features of the November Group grew more distinct on the canvasses of Enckell, a member of the Septem Group, as society was shaken by the conflict. He made two paintings linked with the revolution and civil war, "Chaos" and "Pain," both from 1919. Two sketches for "Chaos" are known. Despite the Expressivist style, Enckell used what were in fact Symbolist means. The pathetic youth in "Chaos" is swathed in a red cape and carries a "Jolly Roger."

During the civil war, Tyko Sallinen remained in Hyvinkää, in his studio, "Hangover," and made one of his most important paintings at the nearby Mutila workers' hall dances: "The Country Dance" (1917–1918). It is a terse composition that relies on the means used by Cézanne and the Cubists; its close cropping and vertical surface perspective seem to topple the group of figures off the canvas.

Soon after the war, Sallinen painted his second major work, "Holy Jumpers" (1919), in Wäinö Aaltonen's (1894–1966) studio in Turku. At the age of 39, Sallinen was finally ready to come to terms with his childhood experiences. Even though religiosity was linked in Sallinen's mind with the strict, contradictory figure of his father – the sadistic disciplinarian, the man of God, the pleasure-seeking periodical drinker – "Holy Jumpers" became not a pronouncement of judgment on the revivalist movement but a gesture of conciliation that embraced all of society. The artist's daughter, the writer Irja Salla, wrote, "Father has painted Jesus blessing, spreading his hands ... When his hands are not nailed to the cross, he is able to bless. He blesses the congregation and the angel brings a frond from the palm of peace."

The basic structure of "The Country Dance" and "Holy Jumpers" is the same: the same rapturous movement flows from right to left. Sin and its devils hover in the upper part of the sketch for "The Country Dance," while a crucifix and angel are found in "Holy Jumpers."

Pride and prejudice in an independent land

Discordant harmony

Independent Finland made uneven progress at first. The "rump" Parliament that met after the civil war declared Finland a monarchy. It was believed that political support and even a king would come from Germany, but when Germany lost the Great War, Finland's dreams of a monarchy dissolved.

Culturally, Finland went through difficult times. There was no question of forming close ties to the Soviet Union, and the passionate advocates of "genuine Finnishness" wished to distance the country from Sweden, even though this western neighbor was considered an enviable model of progress. Scandinavianism and national radicalism were in fact on the warpath during the whole inter-war period.

In the Baltics, the Estonians, especially, were considered a sister nation, and Finland was able to see itself as the active partner in cooperative efforts.

Before the final enactment of the republican constitution, the royalist hero of the "white" forces, C. G. E. Mannerheim, served as chief executive. As one of his aides he had chosen Gallen-Kallela, who designed the first Finnish uniforms.

A national identity was created in an atmosphere that despite its energy easily leaned towards surveillance and a narrow moral outlook. This new puritanism received the political support of the large rural population. Even opera was considered a ribald urban art form, and there was a move to cut down on state subsidies to theaters.

Cultural circles tried to seek new impulses from the past. The heroes of the golden age, from Sibelius to Eliel Saarinen, from Robert Kajanus to Gallen-Kallela, from Pekka Halonen to Eino Leino, were mobilized around the charter of the national awakening, the *Kalevala*.

After their "symposium," the carousers met once again to celebrate the plans to found the Kalevala Society in 1920, but now they could be seen sitting upright in evening dress together with the cream of Finnish society, including President K. J. Ståhlberg himself.

In 1921, Eliel Saarinen drew up plans for an enormous Kalevala hall with a tower that would rise to a height of 90 meters. The building would house a museum, archives, a research institute, and above all a pantheon intended as the final resting place of the great men of the republic. The plans were never carried out, but the idea was later revived in different forms.

The old generation felt ill at ease in the midst of the new "materialism." Gallen-Kallela lost his temper at times and in 1923 thundered that art in the old sense had lost its meaning "thanks to the Bolshevist mental attitude and the bluff of art dealers." The target of this venomous declaration was naturally Gösta Stenman, the radical patron of the November Group.

The taste of the Finnish art public was reflected in its attitude to Helene Schjerfbeck's major exhibition at Stenman's salon in 1917. Stenman noted with disappointment that 99 out of one hundred visitors consid-

Helene Schjerfbeck:
Tapestry. 1914–1916.
Oil, 89.5 x 92 cm.
PRIVATE COLLECTION, STOCKHOLM.

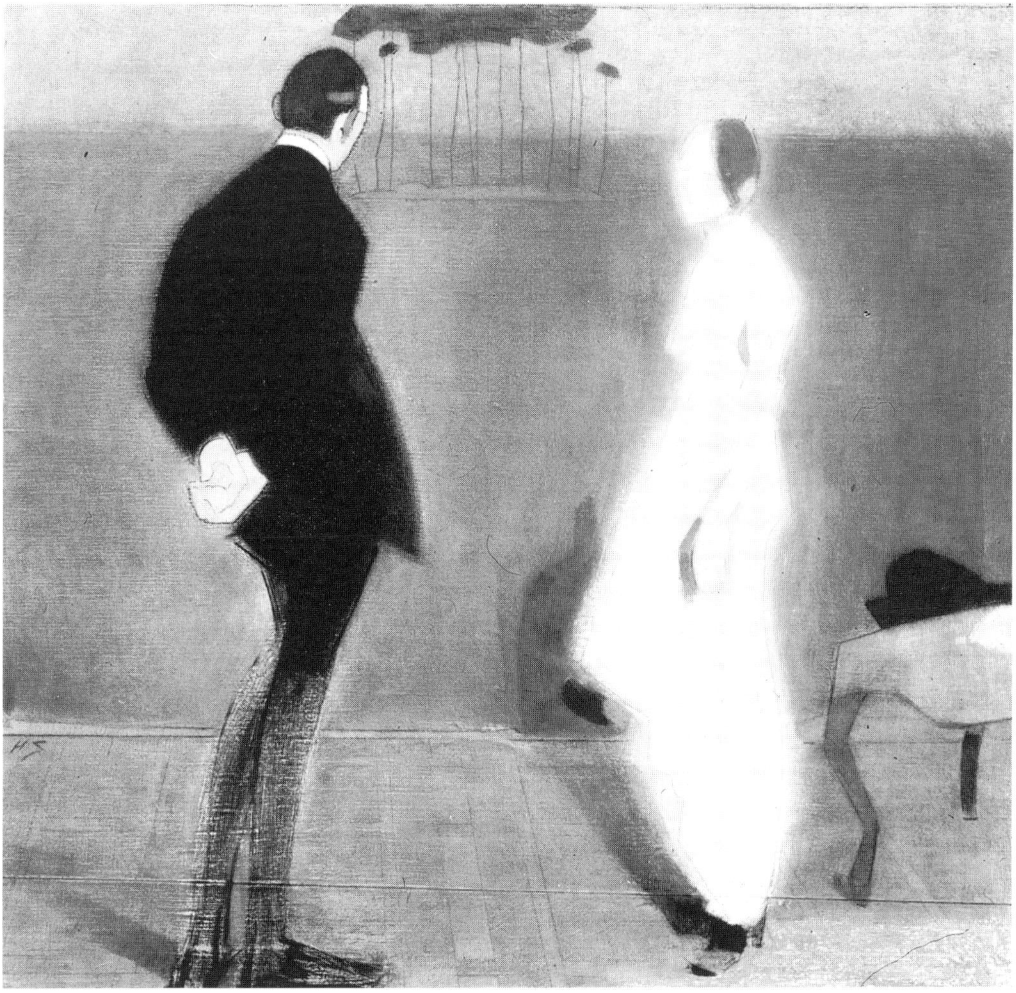

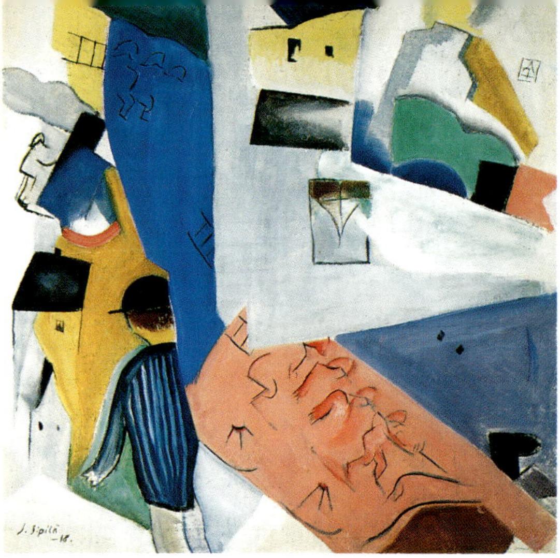

Sulho Sipilä: City View. 1918. Oil, 74 x 67.5 cm.
TURKU ART MUSEUM.

ered Schjerfbeck's old, naturalistic paintings best, while only one defended her Modernist pieces. Stenman moved to Sweden a decade later.

The young generation of artists did not, however, cherish the delusion of national self-sufficiency. A few painters had already been experimenting with far-reaching abstractions at the threshold of independence. The versatile Sulho Sipilä (1895–1949) painted Chagall-like, spaciously sectionalized geometric surfaces beginning in 1917. In the following decade, his style became more Naivistic. Sipilä never managed to produce very much since he became a naval officer in order to make a proper living.

Wäinö Aaltonen made a few Cubist drawings in 1917. He did not want to exhibit them, however, though his colleagues urged him to do so. Aaltonen made his first Cubist collage, "The Face," in 1920, but the true Cubist period in his production did not start until the mid-1920s. Experience with geometrically composed paintings and drawings was transferred to the bold angles and volumes of sculpture, climaxing in true Cubism in "The Dancer" (1928), and in the designs for the monument to Aleksis Kivi in Helsinki. The Finns would hardly have tolerated a Cubist version of their national writer, so Aaltonen took a realistic approach for his sculpture of the poet, pondering the melancholy of creativity.

The greatest asset of Aaltonen's work from the very beginning was its concentrated, magnificent plasticity. "Nude Boy" (1917–20) made him famous as a master of the archaizing sculptural "Egyptian" style. Grandeur was much in demand as the young nation took shape, and granite, Aaltonen's favorite material, signaled durability and solidity in itself.

The new republic's most extensive art offensive was waged to create the monuments of the civil war, or in the terminology of the day, literally the war of freedom. Aaltonen sculpted the best monuments from an artistic point of view. He made a bold design in 1918 for the memorial sculpture to commemorate the liberation of Tampere. It comprised a four-stepped ziggurat-like base and a Hellenic warrior kneeling in prayer. Onni Okkonen, who had become one of the key arbiters in national art, praised Aaltonen's design, noting that it had "the concept of a colossal monument which involuntarily makes one compare it to the statues of the Pharaohs of Egypt and the Buddhas of the East."

Aaltonen's design seemed too modern to the competition jury, and it was placed in the third group, to be rejected. Nonetheless, Aaltonen was commissioned to make the "Savonlinna War Memorial," and was able to make his praying soldier in 1921, though in truncated form. The face of the figure shows the impressive profile of the poet Aaro Hellaakoski, but the kneeling position is based on a miniature sculpture portraying the artist's sister, Elsa. It was also executed in a monumental version, the "Alastaro War Memorial" (1919), the figure of a maiden holding the sacrificial urn of life.

The citizens of Tampere made up for their earlier rejec-

Wäinö Aaltonen: Nude Boy. 1917. Granite, 128.5 cm.
ART MUSEUM OF THE ATENEUM.

Wäinö Aaltonen: Aleksis Kivi, study. 1932. Ceramics, 24 cm.
ART MUSEUM OF THE ATENEUM.

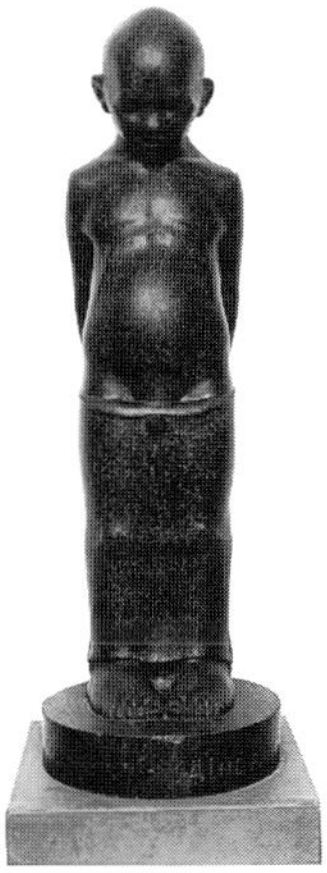

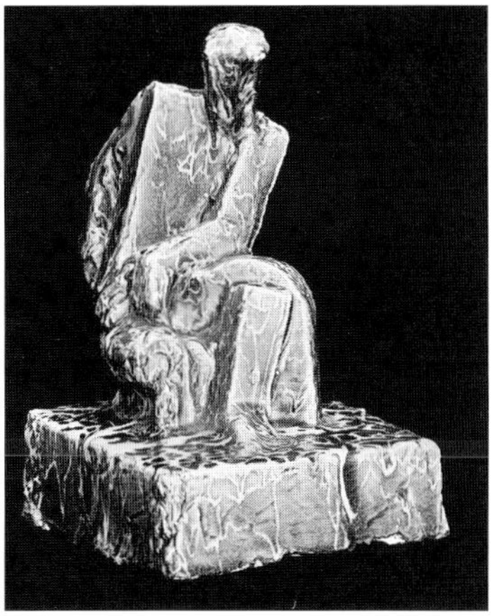

tion of Aaltonen at the end of the 1920s. Aaltonen made the town's Aleksis Kivi memorial, and most important, the statues for Hämeensilta bridge, paid for from a donation by the industrialist Rafael Haarla. They depicted the ancient power of the people of Häme in the form of "The Hunter," "The Maid of Finland," "The Tax Collector," and "The Merchant."

The critic from the Swedish daily *Svenska Dagbladet*, H. Hedeman-Gade, touched a sensitive spot when he wrote of the exhibition of Finnish art held in Copenhagen in 1919. He noted that Aaltonen's marble head of a girl was an enchanting work of art and a monument to the Finnish race: "The nature of race has not been suppressed here any more than it has been in Sallinen's paintings. But we should not speak of a caricature."

The Finns were sensitive to claims that they were Mongols, and they longed for a noble national portrait in place of the November Group's barbarians. It didn't help matters much when the exhibition in Copenhagen proved the November Group's triumph, while the refined Septem Group received less attention. Aaltonen knew better than anyone else, however, how to elevate the Finnish "race" in the spirit of classicism, especially fulfilling Onni Okkonen's wish for a national art based on tradition.

Once again the familiar themes from the *Kalevala* were chosen. Aaltonen sculpted numerous pieces with motives of wading maidens, one, started in Rome, called "Aino" or "Maiden Going Wading" (1923). The streamlined form cut from the white marble brushed aside the tragedy of the myth of Aino and replaced it with the Aphrodite-like purity and beauty of Finnish womanhood. Later Aaltonen conceived innumerable incarnations of the Maid of Finland. Together with the manly gymnast and athlete, they served as the models for the Finnish ideal.

Aaltonen was conscious of his abilities and his position, and he was not saved from attacks of hubris. In Rome in 1923, after seeing with his own eyes the work of antiquity that he had admired, he wrote, "The statue of Ramses II and things like that are fine, but not at all of a kind that couldn't be surpassed. And the old Greeks give the same impression."

There were fresher experiences to be gained in Rome, too. Aaltonen met Futurism, but it did not influence his art, which was dominated instead by a union of Cubism and Classicism. The principles of a subdued form saturated the whole field of art and also tamed the members of the November Group, including Aaltonen.

In spite of all the opposition, the group's ideology had been accepted fairly well in the young republic. Its art was not, after all, a monolithic entity. The Vulcan-like Sallinen had become more like Cézanne, but his work seemed heavy indeed alongside the soulful and masterly paintings of Alvar Cawén. Both developed their own styles, though at different stages, through gossamer brush strokes that left the ground visible.

Marcus Collin was actually the artist who presented the most austere views of the Finn-

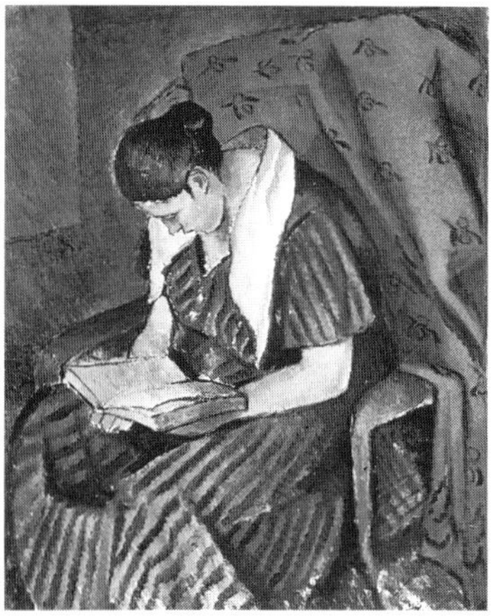

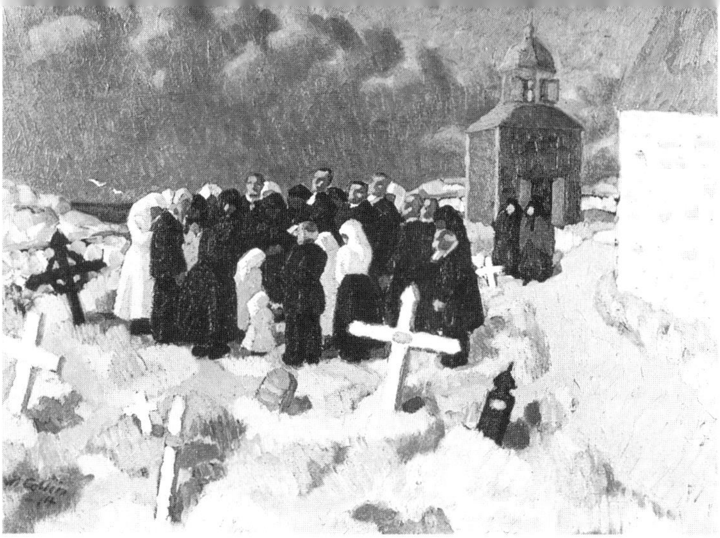

Alvar Cawén:
The Artist's Wife. 1924–1925.
Oil, 100 x 81 cm.
PRIVATE COLLECTION.

Marcus Collin:
Funeral at Kökar. 1914.
Oil, 59.5 x 72 cm.
TURKU ART MUSEUM.

Ragnar Ekelund:
Notre-Dame. 1925.
Oil, 65 x 54 cm.
ART MUSEUM OF THE ATENEUM.

Edwin Lydén:
Golgotha
(center panel of a triptych). 1927.
Oil, 88 x 120.5 cm.
TURKU ART MUSEUM.

ish people. His work is tinged with moving humor, but gives a fairly discouraging picture of both the toilers in the countryside and the drudges in the factories. The public became so accustomed to Collin's deep, dark tones that he was criticized when he changed over to a slightly lighter pallette.

It is difficult to find any unifying factor in the work of the November Group during the 1920s except a docile Formalism leaning towards a cultivation of form. Ragnar Ekelund's strictly geometric art that favored depictions of architecture got the better of all Expressivist approaches. In his wake, for example, the work of Väinö Kamppuri (1891–1972) seemed picturesquely bland. The November Group's last exhibition was held in 1924.

The radicals of the Red Room

Romantic and Modern trends have traditionally thrived better in Turku than they have in Helsinki. The reason is undoubtedly the proximity of Sweden.

Beginning in 1905, a group of young artists gathered fairly regularly in the Red Room at the Pinella Restaurant: Ilmari Kaijala (1886–1944), Edwin Lydén (1879–1956), Emil Rautala (1883–1948), Santeri Salokivi (1886–1940), and Ragner Ungern (1885–1955). At these meetings, they planned exhibitions and discussed the great questions of life.

Lydén depicted the group's meeting in a drawing that caricatured Gallén's "Symposion." There are two versions, one with a book on the table bearing the word *ALSO*. Nietzsche was one of the household gods of the day in Finland, too, though most people had not themselves read *Also sprach Zarathustra*, let alone the rest of the venerated philosopher's writings.

Lydén, Salokivi, and Ungern had studied in Munich at the *Königliche Bayerische Akademie der Künste*. The group's links with Germany remained strong, and all but Kaijala revisited Munich in 1908. The artists' style became more Colorist, and the art public began to speak of "Munich-style Turku art."

The painters of the Red Room went through an intense Neo-impressionist phase. Lydén was quick to make a change, however, and began to make socially committed paintings from 1912. In addition, he made cartoons for two publications, *Punanen viesti* and *Sosialisti*. The group disbanded during the First World War, and the members joined the short-lived

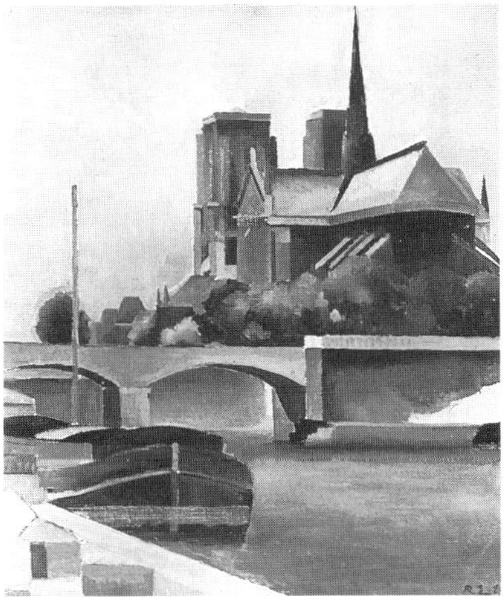

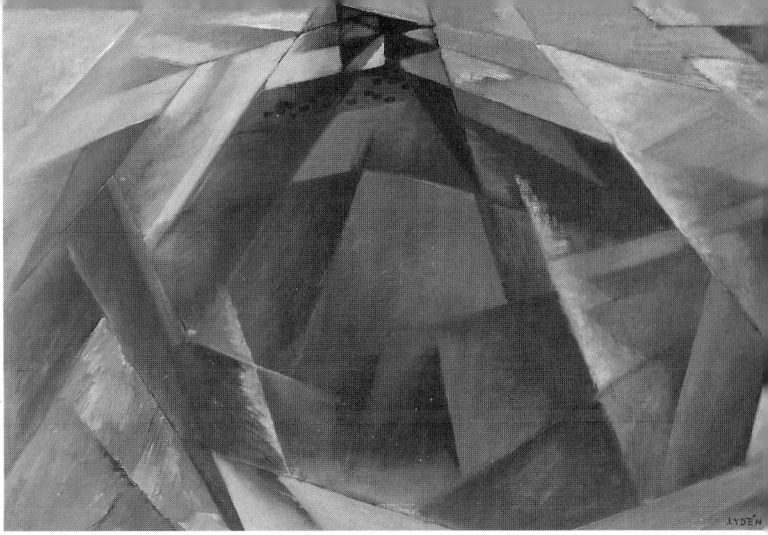

Aura artists' union in Turku.

Lydén returned to Munich in 1919. According to the art historian Raimo Aarras, he met Paul Klee and Rainer Maria Rilke through Lou-Lou Albert-Lazard (Lou Andreas-Salomé). Klee's art became a guiding light in Lydén's search for innovation. He began to paint with watercolors, like Klee. Stylistically, however, Lydén sought his own spiritualist approach. "Rain" (1920) and "Neunte Welle" (1920) were among his finest work done in Munich.

On his way back to Finland, Lydén saw the German Kurt Schwitters's exhibition in Berlin. It made a profound impression on him, and Lydén even bought a little "Merzbild" at the exhibition. Schwitters and Lydén kept in touch. Lydén subscribed to *Der Sturm* and was able to follow developments on the Continent. Lydén made his first collage, "A New Life," in 1921.

Despite all the new stimuli, Lydén's art remained Expressionist. Some of his work shows glimpses of Robert Delaunay's Orphism, but the spirit of Franz Marc is clearer in the swirling movement of great volumes, shown in the cosmic tumult of Lydén's compositions, especially in the "Thunder" series.

Lydén was not certain whether he should paint in a completely abstract fashion. He thought that the connection between the work of art and reality would provide the viewer with the necessary key: "If there is nothing of this reality, a picture is only a decoration." The statement echoes the typical platitude of the day that abstract art is purely decorative. At last Lydén defied the link between viewer and work of art and painted a geometric abstraction called "Sunbeam" (1924). It cannot be considered non-figurative, however, even though Raimo Aarras has linked the work done during this period mainly with the influence of Laszlo Moholy-Nagy. After making his first Concretist composition in 1933, Lydén cautiously and perhaps ironically entitled it "Decorative Painting."

Lydén's *Der Sturm*-like synthesis is a religious triptych completed in 1927. Its central section, "Golgotha," is cleft by Futurist power lines. In the upright forms of the right wing, "Tuonela," the Gothic groins of Delaunay's "St-Severin" and the vaults of Turku Cathedral intersect. The center of the left wing is dominated by the figure of Christ, hovering apart from his cross. The artist got the idea for the triptych after listening to the Danish composer Otto Malling's three-movement organ piece "Gethsemane-Golgotha-Sunday" at Turku Cathedral.

Lydén had a major influence on trends in the Turku art world for decades. He was respected as an authority on Modernism, and he also expressed his opinions as a critic. When internal dissent in the Turku artists' union led to the founding of the little Pro Arte Group in 1933, Lydén held with the young artists and became their theoretical advisor.

The Torchbearers

The Torch-bearers (1924–1930), a group of writers and artists, undertook to modernize

Finnish culture, inspired by an infatuation with modern life. The group's manifesto, published in 1928, declared: "See: how wonderfully young our country is, and how full of power! Come; don't be afraid. You have been chosen to create something new and great."

Olavi Paavolainen (1893–1964), the most conspicuous member the Torch-bearers), published his hilarious series of essays, *Nykyaikaa etsimässä*(In search of the present), in 1929. He wanted to shake up Finland's old-fashioned art world. Paavolainen extolled the urban way of life and the cult of machines: "Express trains, radio messages, and new ideologies leave from and arrive in the cities. The cities are where revolutions, politics, art trends, and the latest jazz hits are born, spread, and buried."

Paavolainen imagined the reaction of the artists who hung out at the Bronda Café when they heard of the young art historian Bertel Hintze's demand in 1924 that aimless still-lifes and unintelligent nudes be rejected. (Hintze later became director of the Helsinki Art Hall.) He thought he knew what they would say. "Were these the fellows who were supposed to create imaginative visions, depict machines and symbols, give shape to endeavors and emotions, and present these 'people whose true expressions can be seen only in modern technology and its creations'? After all, they are 'fine artists.' They're the ones who know how to 'paint' and have their 'fine values' (oh! this magical word value!), their 'pure brush strokes' and 'unfailing skill at matching colors ..."

Finnish art as a whole looked anemic indeed when it was compared as Paavolainen did to Futurism, Dadaism, and the Russian avant-garde. But he did not consider the situation completely hopeless, since he mentioned Väinö Kunnas (1896–1929), one of the youngest members of the Torch-bearers, who deserved praise for the modern feel of his "Dance" series. Paavolainen also mentioned some of the artists who had been forgotten by the critics, "H. Ahtela (the alias of Einar Reuter, 1881–1968), a "melancholic lyricist"; Sulho Sipilä, a Rousseau-like "child and poet"; Lauri Saari (1888–1953), "possessed by devils"; Maria Tamminen, a "sleep-painter" comparable to Kandinsky; and Edwin Lydén. He was kind enough to include the bold Alvar Aalto (1898–1976) in the forefront of architects.

Paavolainen's list is still worth looking at, since we know little of the work of Ahtela and Saari, and nothing at all of Tamminen's. Paavolainen did not try to present all young art, but he could have supplemented his list by mentioning Einari Wehmas (1898–1955), who had studied under André Lhôte, and his Cubicizing painting. Wehmas did, after all, produce pictures and posters for the Torch-bearers' magazine *Tulenkantajat*. Another one of Lhôte's pupils, Carl Wargh (1895–1937), would certainly have made a good addition, as would Yrjö Ollila, who arrived at the *Neue Sachlichkeit* by way of Ingres. One of the popular artists of the day was Martti Ranttila (1897–1964), but

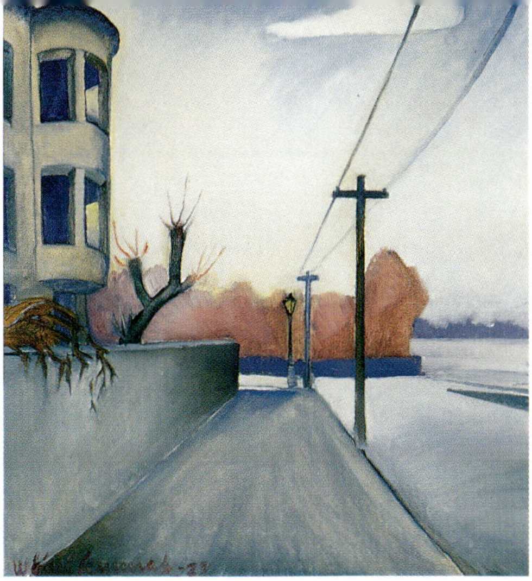

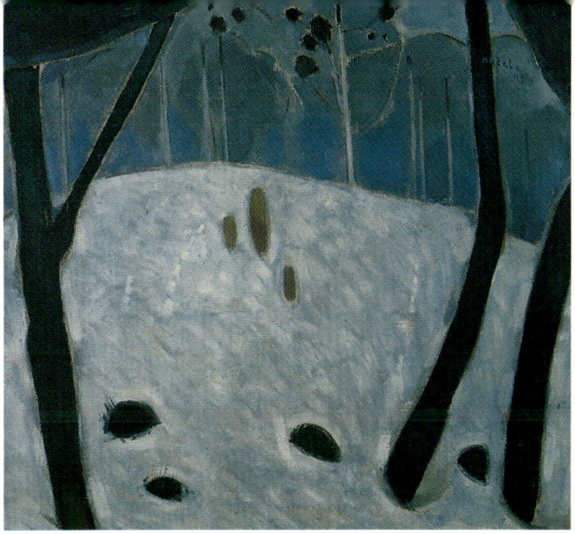

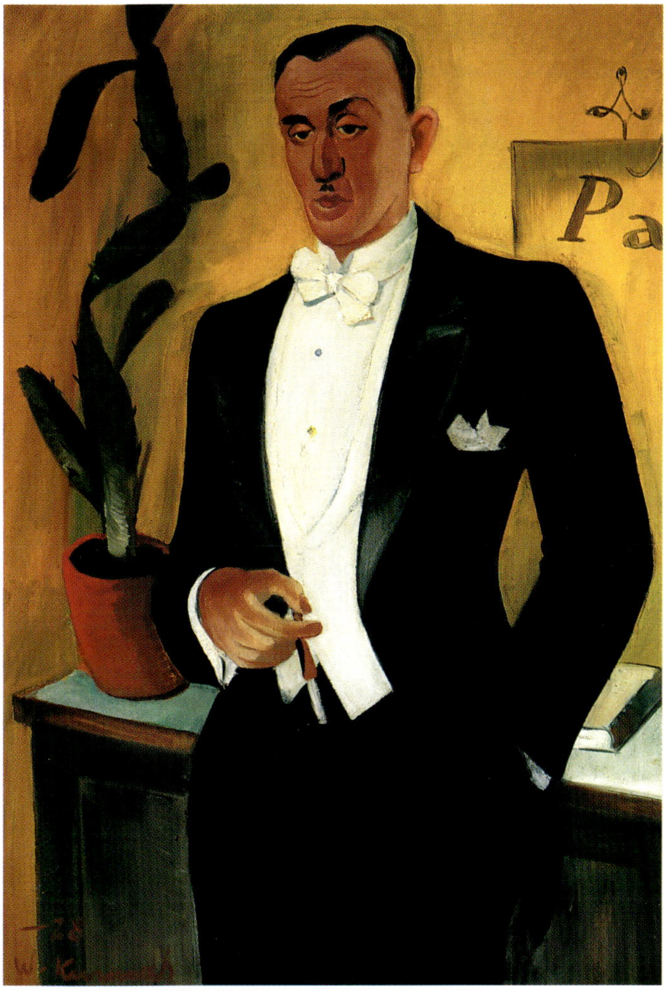

Väinö Kunnas:
April. 1928.
Oil, 58 x 49 cm.
PRIVATE COLLECTION.

H. Ahtela:
Winter Landscape. 1919.
Oil, 83 x 76 cm.
KEMI ART MUSEUM.

Väinö Kunnas:
Olavi Paavolainen. 1928.
Oil, 125 x 80.5 cm.
WSOY.

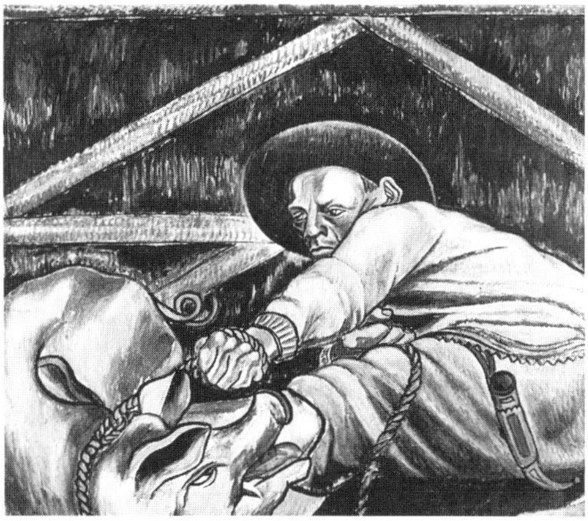

Vilho Lampi: Hanging the Pig. 1930. Oil, 101 x 106 cm.
PRIVATE COLLECTION.

the "new objectivity" of his art was very far from the Torch-bearers' urban enthusiasm for life.

The effects of the *Neue Sachlichkeit* were visible in the paintings of Kunnas and Sipilä, and slightly later in the work of Vilho Lampi (1898–1936). The production of this melancholic artist ranged from ferocious Expressionism to a meticulous style that approached Naivism.

The battle of the spirits

The Torch-bearers' fire did not warm the hearts of the guardians of art. In his review of Paavolainen's book, Onni Okkonen wrote that "healthy national instincts speak against surrendering to foreign influences." It was, however, quite all right to surrender to international Classicism, which permeated the architecture of the 1920s, and became almost an official style when J. S. Sirén (1889–1961) won the architectural competition for a new Parliament House in 1924.

Sirén designed the most important parts of the interior, but there was enough work for some of the country's best interior designers as well. Finland's Parliament House (1926–1931) was one of the last buildings crafted completely by hand. A competition was held for the design of sculptures to decorate the chamber, both open to all entries and by invitation. It was won by "Work and the Future," a proposal submitted by the favorite, Wäinö Aaltonen. Yrjö Liipola (1881–1971), who had done well in Hungary, placed second, and Emil Wikström third. Carl Wilhelms's (1889–1953) entry was purchased. In retrospect, Wilhelms's Art Deco-like design would have been best suited to the style of the building, but at the time, architecture and art were viewed from slightly different angles.

The granite sanctuary of democracy was not even ready when the supporters of the extraparliamentary ultra-right Lapua movement marched by on July 7, 1930. The movement, which relied on supporters from among the farmers of Ostrobothnia, committed various terrorist acts and kidnapped communists, driving them off to the Soviet border. The movement threatened to carry out a coup, and its demands for enacting strict anti-communist legislation were met. Left-wing and liberal intellectuals were in a difficult position, but Gallen-Kallela's last pet project was to make the Lapua movement influential in art as well. In practice this meant labeling almost everything that looked new and strange as "Muscovite."

But Finland did not plunge into a dictatorship or chaos. Liberal cultural forces grew steadily throughout the 1930s, and they won the "battle of the spirits" when a secret police memorandum was leaked to the public in 1936. The memorandum classified as dangerous dozens of cultural personages, including even the Nobel Prize winner F. E. Sillanpää. Prime Minister T. M. Kivimäki's government was toppled.

From regression to new heights

Architecture was rejuvenated more quickly than pictorial art. The Functionalism of Alvar Aalto was already well developed when Parliament House was being built. Paimio Sanatorium, one of Aalto's most important designs, was built between 1929 and 1933. A recession slowed down developments in pictorial art, since private buyers tightened their purse strings, and public interest in art dropped sharply. State subsidies were increased, but did not completely make up for the decline in other resources.

Basic institutions in the art world were created at the beginning of the 1930s, despite difficult times. Uno Ullberg's Classicist museum and art school was built in Viipuri; the granary designed by Engel was turned into an art museum in Tampere; and premises were acquired in Vaasa for an art collection. Private donors went into action. The Kordelin Foundation began its operations, and the Lallukka Artists' Home was opened in 1933.

The idea of founding an association of graphic artists, which had been in the offing for years, was realized in 1931. It had been one of the favorite plans of Lennart Segerstråle (1892–1975), a man with many irons in the fire. He believed that something should finally be done to raise graphics to their rightful place, since the public did not appreciate etchings, woodcuts, and lithography, and did not at all understand the difference between a sheet of graphics and an ordinary reproduction. Nearly the whole cream of the world of graphic art was placed on the new association's board: Segerstråle was made chairman, Mikko Oinonen (1883–1956) vice-chairman, Santeri Salokivi (1886–1940) secretary, Kaarlo Hildén (1886–1963) treasurer, Marcus Collin and Henry Ericsson (1898–1933) members, and Werner Åström and Erkki Kulovesi (1895–1971) alternates. Actually, the group was only missing the skillful Oscar Parviainen (1880–1938) and Aukusti Tuhka (1895–1973), an important teacher. Younger artists were still looking for their niches. Tapio Tapiovaara (1908–1982) became famous for his politically committed work, but the passionate visions of Aleksanteri Ahola-Valo (b. 1900), who had studied in Vitebsk and Odessa, were not known in Finland until the 1970s.

The public demand for sculptures grew, partly because of the interest in Aaltonen's art. The City of Helsinki arranged a competition open to five sculptors "to beautify public places." It was judged in 1931, and the same year the city unveiled "Convolvulus" by Viktor Jansson (1886–1958), and "The Boxers" by Johannes Haapasalo (1880–1965). They were joined by "Bear on an Ant-hill" by Jussi Mäntynen (1886–1978). The most artistically significant public sculptures, however, were Gunnar Finne's (1886–1952) monument to Topelius, "Myth and Truth" (1832), and "Three Smiths" (1932) by Felix Nylund (1878–1940).

The two allegorical maidens on Finne's monument caused public indignation, but it was not so much for their nudity as for the stark simplicity of the design. Yrjö Liipola's javelin-throwing nude "Tellervo," or "Diana at the Hunt" (1929), was accepted without a murmur, but it was intended to embellish a little park, and not to serve as a monument to a great man.

As artists' admiration for Italian and German trends increased, Paris became the bane of the conservatives. The old "Parisian" Uuno Alanko rose to oppose the approach defended by Okkonen and his like: "In the eyes of the uncomprehending, the forge of the smith of vibrant, colorful art – Paris – is dangerous." Not even Sweden's creations were good enough for Ludvig Wennervirta, who had become a straight-laced right-winger. He lashed out against the exhibition policy of the Helsinki Art Hall in 1934: "Both this Bolshevik propaganda exhibition and the Halmstad Group's international Surrealist exhibition that preceded it were obvious mistakes."

The ever-present movement to keep art in line did not quash experimentation. Olli Miettinen (1899–1969) made a non-figurative painting inspired by his experiences in Paris. Its name, "Still-life with Ryecrisp" (1931) is often better remembered than the painting itself. It symbolized the active desire of young artists to let fresh winds in to put an end to Finland's national stagnation. Miettinen was invited in 1934 to take part in the exhibition arranged by the "1934 Group," headed by Kalle Kuutola and Atte Laitila (1893–1972). It presented the art of Lhôte and his pupils, and the reception was negative, to say the least. "Academic naturalism disguised as Cubism" was considered unsuitable for Finnish conditions.

The Helsinki Art Hall's liberal policies offered young Birger Carlstedt (1907–1975) the opportunity in 1932 to exhibit a broad spectrum of both paintings and designs for decorative art. The controversial exhibition was exceptionally diverse: weaving patterns, ready-made curtains and rugs, Neo-plastic designs for the interior of the Chat Doré (the café owned by the artist's mother), at least one chair designed by Carlstedt, and paintings whose style ranged from Expressionism and Cubism to Surrealism.

The reviews of the Swedish-language papers were objective enough, but Edvard Richter, the critic of the largest daily, considered the exhibition sick. "The nature and style of the drawings are usually mostly in the spirit of the Swede E. Josephson's period of insanity, without any real addition of his own in the abrupt, perverse, or extravagant treatment of line. The artificial eroticism of these pictures might be personal, if we did not know that it has been fashionable in Europe for quite some time to be erotic in this way, right down to the orchid."

Carlstedt's pioneering work especially included Finland's first Constructivist composition, "Circle and Triangles" (1932). At the end of the 1930s, his style sought out exotic subjects and expressionistic colorism.

The artists' desire to rebel at times manifested itself as joint action. Artists whose work had been rejected for the annual exhibition arranged their own in

Otto Mäkilä:
Summer Night. 1938.
Oil, 70 x 90 cm.
ART MUSEUM OF THE ATENEUM.

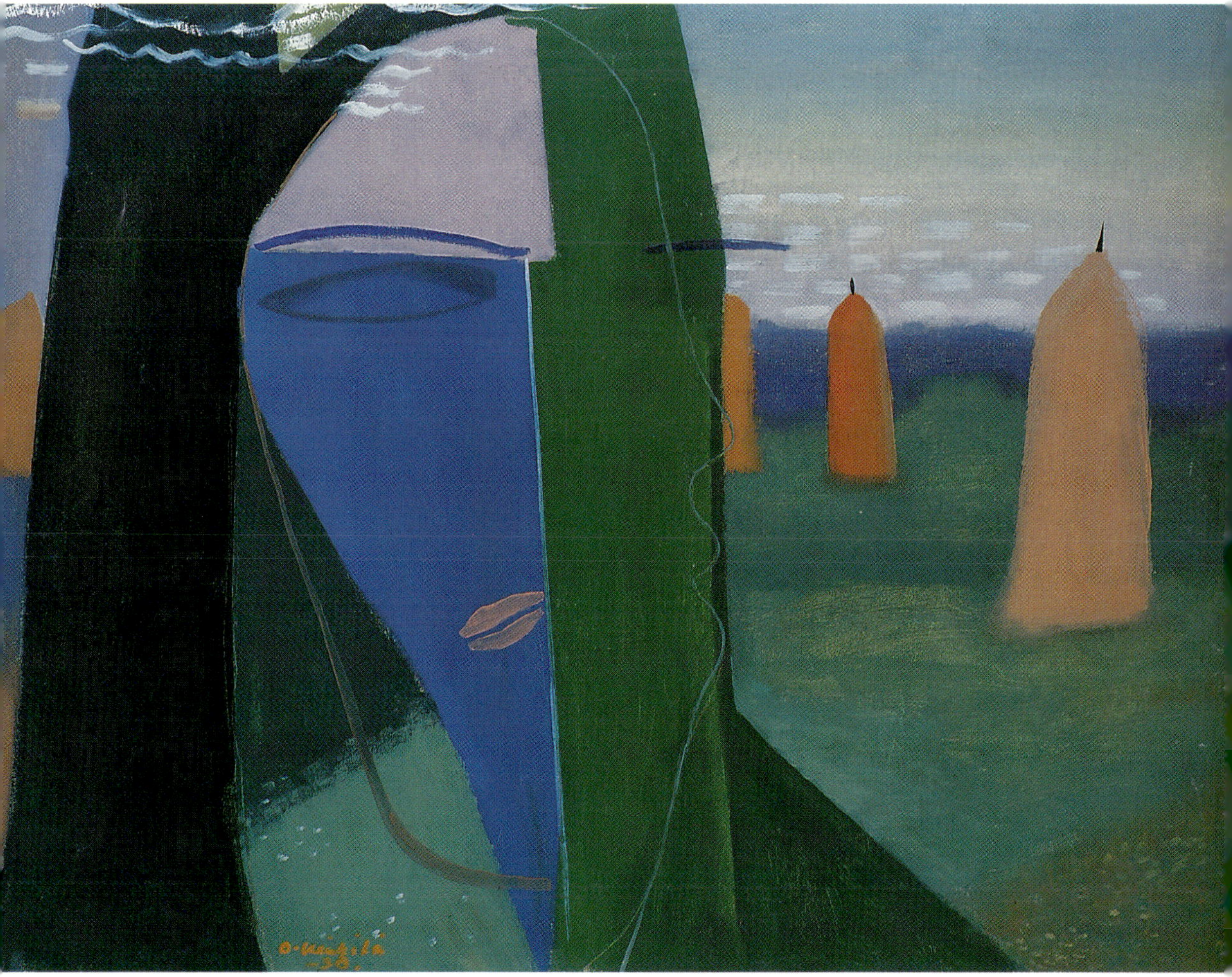

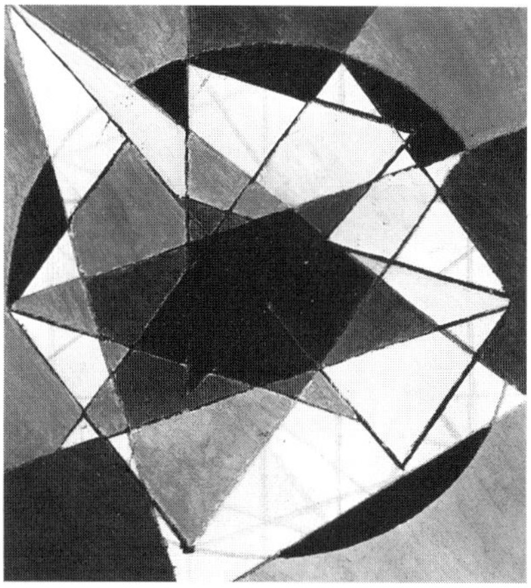

Birger Carlstedt:
Circle and Triangles. 1932.
Oil, 55 x 46 cm.
AMOS ANDERSON ART MUSEUM.

1933 and received moral support from the legendary Colorist Eemu Myntti (1890–1943). The success of the exhibition encouraged Ernst Krohn (1911–1934), Sakari Tohka (1911–1958), and Sven Grönvall (1908–1975), who had studied together, to found the October Group. The names originally proposed for the group reflect its conflicting goals: the Tyko Group (after Sallinen), the Neo-expressionists, Antica Nova, and Vita Classica. The group's first showing in 1934 was transformed into a memorial exhibition for Krohn. His melancholy style, cultivating black, had been influenced by Morand and Carrà, and by the Classicist spirit of the *valori plastici* movement.

From the depths of the mind

Modernism clearly received better treatment in Turku than it did in the capital. Critics like Antero Rinne were more understanding of both Lydén and younger Modernists. Reitala noted that the exhibition designed by Alvar Aalto and Erik Bryggman for Turku's 700th anniversary in 1929 proved a manifestation of the prevailing liberal spirit in the town.

Otto Mäkilä (1904–1955) soon became Turku's most important Modernist. He began studying at the Turku Arts Society's school at the early age of 16. Lydén's inspiring example led him to break with customary Finnish patterns. After receiving a grant, Mäkilä studied in Paris at the Académie de la Grande Chaumière and the Académie Colarossi in 1930 and 1931. Trips to the Netherlands and Switzerland reinforced his orientation towards Modernism.

The art of Chagall, Picasso, Braque, and Matisse made the greatest impression on Mäkilä, but he was nonetheless drawn most of all to Surrealism. Mäkilä did not develop into a provocative Surrealist; his form of expression remained poetic and picturesque. After participating in the exhibition of the Swedish Halmstad Group in Lund in 1937, the artist himself noted that he had seemed Naturalistic among the Surrealists.

The influence of *pittura metafisica* can often be seen in Mäkilä's work, and some of the paintings can be traced from de Chirico to Böcklin. Illustrative examples are "The Sea" (1938) and "Shipwrecked" (1939). While de Chirico painted horizons bordered by deserted buildings, Mäkilä arranged boulders along the edges of his pictures. The figure standing on the shore in "Shipwrecked" brings to mind the mysterious figures on Böcklin's "Island of the Dead" and "Ulysses and Calypso."

"Poésie" (1938), one of Mäkilä's most important paintings from the 1930s, is very different indeed from Surrealism. As the art historian Ulla Vihanta noted in her recent study, Chagall's "Poète" might be reflected in it. Mäkilä's poetical red horse has its own distinctive style, however, and it has been pointed out that even the landscape in the picture was visible from his window.

Surrealism's basic ideals were familiar to Mäkilä, but he did not draw any extreme con-

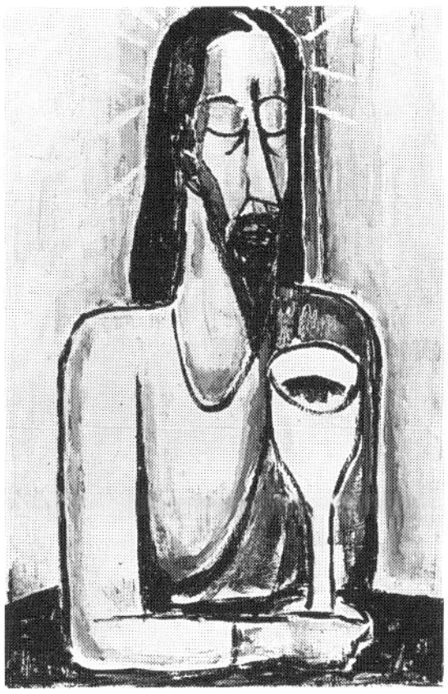

Ernst Krohn: Christ. 1934. Oil, 80 x 52 cm. PRIVATE COLLECTION.

clusions from them. He considered the artist's view in general to be fanciful, superrealistic, and he spoke of creating pictures based on involuntary flights of imagination.

Finnish Surrealism gained a second noteworthy representative at the end of the 1930s: Arvid Broms, whose early work shows an interest in social subjects: "The Unemployed," "The Individual and the Masses" (1938), and "Prisoner" (1939).

Opening up contacts

The founding of the "Free Painting School" (later called the Free Art School) in 1935 built a new bridgehead to French influences. It was truly a "piece of Montparnasse in Helsinki," since its first teachers, William Lönnberg and Carl Wargh, ensured that the students knew the work of Cézanne and Lhôte. At the same time they were taught to understand the Pointillist theory of complementary colors. Frosterus's approach consequently did not disappear with Neo-impressionism.

The school was started at the instigation of Maire Gullichsen, the radical daughter of a wealthy industrialist family whose extensive cultural interests and international contacts gave the impetus for other important reforms. Together with Aino and Alvar Aalto and Nils Gustav Hahl, she founded the applied arts company Artek in 1935.

Artek sold products designed by the Aaltos both in Finland and abroad, mostly to England. The company also began to organize exhibitions of art and applied art.

The Fernand Léger and Alexander Calder exhibition in 1937 aroused the curiosity of the Helsinki public, but also left them at a loss. And not even all the critics were able to explain the secrets of abstract forms or mobiles. Léger delivered lectures in conjunction with this exhibition and also made trips outside the capital. He was enraptured with the paintings at medieval Hattula church.

Raoul Palmgren described the left-wing intelligentsia's feelings towards Léger at a banquet arranged in his honor at the Savoy Restaurant. The welcoming speech was made by the socialist-agrarian government's minister of education, Uuno Hannula. "And when we now sit down at the banquet table around the French master and his enchanting young mistress, and the minister of education, in his first speech in French, welcomes the French Communist artist on behalf of the state, then in the midst of the malicious expectation of scandal that hovers over the rest of the party, there is at least one group of people whose undivided sympathy is on the side of the clumsy minister ..." (R. Palomeri: *30-luvun kuvat* (Pictures from the '30s).

The Functionalist integration of French Modernism and the arts became the key characteristic of those involved with Artek. They also arranged an exhibition of French Modernist painting at the Helsinki Art Hall in 1939. It presented art that was still relatively unknown in Finland by such masters as Bonnard, Braque, Chagall, Derain, Laurencin, Masson, Matisse, Picasso (including "Three Musicians"), Utrillo, and Vuillard.

Alvar Aalto had time to do some painting and sculpting between his other work. As he designed furniture, he experimented with the use of bent plywood in composing abstract wooden reliefs. They were light years ahead of all Finnish art in the 1930s.

Allegories of the republic

After the turn of the century, monumentality suffered from a shortage of commissions and architecture that favored little ornamentation. Functionalism, even more unequivocally than Classicism, rejected the contribution of painters, a contribution that was undoubtedly often far from harmonious.

Yrjö Ollila was commissioned to decorate the ceiling of the National Theater (1932), but excessive Realism detracted from the artistic importance of the result. Parliament House proved a complete disappointment to painters. No first prize was even awarded for the murals for the large committee room. A second prize was given to Lennart Segerstråle's entry, "Navis Republicae." Not a single proposal was carried out.

Not until the end of the 1930s were there any initiatives to embark on new projects. The exhibition of Norwegian monumental painting at the Helsinki Art Hall in 1937 showed that Finland was sadly behind the times. In 1938, the Bank of Finland commissioned Segerstråle to make two large frescoes for its foyer. The artist himself was able to choose the subjects of his work, and from the beginning he titled one "Finland Awakes" and the other "Finland Builds." The war years changed the tones of the paintings, which came to symbolize Finland's struggle for existence and its period of reconstruction.

War-time Karelianism

The effects of the Second World War – for Finland, actually two consecutive wars, in 1939–1940 and 1941–1945 – on art were not immediately visible, except for the hundreds of memorials that kept sculptors busy. Only to a very limited extent was the war depicted in art, in contrast to literature.

The territorial gains that were first made between 1941 and 1945 engendered a new enthusiasm for Karelianism for a while, and military artists who belonged to the information company worked at the front making illustrations of Karelian villages and their inhabitants, with the emphasis on ethnography. Their depictions of battle were not very successful, in contrast, even though some of the artists were skilled professionals. They included Erkki Tanttu (1907–1985), Erik Enroth (1817–1975), Aarne Nopsanen (b. 1907–1990), Björn Landström (b. 1917), Kari Suomalainen (b. 1920), and Henrik Tikkanen

Yngve Bäck:
The Melody of War. 1944.
Oil, 144 x 114 cm.
ART MUSEUM OF THE ATENEUM.

Yrjö Saarinen:
Resting. 1942.
Oil, 130 x 162 cm.
ART MUSEUM OF THE ATENEUM.

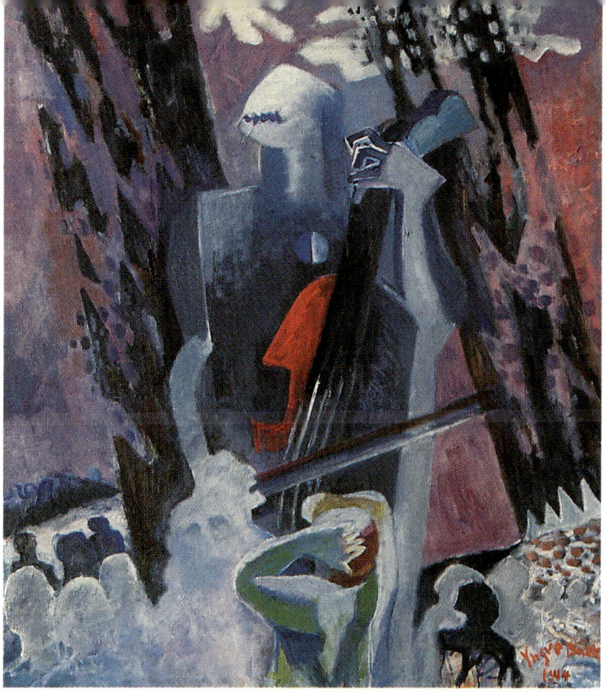

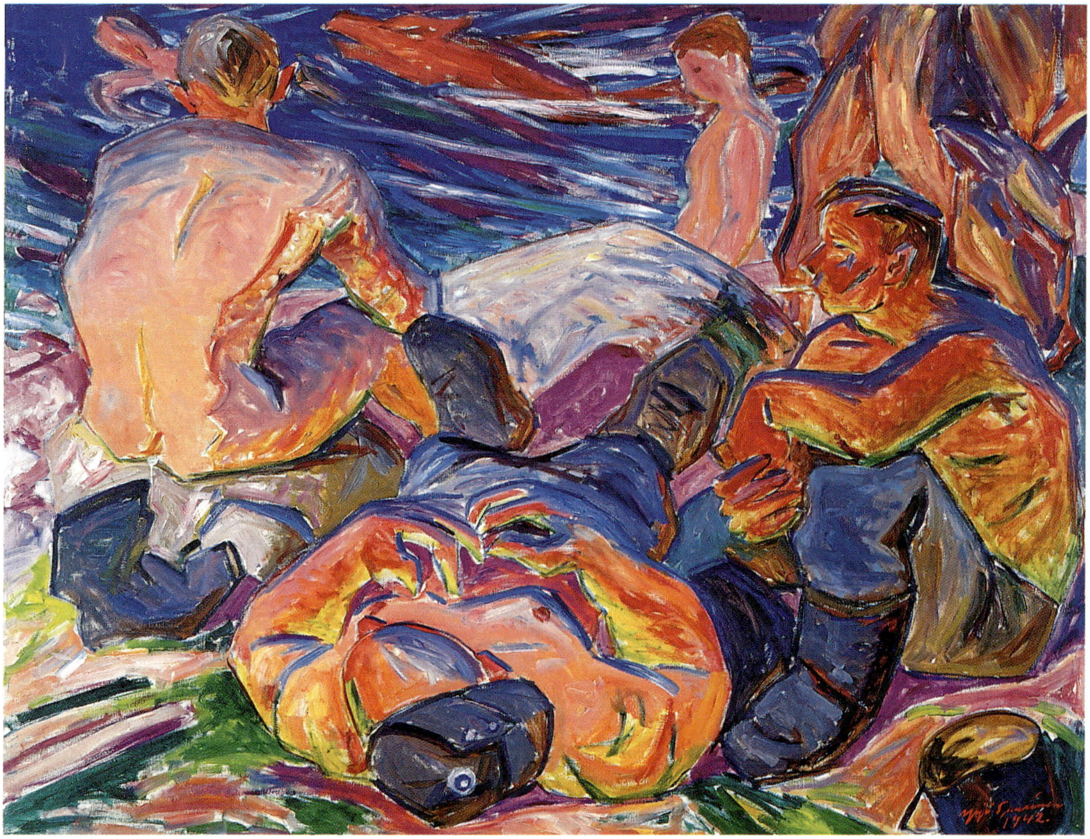

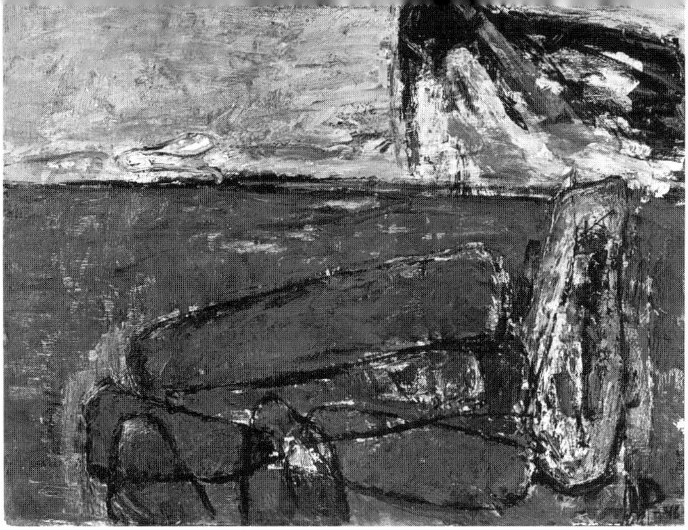

Helge Dahlman:
Landscape. 1946.
Oil, 50 x 61.5 cm.
MODERNA MUSEET, STOCKHOLM.

(1924–1984). Towards the end of the war, the work of the artists at the front was headed by Olavi Paavolainen.

The most important paintings linked with the war were made by Yrjö Saarinen (1899–1958), whose lusty Expressionism depicted Karelian women and the everyday tasks of soldiers in the trenches. We should also remember Otto Mäkilä's allegory of Finland crucified and Yngve Bäck's (1894–1990) robot-like cellist of death in the painting "The Melody of War" (1944).

People mostly settled their personal accounts with the war after peace had come. Unto Pusa (1813–1973) painted "The Fallen Soldier" in 1938 in memory of his brother. The influence of Picasso's "Guernica" can be clearly seen in Gösta Diehl's (1899–1964) "The Bombed Village" (1950) and more distantly in Helge Dahlman's (1927–1979) Expressionist "Composition (War)," 1846–1948. The most impressive sculpture is "The Invalid" (1945) by Aimo Tukiainen (b. 1917–1996), a bronze head with the mangled face of a war invalid.

Longing for internationalization

The frenzy and metaphysics of expression

"The trend that dominates at present, picturesque Realism, at least has the advantage that it is generally genuine, honest, and serious, even though it can also be fustily narrow-minded and intellectually intractable," E. J. Vehmas consoled his readers in 1946 in the aftermath of the war. He did not believe in new "ism periods" and it seemed to him that Surrealism was withering away. Vehmas thought that even the new abstract painting seemed vapid.

In spite of its depression, the art world recovered from the war with surprising speed. That new political creation, the Finnish People's Democratic League, enthusiastically wrote cultural programs and took upon itself to open relations with the east. It considered itself at the vanguard of developments. Passive resistance by intellectuals proved strong, however. The political renaissance of communism was expressed most clearly in literature and least of all in pictorial art. The old constellation of conservatives versus liberal modernism was largely able to satisfy the pictorial artists' desire for revolt.

The October Group was resuscitated, but it never became very active. What it did do, however, was to put art back on the road to national themes and an involvement with nature. The development of the young Expressionists had been interrupted in the 1930s, and now they returned to the art scene, headed by Aimo Kanerva (1909–1991).

"I came from the war and of course was wickeder than usual," Kanerva reminisced about his periods with what he called "speed painting." His post-war style can be studied as an outburst of aggression just like the paintings of Willem de Kooning, but we can just as easily interpret Kanerva's energetic style as a proclamation of joy and victorious rejoicing. The artist did not give up his subjects from real life, even though the abstractness of his work at times in fact approached the non-figurative. Take for example "Yellow Landscape" (1945), "Hot Day" (1947), or the starkly geometrically conceived "Stone Quarry" (1947).

Aimo Kanerva and Yrjö Saarinen (1899–1958) painted together a great deal, but their Expressionism did not take the same approach. Kanerva's was soon transformed into an increasingly sensitive depiction of nature.

Mauno Markkula (1905–1959), a Romanticist in his use of color, was in a class all his own among the Expressionists. His work, radiating a mystical atmosphere, has often been compared to the production of Carl Kylberg and Emil Nolde. Åke Mattas (1920–1962) developed a totally new Expressionist idiom, concentrating on creating psychologically merciless portraits. In his cadaverous self-portraits, Mattas also depicted the destructive phases of his own alcoholism.

Erik Enroth's post-war production is Expressionist in spirit, but geometric and monumental in form. To Enroth, reconstruction meant almost religious

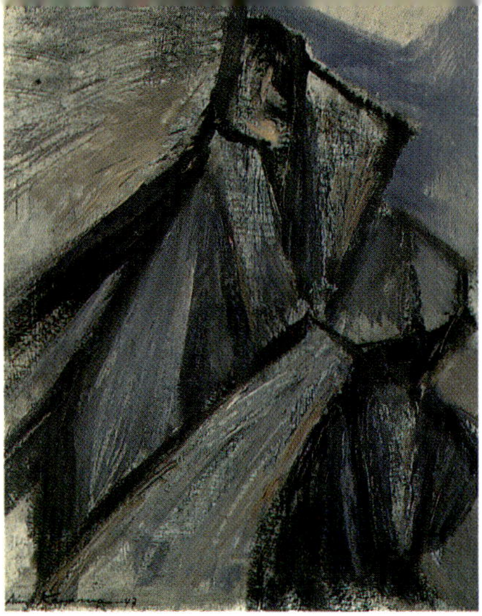

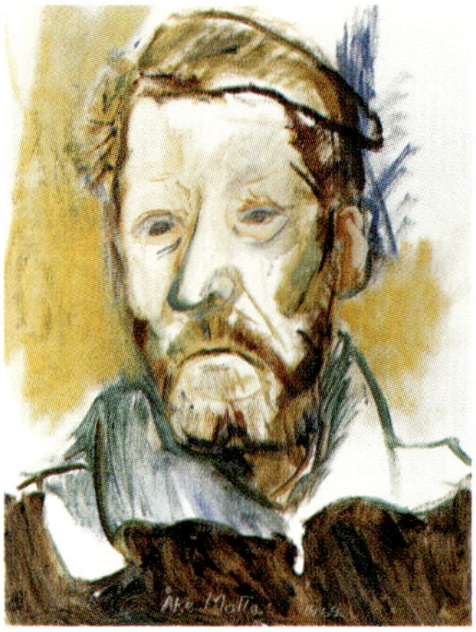

Aimo Kanerva: The Quarry. 1947. Oil, 82 x 62 cm.
PRIVATE COLLECTION.

Åke Mattas: Self-portrait (Tired). 1962. Oil, 55 x 38 cm.
TURKU ART MUSEUM.

visions of the birth of a new, powerful man, the Prometheus of an industrial society.

The metaphysical trend during and after the war has been discussed very little, even though it was highly obvious. The Turku artist Hilkka Toivola (b. 1909) cultivated Christian thematics in her metaphors of loneliness and exhaustion. Elga Sesemann (b. 1922), Elvi Maarni (b. 1907), and Viljo Ranta (b. 1906) also worked with dream-like symbolic themes. Birger Carlstedt's painting underwent a rejuvenation in the 1940s, partly thanks to the Halmstad Group. Carlstedt nonetheless adapted the *pittura metafisica* and at times Surrealist material to create his own personal style. It has not always been possible to interpret his paintings. "They are permeated by the inhuman emotion of the painter of our day, the coldness of the universe, " wrote Helvi Hämäläinen. Critics failed to notice the plastic power of Carlstedt's work combined with an erotic and atmospheric resignation.

The metaphysical silence of a deserted beach was interpreted most successfully by Unto Koistinen (b. 1917–1994). His paintings could be called existentialist landscapes. Otto Mäkilä developed into a true Surrealist at the end of the 1940s and beginning of the 1950s. His world of form became freer, and began to come alive with abstract biomorphy and even adaptations of Henry Moore's nested forms. At the beginning of the 1950s, Mäkilä shifted entirely to non-figurative painting.

The Turku artist Ole Kandelin (1920–1947) tried to combine devotional subjects with a vapidly decorative style, but after seeing paintings by artists like Miró in art journals, he was inspired to paint non-figuratively. Kandelin's refreshing late production shone like a lone jewel in the the wilderness of the post-war art world.

Modernism made its final breakthrough in the 1950s. All fields of art underwent a reform. Poetry lost its meter. Non-figurative art was accepted, and simplicity dominated triumphant design. Architecture progressed at a more even pace since it was able to rely on the past.

The prism of structures

Post-cubist stylization strengthened its position in the 1940s. Its significance was judged in the mural competition arranged at Marie Gullichsen's initiative. In 1946, the Ahlström Company (Maire Gullichsen's maiden name was Ahlström) invited seven artists to paint a draft for its Kauttua factory dining room. The artists were chosen from among the Modernists of the day: Yngve Bäck, Birger Carlstedt, Torger Enckell (b. 1901–1991), Sven Grönvall (1908–1975), Olli Miettinen, Unto Pusa, and Sam Vanni (b. 1908–1992). Vanni and Pusa won the shared first prize, but the job was given to Carlstedt, whose Post-cubist proposal was carried out. He worked on the large (2.7 x 12.5 m) canvas for about three years, and after it was finished, went over completely to non-figurative, geometric compositions. His estrangement from a figurative basic conception was gradual. At around the same time, Lars-Gunnar Nordström

Lars-Gunnar Nordström:
Dimensional Diskology. 1956–1960.
Oil, 160 x 160 cm.
ESPOO CITY COLLECTION.

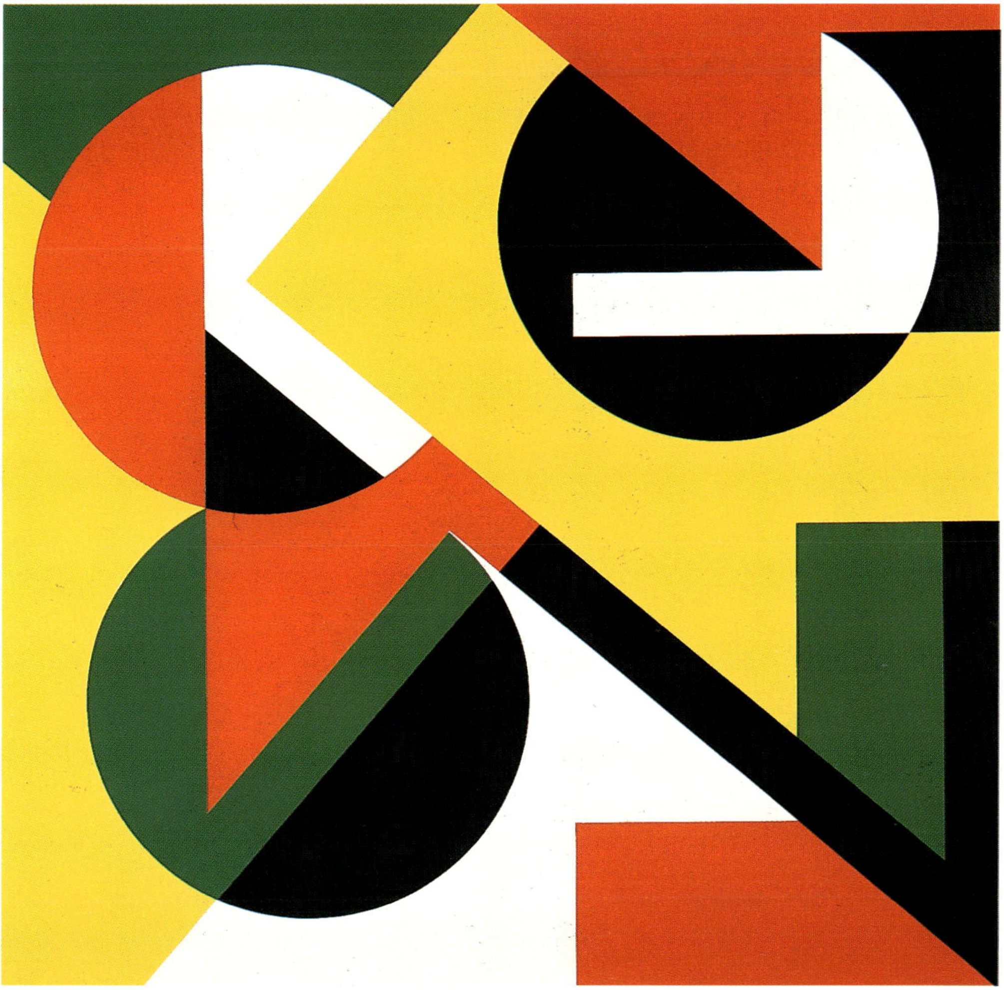

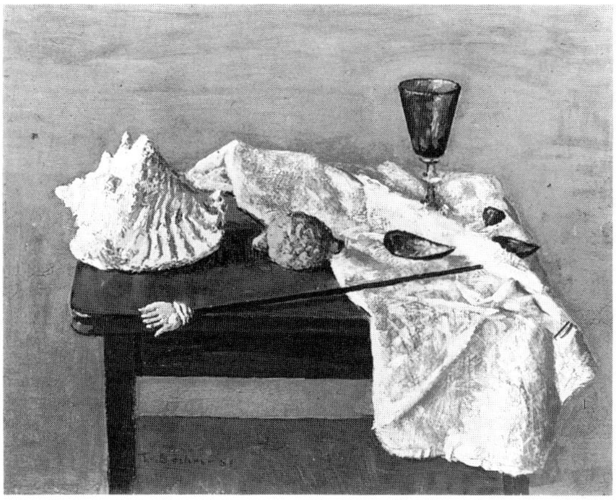

Tuomas von Boehm:
Green Glass. 1951.
Oil, 46 x 55 cm.
PRIVATE COLLECTION.

(b. 1924) moved towards concerted Constructivism. Sam Vanni took up non-figurativeness soon after the French exhibition in 1952.

Applied art was quickest to shake off the travails of the war. Gunnel Nyman's (1909–1848) fine work with glass created the basis for the international onslaught of Finnish design. Its central figure was Tapio Wirkkala (1915–1985), who was also a sculptor. His aerodynamically designed plywood sculptures, such as "Whirl" (1935), were not initially considered fine art.

Nothing took place in pictorial art that even approached Wirkkala's success at the Milan Triennials. Work was nonetheless being done at the time to promote modern art. Nykytaide ry. (a modern art association) cultivated international exchanges and had the Finnish pavilion, designed by Alvar Aalto, built for Venice's biennial park in 1956.

Maire Gullichsen founded Galerie Artek in 1950. It presented not only early Modernist classics, but also newer work by artists like Vasarely and Robert Jacobsen (1956). The gallery also provided space for Finnish Constructivism.

Gradually, national and international trends in painting went their separate ways in the 1950s. The lines between the styles were nonetheless not at all clear-cut. It was possible for a refined Realist like Tapani Raittila (b. 1921) to appear together with the Constructivist Lars-Gunnar Nordström at an exhibition, but the Prism Group, founded in 1956, was much more selective. It was not interested in national "sauna art," and instead aimed at joining forces with French-inspired Modernism. The idea probably originated with Gösta Diehl, but not until Torger Enckell and Sam Vanni joined up did the project get under way. The Prism Group also included Sigrid Schauman, Ragnar Ekelund (1892–1960), Yngve Bäck, Gösta Diehl, and Unto Pusa, the only monolingual Finn.

The Prism Group arranged two exhibitions in the 1950s, in 1956 and 1957, when the sculptors Mikko Hovi (1879–1962) and Gunnar Elfgren (1896–1976) were invited to exhibit with it. The group's exhibitions toured the country, and the message of Modernism was able to spread to "virgin" territory, as Sam Vanni put it. Turku was an exception, of course. Otto Mäkilä's supporters had organized into Group 9 in 1952. It aimed mostly at abstraction, while Pro Arte, founded in 1957, emphasized Surrealism, its most important members being Alpo Jaakola (b. 1929–1997) and Max Salmi (b. 1931).

The painting of Anitra Lucander (b. 1918), Per Stenius (b. 1922), Erik Granfelt (b. 1919–1990) and Tuomas von Boehm (b. 1916) can be considered a lyrical sequel to Cubism. The influence of Bonnard, in turn, can be seen in the work of Rafael Wardi (b. 1928).

Unto Pusa's art was charged with the tension between national content and universal form. He believed that "in the future, the realization of pure plasticism in tangible reality will replace what we now expect of a work of art." In his teaching, Pusa aimed at theoretical clarity, and a com-

Unto Pusa:
Storehouse III. 1957.
Oil, 100 x 81.5 cm.
ART MUSEUM OF THE ATENEUM.

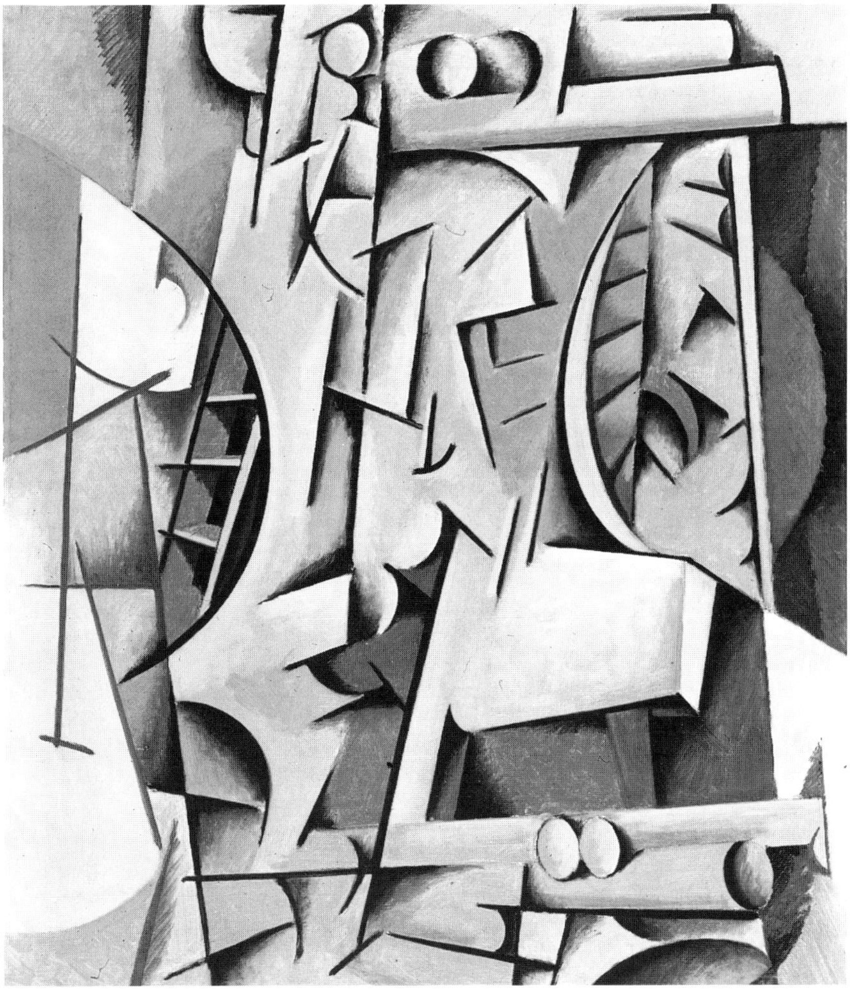

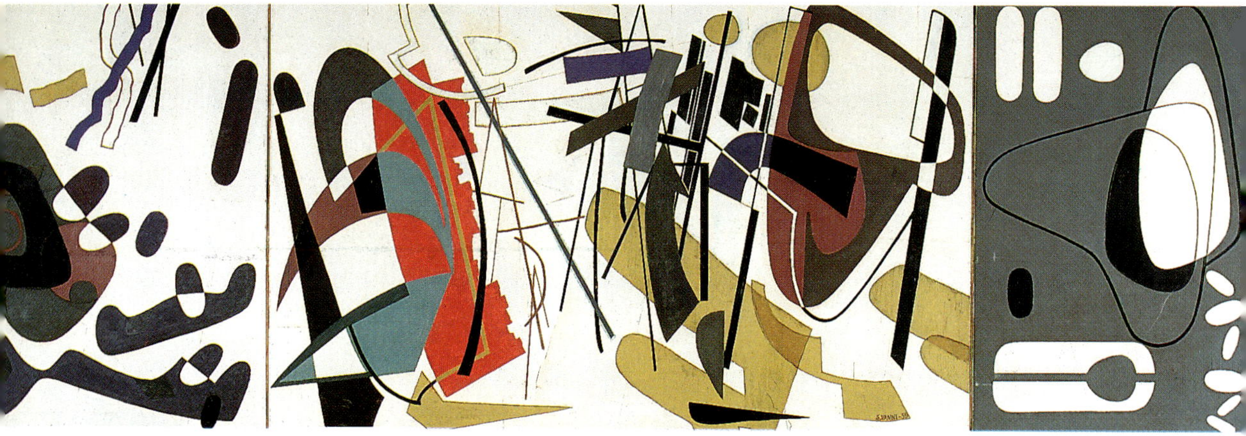

position akin to architecture, free of any "literary" material. He had studied under Lhôte and Léger in 1948 and 1949, and combined Léger's views with a broad knowledge of 20th century art theory. In his own production, Pusa nonetheless retained content and ideology. He was not a socialist, but rather an idealist when it came to Finland's post-war reconstruction, paying homage to the nobility of work and the magnificence of industry.

Under Pusa and Vanni, teaching at the Free Art School rapidly produced results. The students from this this golden decade of artists' groupings, Tor Arne (b. 1934), Erkki Hienonen (b. 1933), Kauko Hämäläinen (1928–1986), and Seppo Kärkkäinen (b. 1935), founded Group 4 at the end of the 1950s.

Sam Vanni made a clear break with the remnants of figurative art, but fused many kinds of influences, from Pillet to Vasarely. One of Vanni's goals was monumental painting. He was not given to compromises, and instead painted pure compositions. At times Vanni had to defend himself against even the most primitive attacks. "Contrapunctus" (1960), the synthesis of his work during the 1950s, was given a good reception by the public, but when it was placed in the lobby of the Helsinki Workers' Institute, one of the indignant teachers said that Vanni was crazy. Vanni, in turn, declared that the teacher was stupid. It is easy to imagine what a shock it was to many people when Vanni was made a member of the Academy of Finland in 1964.

Ernst Mether-Borgström (b. 1917–1996) was initially known more for his graphics with circus themes than he was as a painter, but over the decades, his approach, too, matured in a non-figurative direction. His playful, light-filled idiom differed completely from the seriousness of Constructivism.

Constructivist sculpture was a rare phenomenon as late as the 1950s. Lars-Gunnar Nordström was the first to tackle constructions, but he had to wait for quite some time before they evoked any positive response. At Galerie Artek in 1959, Veikko Eskolin (b. 1936) presented both metal constructions and pieces made from transparent plastic, such as "Cyclical Spiral," made from slats.

The rejected angel

Sculptors were not very enthusiastic about going off into the jungle of non-figurativeness. Young sculptors sought their own idiom by remaining close to nature, using a simplified and linear lightness. Masters of this style included Harry Kivijärvi (b. 1931), Kain Tapper (b. 1930), and Pekka Aarnio (1930–1960).

Kauko Räsänen (b. 1926) delved into forceful plasticity and also took an interest in pierced forms. His work suddenly led to a fierce confrontation between old-fashioned values and an esthetic that emphasized form. Räsänen's "Angel" (1960), derided as "The Hole-ridden Angel" or "Lucifer's Angel," was removed from Lappeenranta cemetery at the insistence of the congregation.

There were continual con-

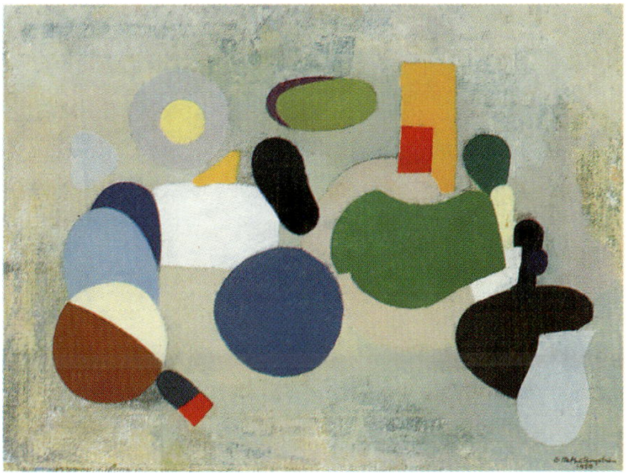

Sam Vanni:
Contrapunctus. 1959.
Oil, 150 x 450 cm.
HELSINKI WORKERS' INSTITUTE.

Ernst Mether-Borgström:
Forms of an Ameba. 1959.
Oil, 33 x 41 cm.
PRIVATE COLLECTION.

Kauko Räsänen:
The Angel. 1963.
Bronze, 170 cm.
ART MUSEUM OF THE ATENEUM.

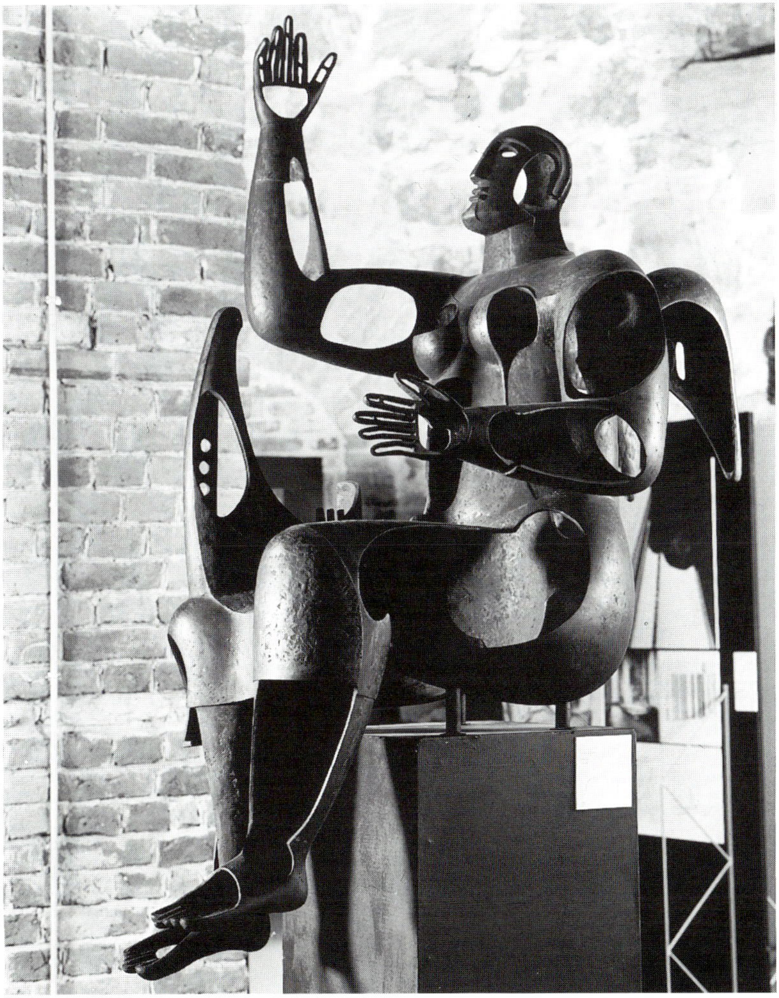

flicts as the free treatment of form impinged on different fields of collective symbolism. Aimo Tukiainen's "Silent Fortress" (1960) was to have been used as a war memorial in Savonlinna, but those who had commissioned the sculpture did not approve of its unusual style. There were no figures at all in this balance-shaped bronze sculpture, and the unaccustomed viewer could hardly glimpse the landscape with its fortress, shattered by cannons, since it was only insinuated. More customary figurative art was expected of the sculptor who had created Marshal Mannerheim's equestrian statue.

Another controversial work of art also had a landscape motive: Kain Tapper's altar relief "Golgotha" (1961–1962), made for Orivesi Church. The rocky landscape, seen from above, merged in the viewer's imagination with a torn curtain. Tapper's sculpture was the first abstract work of art to be placed in a Finnish church.

Eila Hiltunen (b. 1922) studied welding in the mid-1950s, and used it to make line-like bundles in her highly simplified figurative work. Laila Pullinen (b. 1933) experimented with the effects of welded scrap iron in such pieces as "Passion" (1959).

An abstract work of art was occasionally accepted as a public sculpture if its form unequivocally had a visible foundation in reality. Kain Tapper's "Shuttle" was erected in front of the Finlayson mill in Pori in 1958, and Arvi Tynys's (1902–1959) dancing figure, "Up into the Light" was placed in front of another textile factory in Hanko that same year.

Informalism

Trends in art rarely began and ended with decades, but Finland woke up to a new age in 1960. Denizens of the art world returned from the Venice Biennial either annoyed or enthusiastic. Informalism had made its breakthrough. E. J. Vehmas was one of the critics for whom the Biennial was a historic moment. He wrote that at no other exhibition did the visitor feel as if he were standing on the border between two stylistic periods. Vehmas felt that Classicism, which had lasted for half a century, was on its death-bed, while Romanticism was making a triumphal entry. Instinct and spontaneity were replacing logic, and analytical natural science was giving way to pantheistic and cosmic emotions.

Vehmas pointed out Informalism's use of materials, and interpreted the amorphy cultivated by the style as an eternal movement, "just as if it were continually being born, growing, and dying before the beholder's eyes."

Informalism was received with unreserved enthusiasm in Finland. The trend had not, however, come as a complete surprise. The foundation for Informalist ideology had been laid back in 1958–1959 by the "Bronda Attic" group. Olavi Haarala (1925–1978), Wiking Forsström (b. 1931), Arvo Summanen, and the group's spiritual leader, Eino Ruutsalo (b. 1921), who had studied in the United States, experimented with abstract Expressionism and a spontane-

Pentti Kaskipuro:
Portrait of an Esthete. 1961.
Drypoint and aquatint, 19.3 x 18.2 cm.
ALVAR AALTO MUSEUM, JYVÄSKYLÄ.

Pentti Lumikangas:
Waiting. 1964.
Drypoint and aquatint, 24.6 x 39.5 cm.
SARA HILDÉN ART MUSEUM, TAMPERE.

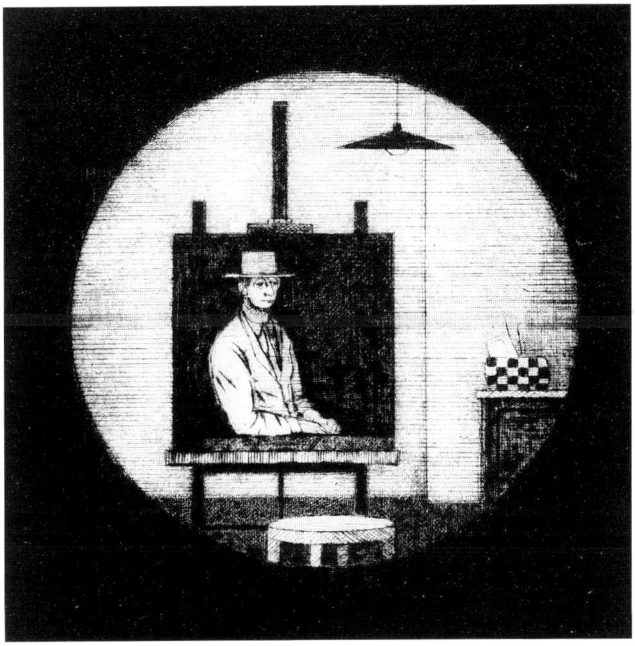

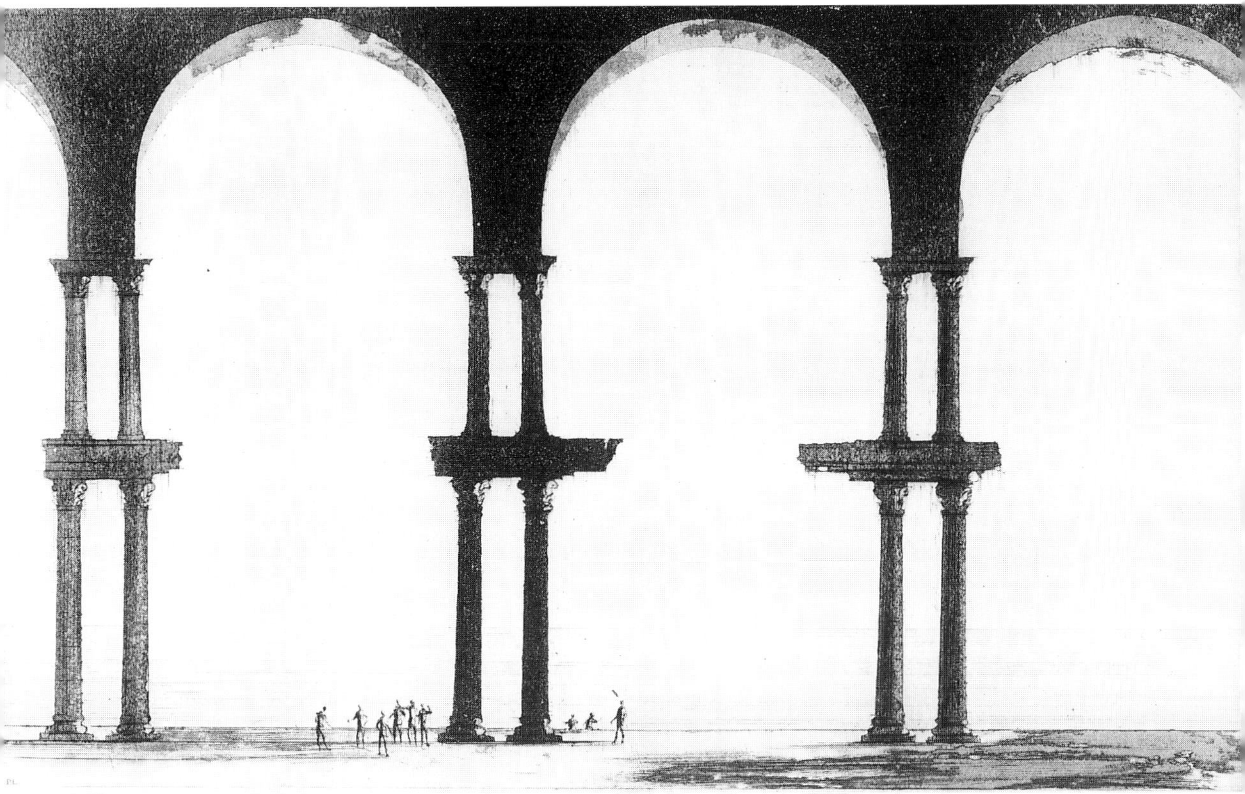

Ulla Rantanen:
Steps. 1966.
Color woodcut, 58 x 35 cm.
ART MUSEUM OF THE ATENEUM.

Jaakko Sievänen:
Painting. 1961
Oil, 150 x 170 cm.

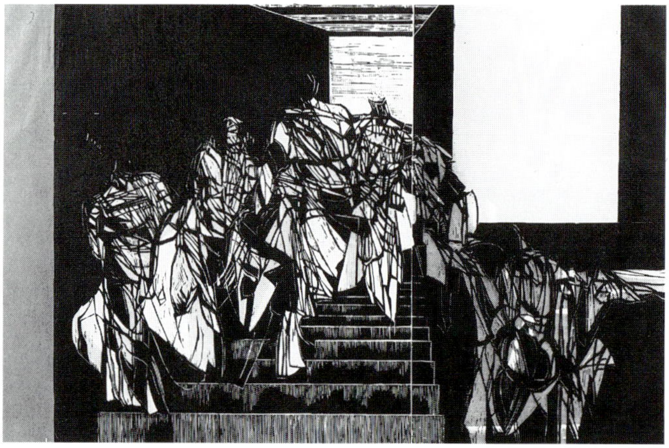

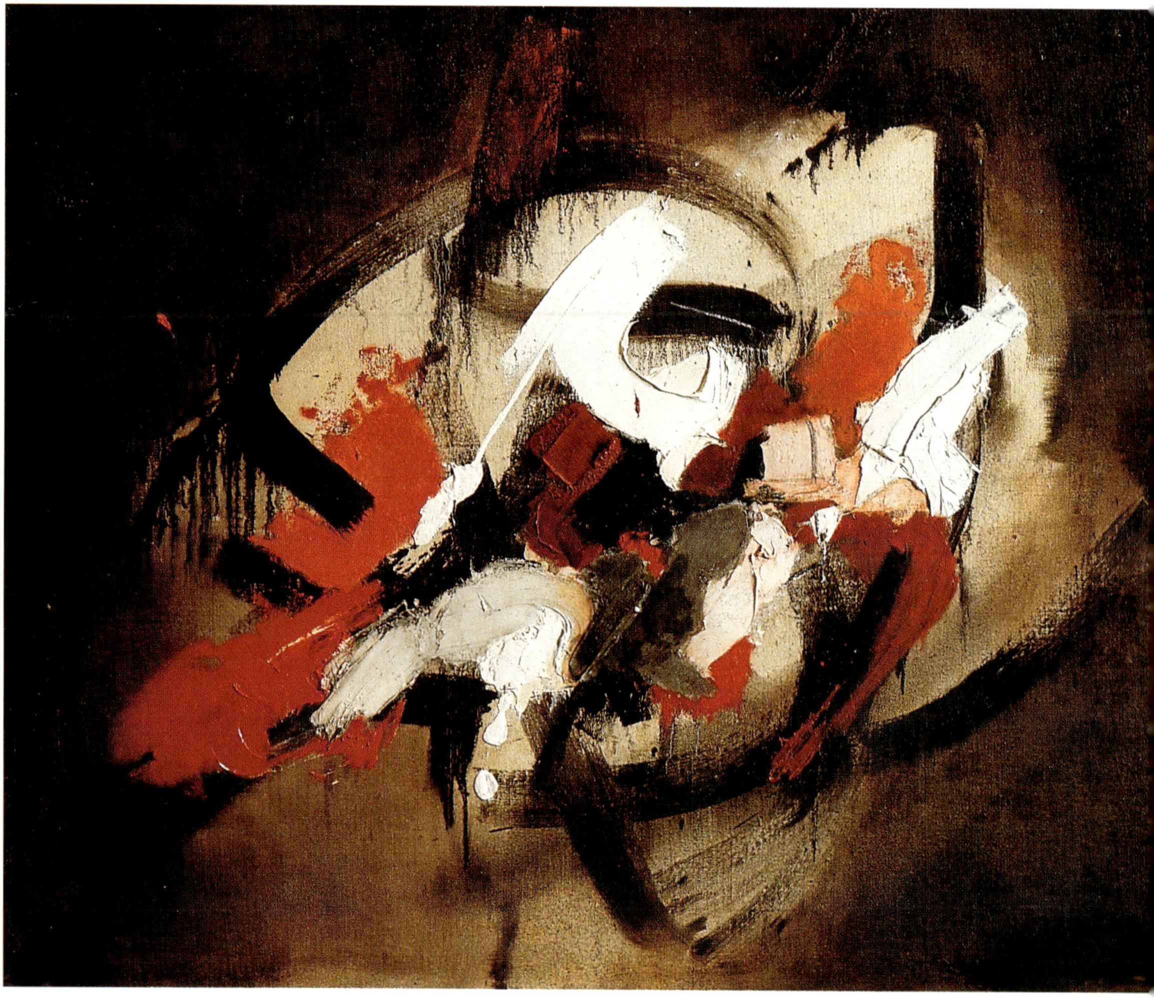

ous work method, "rhythmic automation." Ruutsalo later became one of the key figures in Kinetic Art.

Carl-Gustav Lilius (b. 1928–1998), who was not a member of the "Bronda Attic" group, had a Tachist one-man show in 1958. Paintings and graphics by Jaakko Somersalo (1916–1966) represented a more lyrical form of abstraction. Tuulikki Pietilä (b. 1917) was one of the first graphic artists to experiment with Informalism. Her colleagues, however, mainly remained within the bounds of figurative art. The period's most important work in graphics was done by Ina Colliander (1905–1985), in woodcuts inspired by the angular stylization of icon art. Pentti Kaskipuro (b. 1930), a rising star, made magically realistic metal graphics, and Pentti Lumikangas (b. 1926) constructed refined architectural fantasies.

The authority of Informalism increased with the international Ars 61 exhibition held in Helsinki. It presented the modern art of the Parisian school and of Spain and Italy.

It was now possible to hang up-to-date Finnish art alongside that of Alberto Burri, Luciano Minguzzi, Roberto Crippa, Jean Fautrier, Hans Hartung, Pierre Soulages, Rafael Canogar, and many others. In painting, Lauri Ahlgrén (b. 1929), Mauri Favén (b. 1920), Erkki Heikkilä (b. 1933), Jaakko Sievänen (b. 1932), and Esko Tirronen (b. 1934) could already be considered experienced Informalists. A number of sculptors also emphasized Informalism and abstractions of nature: Eila Hiltunen, Harry Kivijärvi, Kauko Räsänen, Kain Tapper, Aimo Tukiainen, and Marjatta Weckström (b. 1932).

Informalism spread throughout the country. No opposition seemed to arise to check its progress. The reason is that Informalism's concept of form regenerated national Expressionism, and it was easy to combine a free form with landscape abstractions. Finnish Informalists were thus on familiar ground, and at the same time they felt that they had finally attained an international level in modern art.

A statement by Jaakko Somersalo describes the situation that had been created by achievements in nuclear physics and the conquest of space. "Being has become invisible, and it is art's task to make it visible again. Man has begun to look for a picture of the world in art, too, a picture that science has formed with its own means."

The supporters of Constructivism could not bear the Romantic-Expressivist tidal wave. In addition, the trend was already a thing of the past internationally when Finland was discussing who would represent Finland at the 1962 Venice Biennial. Maire Gullichsen acidly described the achievements of Informalism as "the sniffles on canvas."

Informalism gave birth to a great deal of commonplace abstractions, but the most important work done in the style has retained its value. Perhaps Informalism's most fruitful influence was after all a shattering of traditional patterns in sculpture and an opening up of new plastic potentials. The services

Kain Tapper:
Spring Brook. 1967.
Wood and glass, 43.5 x 52 cm.
ART MUSEUM OF THE ATENEUM.

Harry Kivijärvi:
The Portal. 1966.
Diorite, 84 x 61 x 28 cm.
COLLECTION OF THE ARTIST.

rendered by the trend also include a change in esthetic concepts.

Informalism made it much easier to understand the relative independence of form from external reality than any other abstract style. It did not, however, mean that severing ties with nature was accepted in all contexts and by all segments of the public.

Sculptors were the ones who were most open to attack as a result of the stylistic revolution. Tapper's "Funeral March" (1962) was openly mocked by those who only saw three blocks of wood. It was impossible to even imagine that an *objet trouvé* could be exalted into a work of art. Tapper had nonetheless worked over the material of his sculptures just as Laila Pullinen had done. His free-form work, however, was sparking off the great debate "Is a tree stump a work of art?" The actor Tarmo Manni defended Tapper's sculpture and said that the artist had conceived the idea for his sculpture as he listened to what had become a classic of Finnish folk music, "Peltoniemen Hintriikan surumarssi," a funeral march from Ostrobothnia.

Today Eila Hiltunen's Sibelius monument (1961–1967) is one of the inevitable stops on Helsinki's tourist routes, but a heated debate raged about the sculpture when it was unveiled. Giving in to public pressure, the sculpture committee placed a relief of Sibelius's face near the rhythmic "clouds" of Hiltunen's sculpture.

The return of the figure

The most important Informalists were not satisfied with composing cosmic visions of materials for very long, and gradually returned to figurative painting. Others chose a loose abstraction or non-figurative approach.

Jaakko Sievänen entitled a series of his newest work "Rediscovered Figures" (1962). Esko Tirronen (b. 1934) began to make paintings that sought to achieve an urban atmosphere; their fashionable female torsos became the emblem of his art. Ulla Rantanen (b. 1938) had no difficulty joining the Neo-figurative artists, even though she had not experienced the intoxication of Informalism.

The exhibitions of the March Group documented Informalism and its process of transformation beginning in 1961. The group was founded by Lauri Ahlgrén (b. 1929), Erkki Heikkilä (b. 1933), Laila Pullinen, Jaakko Sievänen, and Esko Tirronen, but later the group was expanded and had a different composition from one exhibition to the next.

Sculptors who embraced Informalism were loath to return to figurative art, and developed more allusive forms of expression. Laila Pullinen's magnificently flowing bronze draperies did indeed intimate the concept of a figure, but it is present more as a movement than as a tangible form.

Heikki Häiväoja (b. 1929) often placed the events depicted by his sculptures inside rectangular pieces or between two opposite pieces. The works of

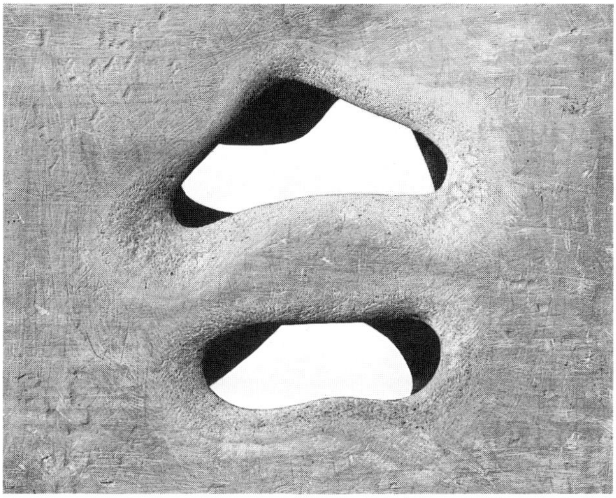

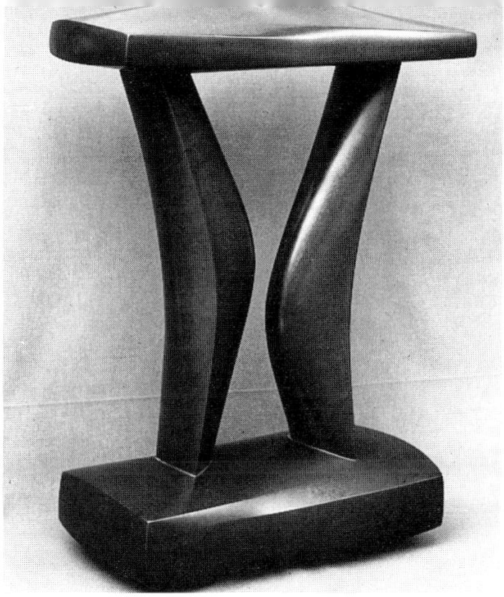

art bring to mind implosions, or an idea of movement inside form. Mauno Hartman (b. 1930) built log structures whose generous form was sensitized by a complex and rich treatment of the surface.

In the 1960s, Kain Tapper developed into the great lyricist of wood sculpture. In his hands, the atmosphere of the Finnish landscape was translated into the idiom of wood, whether it was light filtered through forest or a haze, rain or a thunder cloud rising above the landscape.

The writer Harri Tapper once asked his brother if there is a sculptural form for such an intangible thing as night. The artist answered, "There is a form. The night has a shape. It challenges you to sculpt. You've just got to do it."

In 1957, Tapper sculpted the wooden "Horse Skull," whose deathly grimace conveyed something of an experience he had had as a youth, the sudden death of a horse. Later the skull developed into a plastic basic form and finally into a Minimalist block. The surface structures of the pieces spread like vague landscapes of patina and relief, creating fleeting natural effects.

Harry Kivijärvi, who had studied in Rome, concentrated on stone in the early 1960s. He especially studied the potentials of gently treating the furrowed surface of vertical slabs. The artist might have been influenced somewhat by the slashed fabrics of Lucio Fontana.

One of the essences of Kivijärvi's vertical sculptures is a pressure exerted from within the form. In dealing with sailing as a motive, for example, the artist has even made the weight of the material and a lightness of movement seem simultaneous and reconcilable. Portals as themes and references to primitive architecture often recur in Kivijärvi's sculptures.

Down the last stretch

The 1960s in Finnish art was like the last stretch in a long race. Young artists delved into a forgotten past and discovered Dada and objects. They found out about what was happening on the international scene and learned to use photographs, to arrange happenings, and to combine art forms. In 1960, Helsinki's Swedish Theater hosted a performance by John Cage and Merce Cunningham, with sets designed by Robert Rauschenberg, but the immediate results of the event were negligible.

The "Bronda Attic" group proved Juhani Harri's (b. 1939) most important youthful training ground. It convinced him that the common denominator of European and American avant garde was Material Art. He discovered Rauschenberg's Combine Painting in American art journals, but he found his closest models in Burri's burned paintings and Arman's Neo-realism.

Inspired by Burri, Harri experimented with burning techniques for the first time in 1960. He bought some bottled gas, rented a cellar, and started to mix pigments with metal powder, burning it to the surface of his assemblages. This is the

Juhani Harri.
Cagliostro Sailing. 1965.
Assemblage, 63.5 x 52.5 x 10.5 cm.
TURKU ART MUSEUM.

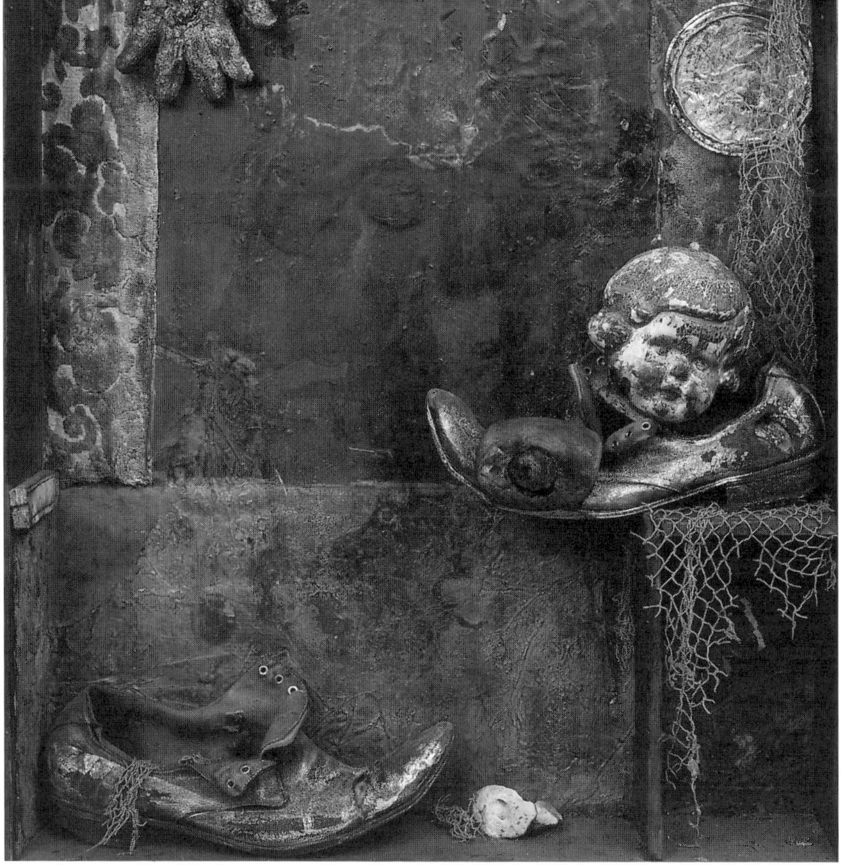

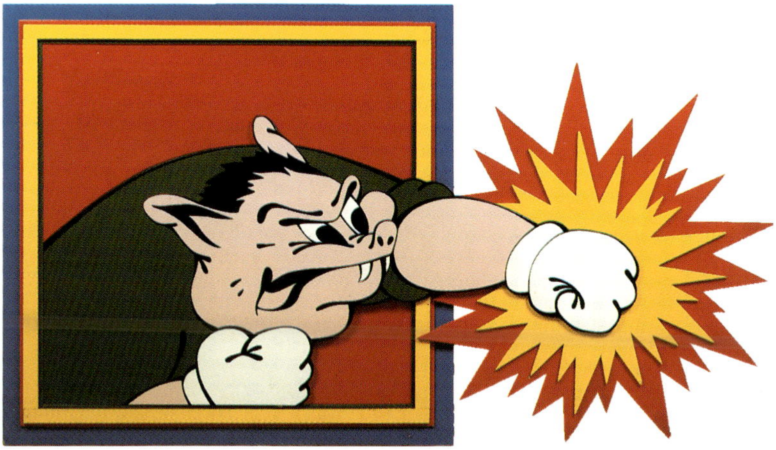

Harro Koskinen.
The Pig Strikes. 1969.
Alkyd paint on wood and chipboard.
140 x 230 cm.
TURKU ART MUSEUM.

method he used to make "The Burnt City of the Birds" (1860) and "The Kingdom of Keys" (1962).

Harri began to use boxes as a stage for his assemblages beginning in 1964. He seems to have gotten the idea primarily from bird cages and the frames for model ships, and only secondarily from the art of Joseph Cornell. Harri used discarded objects and fragments from nature in his boxes, conjuring memories of childhood, the eternal metaphors of the sea, and images of longed-for distant lands.

Harri was not interested in socially committed art, while Ismo Kajander (b. 1939) found a meaning in art in ideology : "Dadaism gave the artists of the bourgeois world a view of the demands for social change: the means for tearing apart what exists."

One of Kajander's first assemblages was the "DADA Cupboard" (1962), made after his trip to Paris, an old washstand whose left side, with objects and photographs, represented the world of men, and right side that of women. The artist's five-year-old goddaughter was responsible for the piece's socially committed contribution. Her little poem was written on the door: "Old Macdonald had a family and it didn't have any food and it died of food since it didn't have any food."

John Cage's idea of eliminating the barrier between art and reality inspired Kajander to carry out experiments, the best known of which was "Music Machine" (1964), made together with the composer Henrik Otto Donner. The two fashioned it from various kinds of junk, the rim of a bicycle tire (a reference to Duchamp), a rake, a birch log, and other scrap.

The Turku artist Kauko Lehtinen (b. 1925) had his first exhibition in Helsinki in 1961 at the Pinx Gallery, which had become the forum for experiments by young artists. Lehtinen's work had elements of Neo-realism and Combine Painting. The artist glued various objects, cardboard, and metal onto canvas, painting the actual subject of the picture roughly on top of everything. Fairly soon, he removed the concrete objects from his canvas and developed a pungently humoristic style that toyed with figuration. It was not true Surrealism, even though the distortion of forms could be interpreted as having a Dali-like ecstasy of paranoid visions. Picasso's influence on Lehtinen's work was nonetheless more important than that of any other artist.

The Finnish underground movement, with its comic strips, poetry, and provocative happenings, was started in Turku. Harro Koskinen (b. 1945) developed his own special "pig ideology," taking its basic idea from a Brechtian theory of alienation: "The pig is familiar to everyone, but when it is put in place of people, doing people's work, the observer begins to ask about the activity's meaning. In working towards an effective, activating visualization, I also ended up with a simplified, clear method of presentation. In choosing the pig in place of man, I thought of the dirty tricks that people do every day: lie, kill, exploit, oppress. I also considered the pig's image, disgustingness, to be important."

Koskinen made a large number of assemblages and even "pig jewelry," but his comic strip-like painted wooden reliefs attracted the most attention. "Pig Messiah," showing a crucified pig (1969), led to a court case that dragged on for years. It concluded with both the artist and the exhibition committee that had chosen to show it being fined for blasphemy. The event was a farcical parallel to the blasphemy case involving the writer Hannu Salama.

Pop Art naturally played a role in the art of the 1960s. Paul Osipow (b. 1939), Leo Lindsten (1943–1988), and Mikko Jalavisto (b. 1937) made fairly free use of loans, while Kari Jylhä (b. 1939) and Raimo Reinikainen (b. 1939) developed distinctive styles. Even farther from the trend was Heikki W. Virolainen (b. 1936), a creator of decoratively painted sculptures. Though his work was thought to have been influenced by Pop Art, it had more to do with the varicolored world of icons.

The power of the grid

The young geometricians felt a need to get together and founded the Aloha Group in 1966. The group included a number of the decade's innovators in Constructivism and free abstraction: Timo Aalto (b. 1941), Jorma Hautala (b. 1941), Juha Soisalo (b. 1941), and Kari-Juhani Tolonen (b. 1945). This quartet was later joined by Risto Vilhunen (b. 1945). The group took its name from the old movie theater where some of the members worked, and when it was torn down in 1969, the group disbanded.

The stringent forms of Constructivism were sometimes combined with free forms, but achieving a kinetic effect became one of the key goals at the end of the 1960s. There were rather few true Op-art pieces, but Martti S. Mäki (b. 1947), for example, painted line compositions set off with contrasting colors. Risto Vilhunen and Göran Augustson (b. 1936) mostly applied the ideas of Vasarely, bombarding the beholder's retina with somewhat lighter contrasts.

Sam Vanni's painting "The Multidimensional Room" (1961) gave an early signal of the future power of three factors. Grids showed that symmetry, repetition, and seriality did not necessarily lead to monotonous painting, but in fact made room for ever fresher constructions of color and form. Ernst Mether-Borgström's black and white towers are a good example.

Göran Augustson found his personal style in abstractions of nature, but Juhana Blomstedt (b. 1937) remained a stylistic nomad, continually investigating various alternatives. Matti Kujasalo (b. 1946), in turn, developed a network of events within a checker-board and squares into an increasingly refined style of painting based on a prechosen system.

The great ideal of Constructivism, collaboration between art and architecture, was never realized. Efforts were made to revive this utopian concept in 1971 at an exhibition where Jorma Hautala, Erkki Hirvelä

Juhana Blomstedt:
Still-life. 1971. Oil, 135 x 190 cm.
ART MUSEUM OF THE ATENEUM.

Raimo Utriainen:
Wave. 1974. Aluminum, 13 cm.
TAMMASAARI DOCK, HELSINKI.

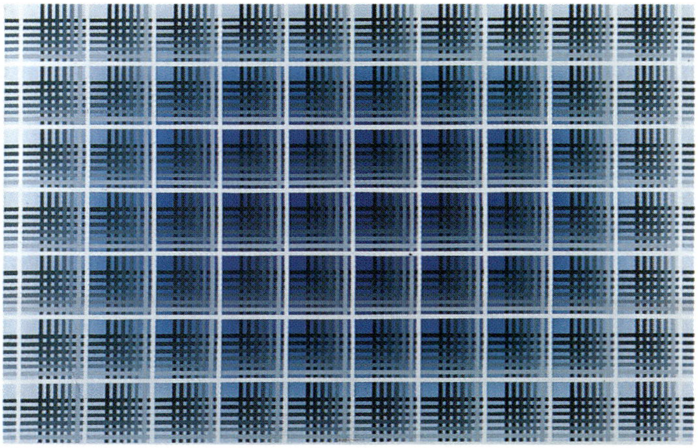

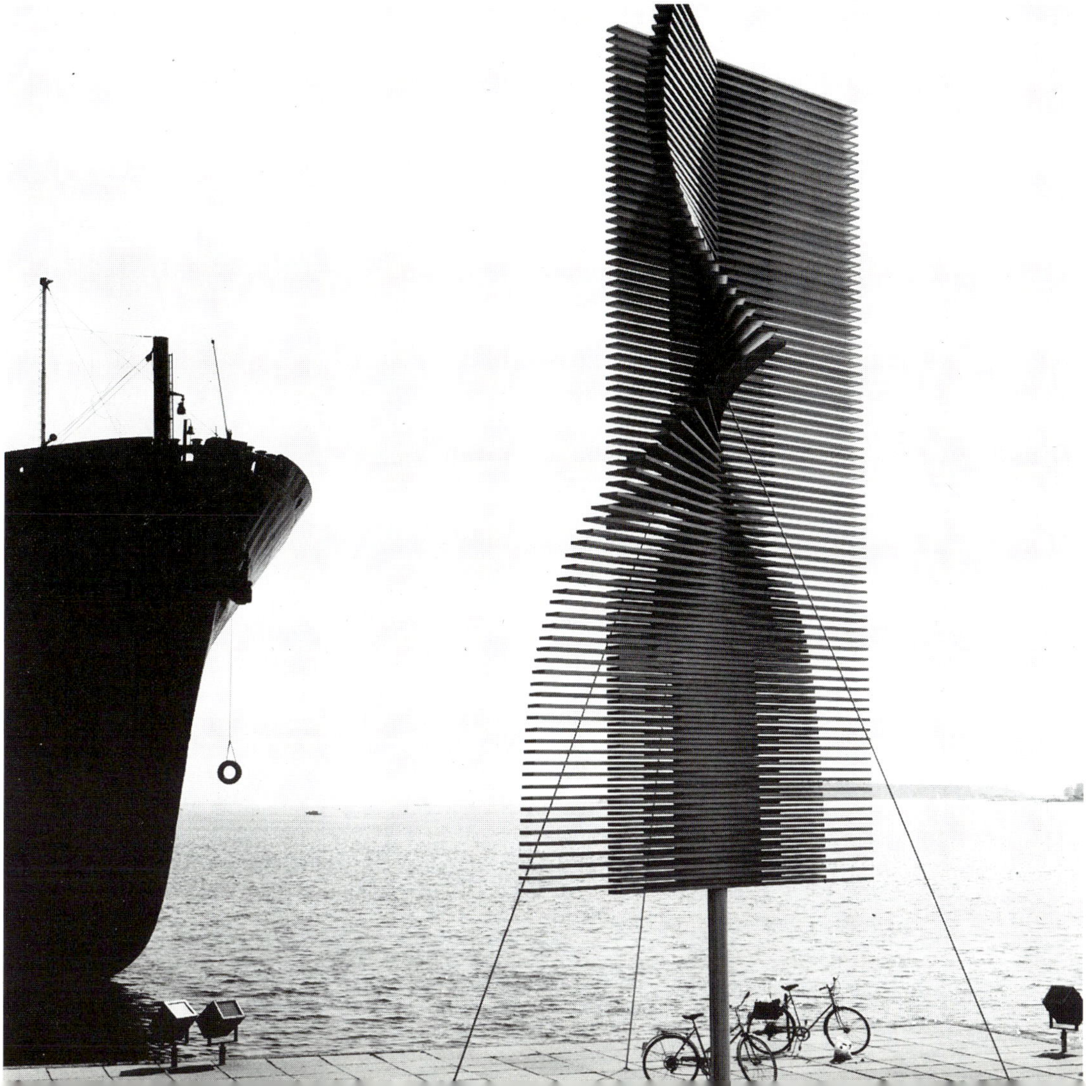

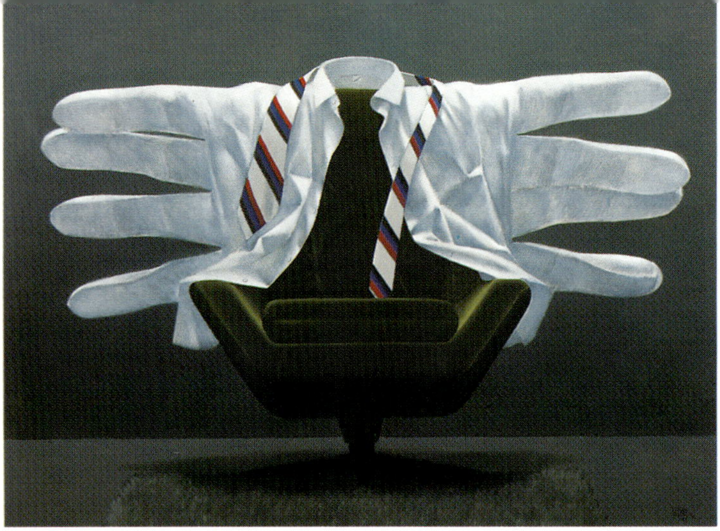

Kimmo Kaivanto: Night (The White Winner). 1972. Oil, 140 x 162 cm.
SARA HILDÉN ART MUSEUM, TAMPERE.

(b. 1937), Perttu Näsänen (b. 1940), Sven-Olof Westerlund (b. 1935) and the cultural activist Kai Linnilä designed imaginary models of the union of sculpture and architecture from cardboard elements.

The sculptor Raimo Utriainen (b. 1927) created his lyrical version of Constructivism at the beginning of the 1970s by joining a meticulous and systematic structure with plastic volumes. The artist arranged overlapping stacks of aluminum slats into sculpturally undulating, transparent surfaces. The complex reflections of the slats reacted to even the smallest changes in light and created a surface that lived along with its surroundings.

Utriainen predicted at the beginning of the 1960s that sculpture would wither away unless it could serve architecture as an overall concept. He was given the chance to test the synthesis of a slat sculpture ("Wave") and an architectonically forceful environment in front of Alko Oy's plant in Helsinki in 1974. The dimensions of the elegant sculpture proved too small, however, when they were set against the enormous mass of the building.

Art's triangle drama

The ideal of diversity dominated young art in the 1960s. Figurative and non-figurative art lived in peaceful coexistence though people still shied away from socially committed work in the middle of the decade. Kimmo Kaivanto's (b. 1932) retrospective at the Amos Anderson Art Museum in 1971, "Fingers in the Game," struck at different note. The far left declared that Kaivanto's art was "bourgeois leaven." Kaivanto didn't go far enough in criticizing militarism in his work; he should have condemned it selectively and found evil in capitalism in particular.

Using fingers, Kaivanto painted, drew, and sculpted metaphors of the link between violence and male sexuality. Perhaps the negative reaction he elicited also held the germs of puritanism: the day's sexual revolution and free love were seen as barriers to the real revolution.

"Fingers in the Game" was the last major show of diversity in socially committed art. Afterwards, liberal views were on the defensive as cultural Leninism, or actually Brezhnevism, took the leading role in public opinion.

Finnish art was pulled by three different currents. One was dominated by "homo politicus," demanding popular realism, with its working-class heroes. The second emphasized "homo faber," the importance of soft technology and a Constructivist view of the environment. The ideal of the third trend was "homo ludens," favoring individualism and the strategies of Conceptual Art. "Homo ludens" was consigned to the thankless position of the opposition, since the two other trends considered it their moral duty to improve society.

The parties in this triangle drama arranged themselves into loose groupings. Those prone to political realism joined the Cultural Workers' Union or its

Osmo Valtonen:
Typography. 1975.
Sand, steel, engine.
COLLECTION OF THE ARTIST.

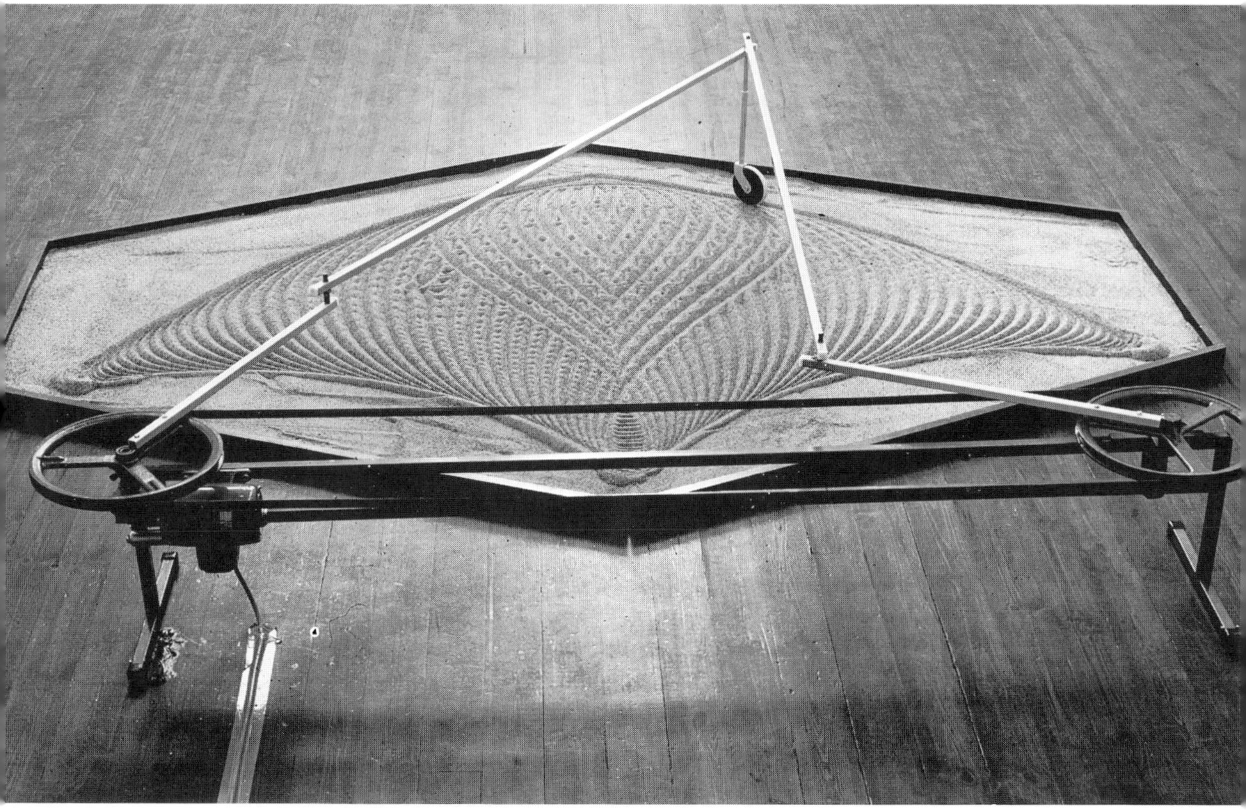

fringes. The Dimension Group gathered together Constructivists and "engineering artists" for their exhibitions. The Reapers took care of the remnants of the happy '60s.

The Cultural Workers' Union was supported by young people from good bourgeois homes and the middle-aged. They felt guilty that they were doing so well, and that this new affluence was unevenly distributed. They also thought they knew how to satisfy the esthetic needs of the proletariat. Realism's history was revived, but the atmospheric art of such modern masters as Aimo Kanerva and Veikko Vionoja (b. 1909) was also respected.

The founders of the Dimension Group dreamed of grandiose collaboration between artists and technology. It seemed that if technology were properly used, it would open up limitless potentials to mankind. The group described its activities as two-directional: "An effort will be made in the group's exhibitions and happenings to illustrate the potentials offered to art by science and technology and the ways in which art can be used to express the phenomena of science and technology."

Inspiration for founding the group was taken from such internationally famous examples as the Groupe de Recherche d'Art Visuel and Experiments in Art and Technology. Dimension's original members had mostly concentrated on kinetics and painting, but gradually the group became more diverse. The group was joined by composers of electronic music and other computer experts. A special subgroup, Pythagoras, worked on the use of computers in art, taking its name from the "composing and painting" computer designed by the sculptor Osmo Valtonen (b. 1929), the engineer Erkki Rajulin, and the composer Heikki Toppila in 1971. The most imaginative representative of Dimension's "green approach" was Olavi Lanu (b. 1925), with his pantheistic illusions of nature.

According to Jan Olof Mallander (b. 1944), the Reapers were founded to bring together the "homeless energies" of art. They were recognizable from pop objects, the pictures and word methods of Conceptual Art, amateur painting, photography, and "paper sculptures" (Mallander's name for picture montages).

The Reapers arranged their first joint showing in 1970, entitled "True Lies." It reflected the members' wish to question the politically simplified relationship between art and reality. The Reapers were ideologically close to the new left, but they were disaffected with both the right and the left, finding the same inflexible system. For six years, the central forum for the group's public appearances was Cheap Thrills, the gallery founded by Mallander in 1971.

Olli Lyytikäinen (1949–1987) was the Reaper who was most successful abroad. His skillful fabulation and sarcastic psychopathological portrayals had more to do with Claes Oldenburg's approach than they did with old-fashioned Surrealism. Another Finnish artist with international success was Ilkka-Juhani Takalo-Eskola (b. 1937), whose "forest theater" and expressive amateur painting can be

Olli Lyytikäinen:
Three Pyramids and a Sphinx. 1974.
Watercolor and pastel, 57 x 80 cm.
PRIVATE COLLECTION.

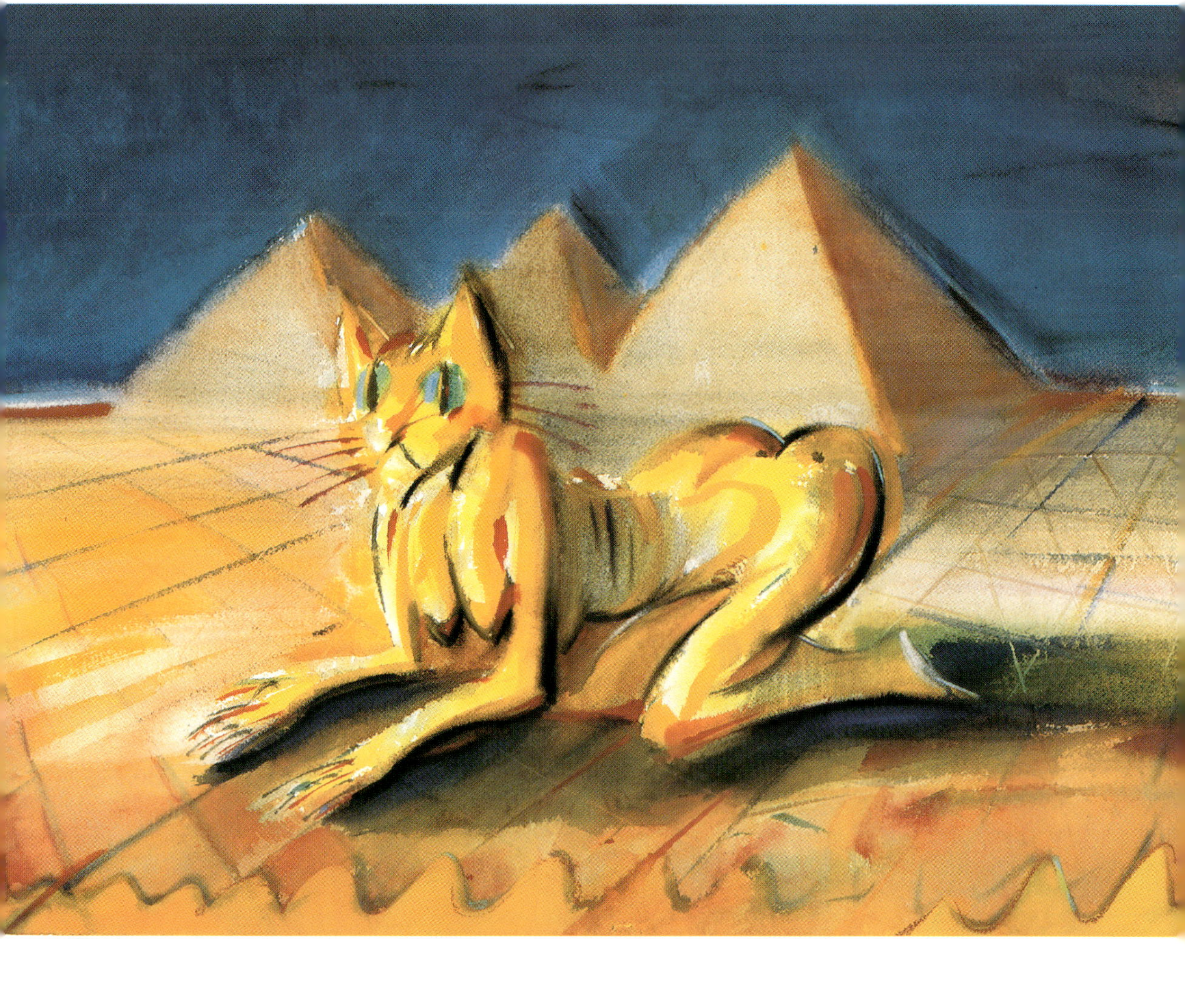

Outi Heiskanen:
Silent Winter. 1981.
Aquatint. 51 x 51 cm.
PRIVATE COLLECTION.

Paul Osipow:
Painting. 1987.
Acrylic, 150 x 150 cm.
PRIVATE COLLECTION.

Tapio Junno:
The Scream I, 1978.
Bronze, 60 cm.
ART MUSEUM OF THE ATENEUM.

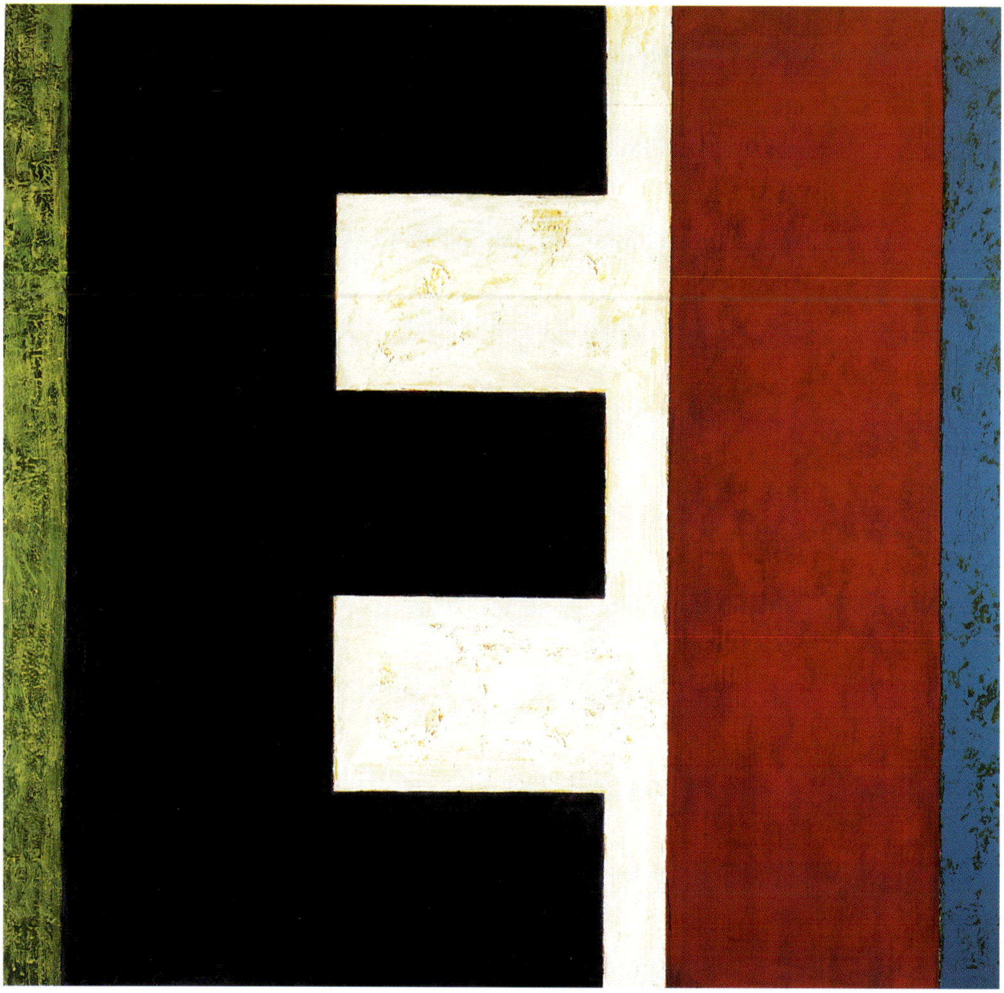

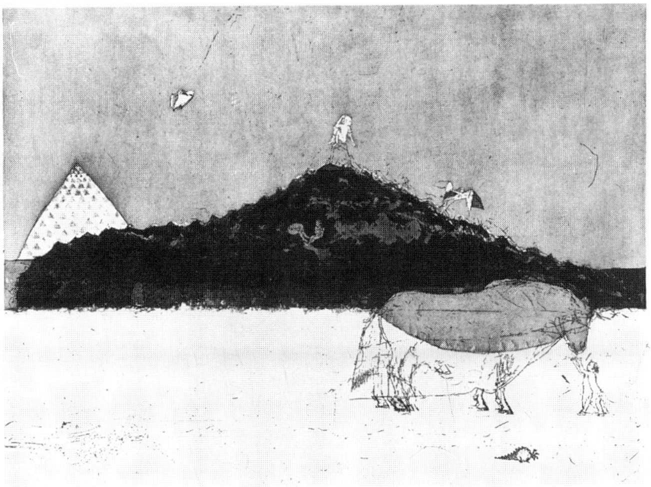

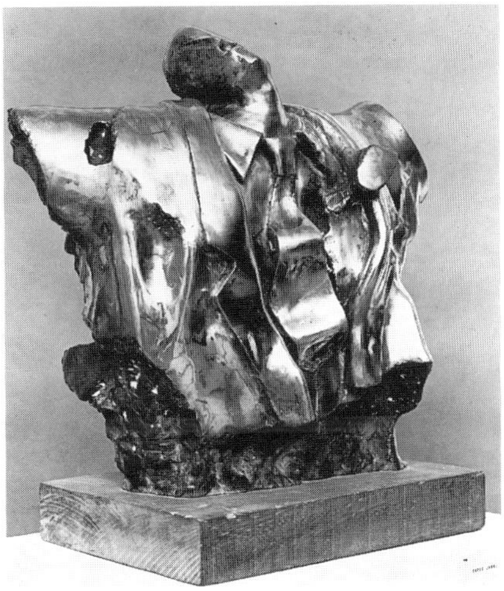

traced back much farther than to the Reapers. His works of art and performances also expressed a belief in the liberation of the individual from ponderous systems and the power of money.

Groups naturally only covered a small part of the whole art world, and important work was done outside them. The young artists of previous decades matured and became "classics." Paul Osipow concentrated on simplified geometry and an emphasis on the materiality of color. Outi Heiskanen (b. 1937) did innovative work in metal graphics using traditional means, and began her distinctive performances in the 1970s long before the great age of Performance Art. Ossi Somma's (b. 1926) *arte povera* and wax sculptures of the Christian apocalypse developed into an impressive manifesto of melancholy humor and moral pathos. The bronze figures of Tapio Junno (b. 1940) interpreted the fears and unexpected dangers of today's affluent society.

The "triangle drama" in art began to fall apart in the latter half of the 1970s when Realism came to a dead end and Constructivism seemed to offer only limited potential. "Homo ludens" moved from the outskirts to the center of art in the 1980s, but young painters inclined towards Expressionism gradually began a process of rejuvenation. Women were the quickest to make new decisions in the 1970s. Marjatta Tapiola (b. 1951) brought a painful psychological Expressionism to painting; Leena Luostarinen (b. 1949) created an exotic, full-blooded Roman-ticism; and Marika Mäkelä (b. 1947) produced powerful Post-modern, abstract painting.

Full-scale Neo-expressionism was one of the phenomena of the 1980s, but architectonic forms and a picturesqueness that studied the ambivalence of the picture surface were also in evidence. Silja Rantanen (b. 1955) and Lauri Laine (b. 1946) went farthest with this approach.

Monuments to great men and designs for them still take the pulse of society's attitude towards art and politics. In the 1970s, Tapio Wirkkala designed a Land Art monument to President Urho Kekkonen in Saivaara, in Lapland, but the proposal was rejected for ecological reasons. Harry Kivijärvi's monument to President J. K. Paasikivi (1977–1980), in contrast, was unveiled without any real protest, as was Pekka Kauhanen's (b. 1954) Post-modern monument to Kekkonen, "A Great Age" (1990). The conservative spirit created by the recession stuck down Veikko Myller's (b. 1951) design for a monument to President Risto Ryti. A number of politicians have tried to prevent the project from being carried out because its Minimalist and Constructivist form supposedly do not express Ryti's life work.

One of the key sculptors of the 1980s, Martti Aiha (b. 1952), won Alko Oy's competition, making one of Finland's largest public sculptures, "Rumba" (1992). Its flaming form and large dimensions were able to provide a sufficient counterbalance to the masses of the industrial architecture that surround it.

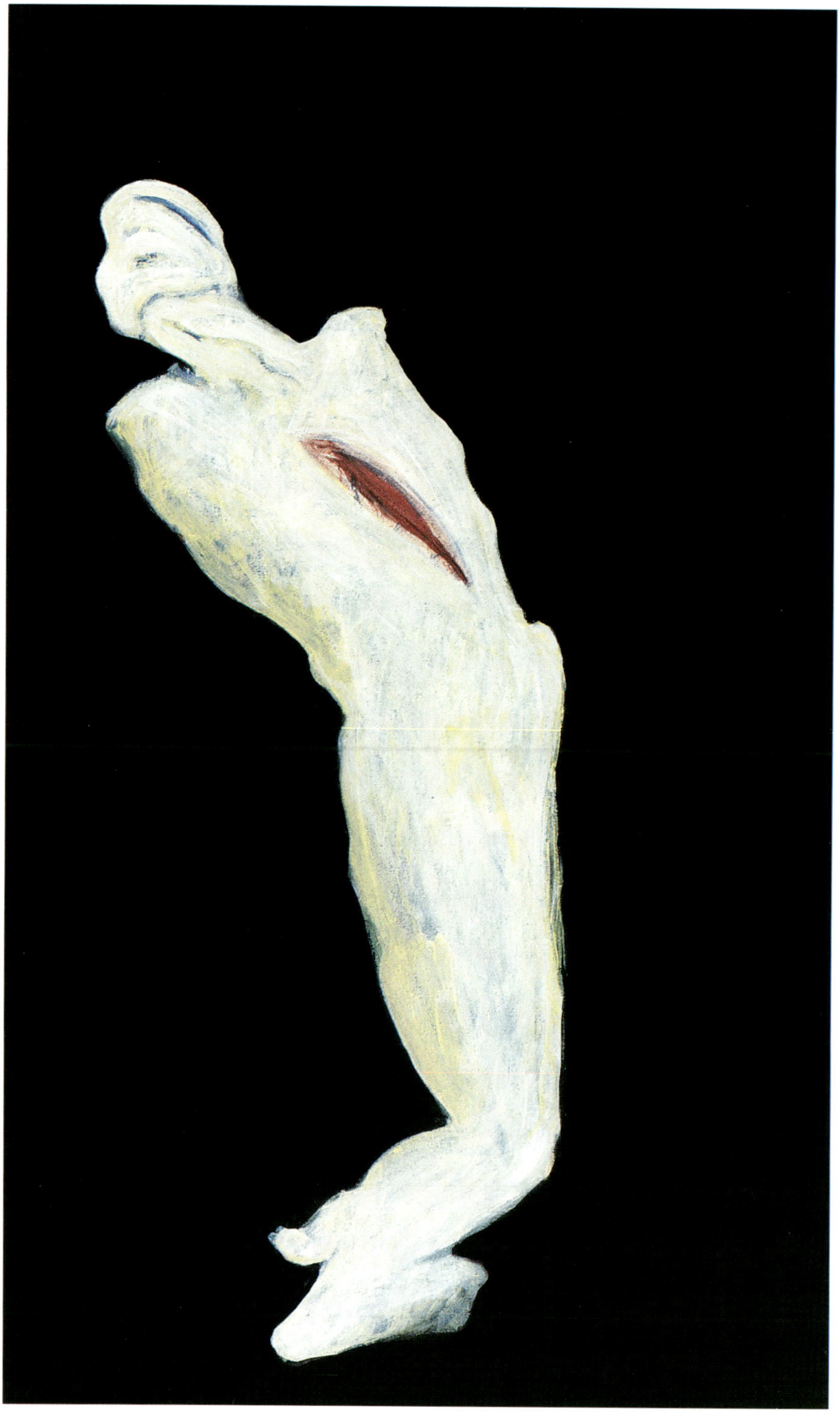

Marjatta Tapiola:
Empty Sleeves. 1986.
Tempera, 165 x 94 cm.
CITY OF VANTAA COLLECTION.

Leena Luostarinen:
Rock Bound V. 1986.
Oil, 130 x 165 cm.
COLLECTION OF THE ARTIST.

Silja Rantanen:
Impression of Mutual Relations from a Certain Distance. 1991.
Oil, 220 x 330 cm.
COLLECTION OF THE ARTIST.

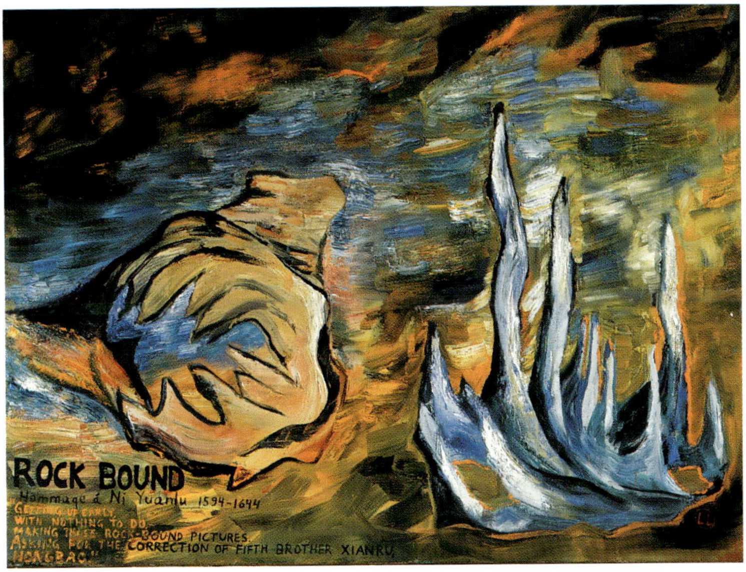

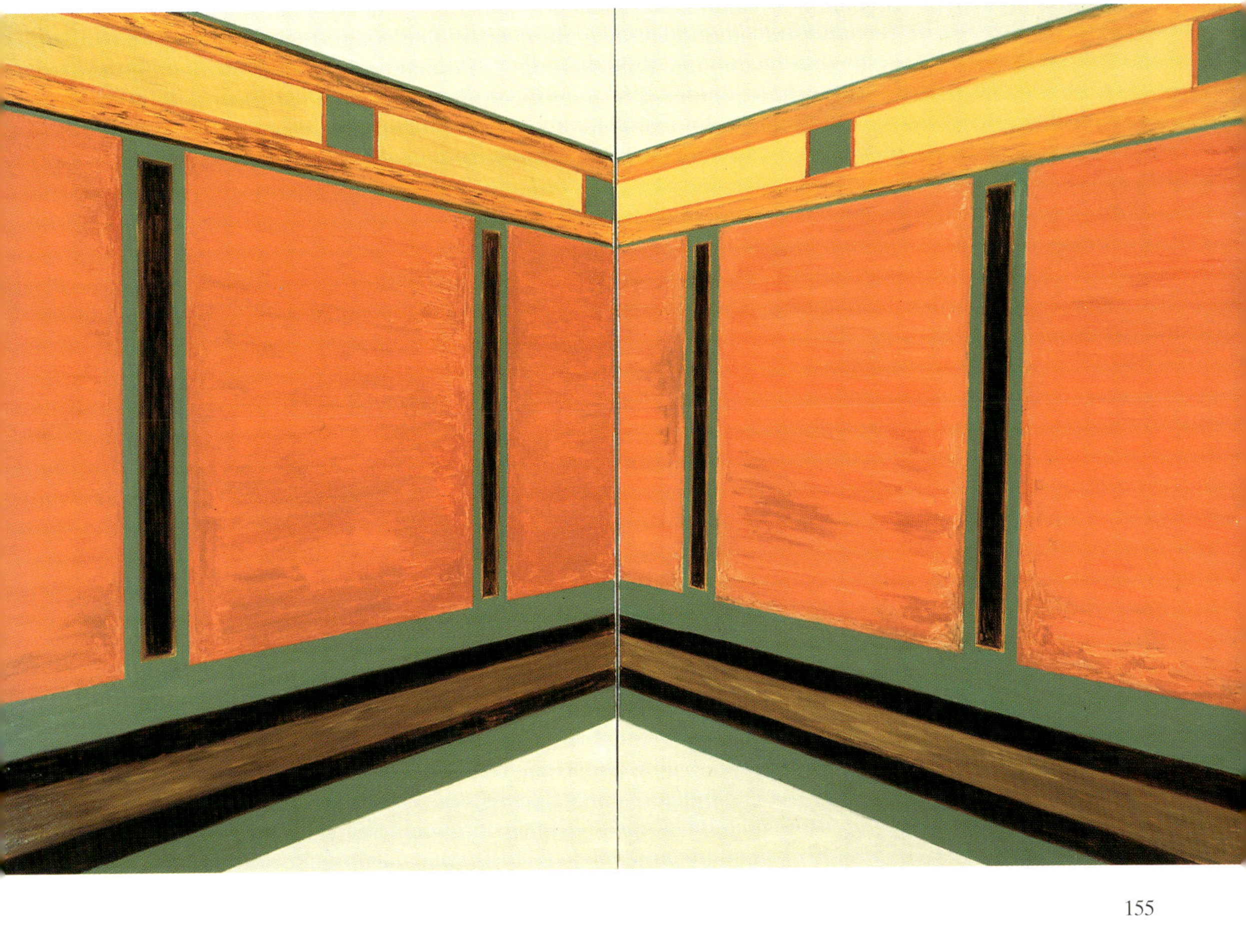

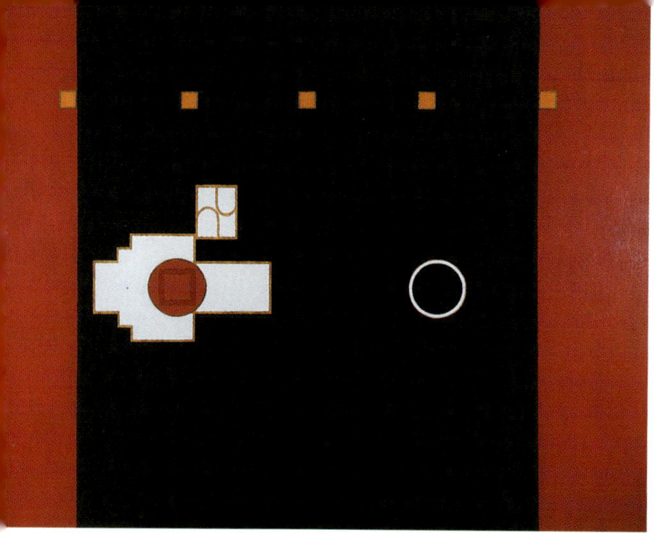

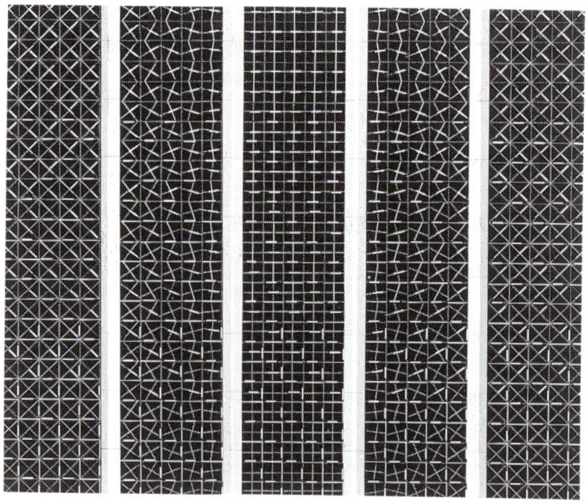

Stories change

In Finland, as elsewhere, the great task of art in the 1980s was presumed to be the destruction of the great "stories" of Modernism, visual utopias aimed at a new society. In reality, the stories have just changed their titles. The greatest story could be called "the free Odyssey in the archipelago of art history," while another could be called "the triumph of the feministic viewpoint." A third story tells of the merging of the artist and the businessman, while the fourth relates the victory of theory over art. The fifth is an old one: all art forms unite (and try to include reality while you're at it).

Did national features disappear in this Post-modern mill? Certainly not, as we can see from the meditative Conceptual Art of Lauri Anttila (b. 1938), the brilliant treatment of wood by Kari Cavén (b. 1954), the *Kalevala*-like shaman cult of Erkki Pirtola (b. 1950), Sirpa Ala-Lääkkölä's female conception of Gallén's "Aino" triptych, or Maaria Wirkkala's (b. 1954) emotional Space and Environmental Art.

A personal contribution to counterbalance the group work and collective efforts (Jack Hellen Brut, Homo $) often required by Performance Art is increasingly gaining ground. Take some of the installations by Marja Kanervo (b. 1958), video work by Marjatta Oja (b. 1972), and family-oriented sculptures by Pekka Nevalainen (b. 1951).

The recession that began at the end of the 1980s quickly strangled the cornucopia of pictorial art. The decline in experimentation has led to increased caution and has emphasized the importance of tradition. The fear that Finland will lose its identity in the European Union might strengthen the national features of art.

International exchanges

The recovery from the recession after the mid-1990's encouraged increased enterprise in the field of culture in Finland and broadened the scope of international exchanges in the arts. The national self-portrait came to be drawn more from a European than from a Nordic perspective.

The exploitation of new technology has revolutionized both our everyday lives and the means available for executing and distributing works of art. Artists are looking into all manner of interactive media, producing their works digitally and conversing with each other via their home pages. The media arts have been accepted as a matter of course, and some associations of artists, such as The Other (Muu ry), have concentrated on developing new modes of expression.

The speed with which these developments have taken place has been greatly influenced by government cultural policy. An ambitious desire has been conceived for creating an "information society" in Finland that is able to react quickly and flexibly to international economic demands, and the economic dimension has also been

Lauri Laine:
Untitled. 1990.
Oil, 200 x 240 cm.
PRIVATE COLLECTION.

Matti Kujasalo:
Five-part Systematic Painting. 1988.
Acrylic, 75 x 87 cm.
PRIVATE COLLECTION.

Maaria Wirkkala:
Tirami Su (Confession Dialogue). 1995.
Outdoor installation.
CAMPO BANDIERA E MORO, BIENNALE DI VENEZIA.

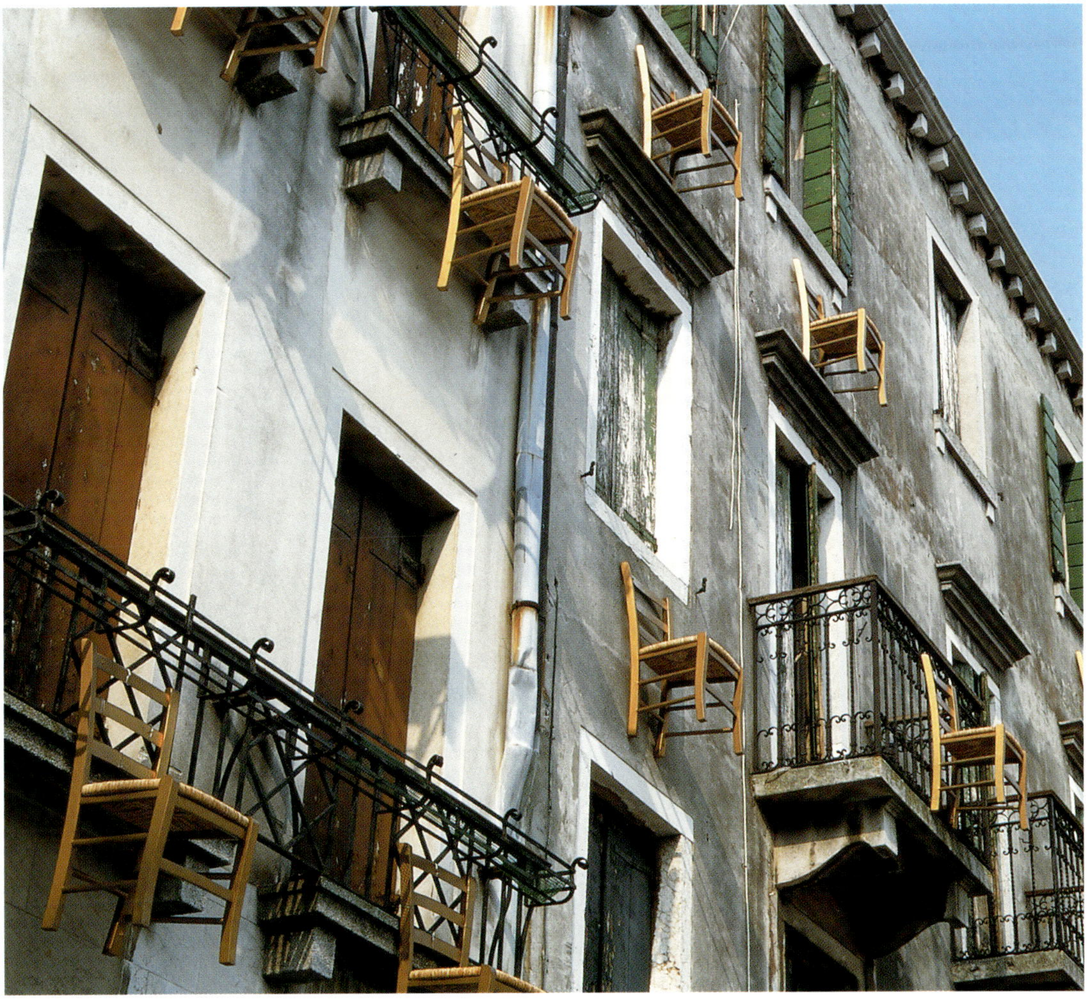

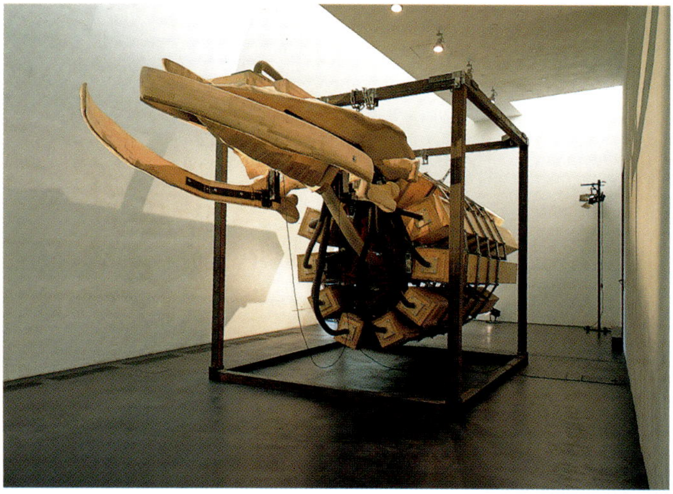

Markus Copper:
Archangel of Seven Seas. 1998.
Steel, wood, organ pipes, electric motor, 8.5 x 2.9 x 3 m.

emphasized in the processes of producing art. A situation is emerging in which works of art are more often group projects than the isolated efforts of creative individuals.

Prospects are not in all respects favourable, however. It has been asked whether the flood of information that greets us in this new society will stifle our ability to make rational choices in matters of values, and whether the attraction of technology may not have the same passivizing effect as mass entertainment. As art has to compete both financially and ethically in these arenas, there is a fear that its function as an alternative view of life and its ability to go against the grain of general opinion will degenerate.

The engulfing enormity of the new field of activity that has opened up, and its fragmentation, may well lead to a loss of independence. Artists will be looking for approval from the public and from their sponsors and will no longer be able to allow their work to arise naturally out of their own subjective views.

Kiasma like a sculpture

The most significant cultural building of the decade, Kiasma, the Museum of Contemporary Art, opened its doors to the public in spring 1998. The building was designed by the American architect Steven Holl. His idea of uniting two separate entities with a kind of plastic joint, a Chiasma, was severely criticized by Finnish architects and by the public, but the protest has now subsided and the building has also been praised in many quarters.

The cramped site and the restrictions imposed by its position in the urban landscape were a great challenge for Holl, and the resulting design gave the centre of Helsinki a new architectural sculpture, the sweeping lines of which skilfully bind together the conflicting architectural styles of the surroundings and the problematical features of the town plan.

Kiasma's location in the very heart of the city could easily help it to become a "living room" for the local people. The museum's policy has partly been based on the media arts and experimentation that crosses the frontiers between different branches of art. The building is also fitted with some of the most up-to-date technology available.

The bitch and her puppy

One of the leading media artists, Marita Liulia (b. 1957), produced her first multimedia work, "Maire", on the subject of Maire Gullichsen, perhaps the most outstanding background figure of modernism in Finland, and her second, "Ambitious Bitch", on women in the contrasting lights of information and the arts. She then made still more ample use of her ironically loaded feminism in "Son of a Bitch", a study of men. "They make up 48 % of the population and they need our sympathy," she says.

Video art comes close to the cinema in the works of Eija-Liisa Ahtila (b. 1959) and Maria

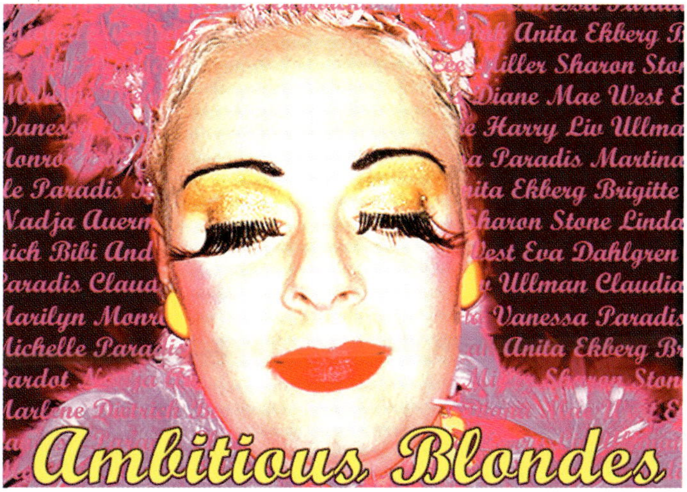

Marita Liulia: Ambitious Bitch. 1996.
CD-ROM, 2nd edit. 1998.
SCREENSHOT: MARITA LIULIA

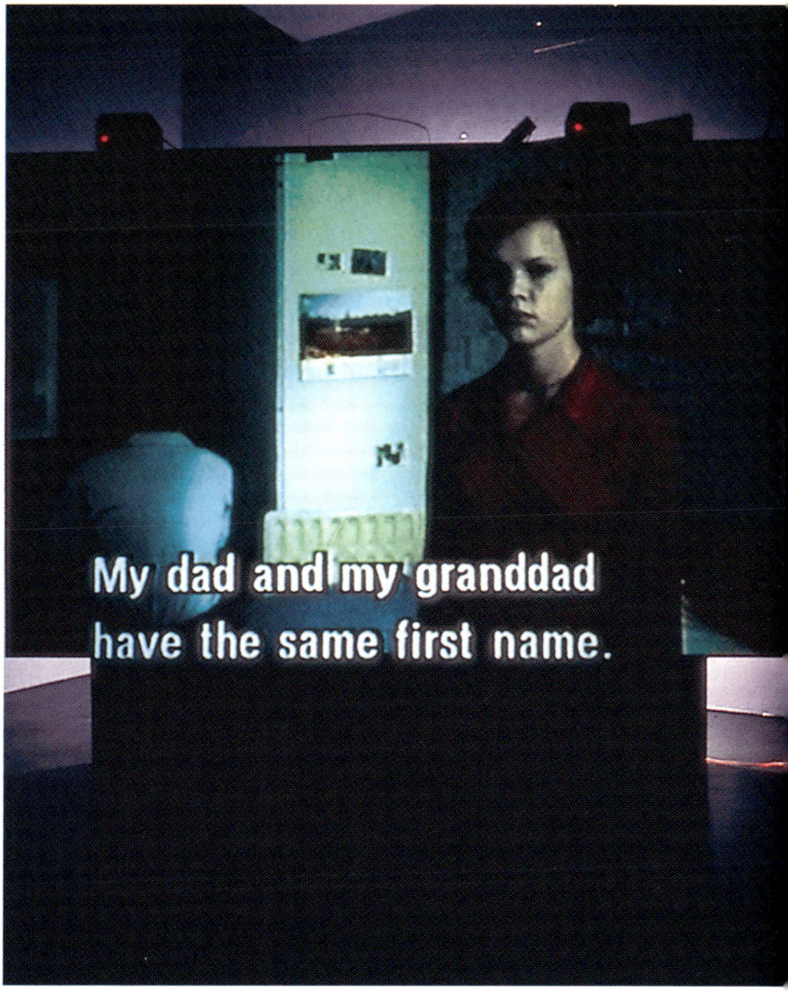

Eija-Liisa Ahtila:
Today. 1996–1997.
35 mm/ Video installation.
Written & directed by Eija-Liisa Ahtila.
COPYRIGHT: CRYSTAL EYE,
COURTESY GASSER & GRÜNERT INC.

Ruotsala (b. 1959), for instance. In fact it is often difficult to draw the line between the two art forms, as many of these works assign a more important role than ever before to a narrative that advances from one event to the next.

Henrietta Lehtonen (b. 1965), in works such as her video "Bambino", examines the messages carried by one precisely delimited series of images. When the work was presented at the Venice Biennial in 1996, where it was located in a functioning church, the image of a child took on a meaning that was firmly grounded in Christian mythology.

Lehtonen has opened up an interesting path to the self-examination that so naturally becomes a part of video art. She allows herself to be hypnotized and then discusses the fundamental questions of creative art with her hypnotist.

Teemu Mäki (b. 1967), in turn, uses video to examine the principles of his own world of values and the possibilities for human existence on the other side of values. The aggressive features contained in Mäki's art have aroused a great deal of

Esko Männikkö:
Kuivaniemi. 1991.
Chromogenic color photograph,
50 x 40 cm.

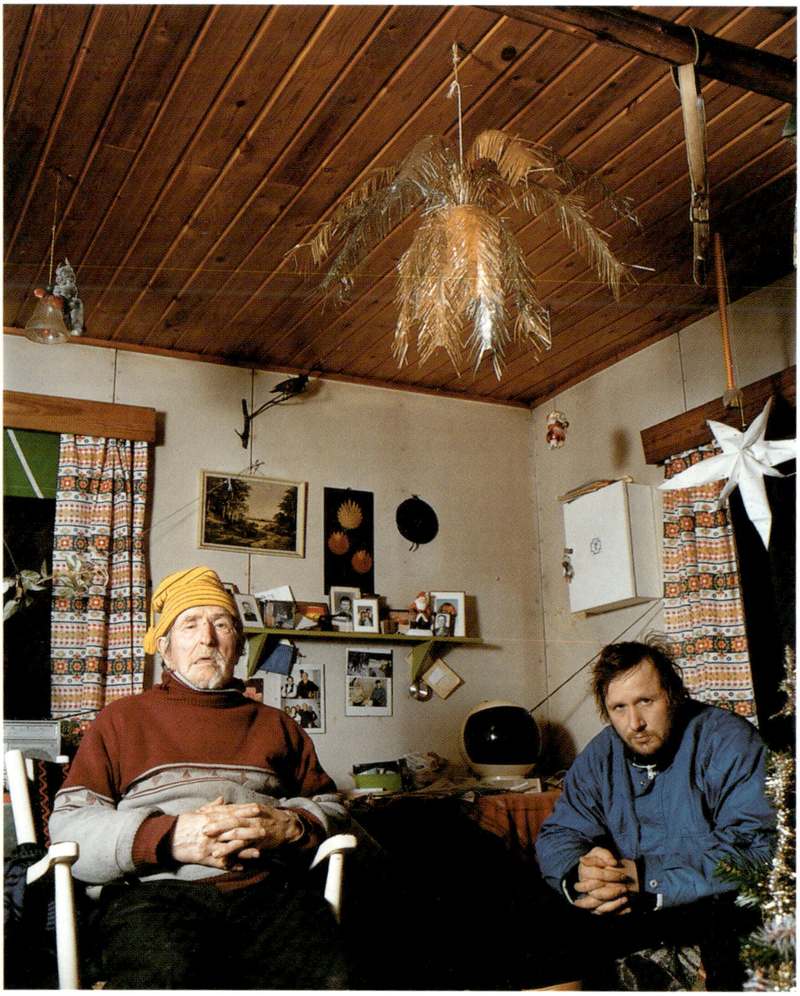

discussion on the ethics of artist production, although the debate has devoted less attention to the other philosophical questions that he raises.

Photographs have come to occupy a position of growing importance in Finnish art, the best known exponent of their use being Esko Männikkö (b. 1959), the "Vermeer of the North", whose photographs reflect the dilatory lives of the people of New Mexico just as much as those of the people of Northern Finland.

The German critic Ruth Diehl writes:

"Esko Männikkö is a photographer of internal conditions, who describes the world of dwellings in his photographs just as much as the world of the dwellers. He finds his subjects in all corners of the earth, and approaches them with a sympathetic gaze, not prying or preaching, but with a tempo that inspires a great sense of peace. Männikkö confronts feigned melancholy with a credible spirit of humanity, and it is this that distinguishes his work from feature photographs."

Extrusion and space traps

The reformers of traditional painting have frequently set out to combine it with photography as a means of presentation, as was done by Jussi Niva (b. 1966), the first Finn to enter the Kassel Documenta, in 1992. The objects of his interest vary from questions regarding the concept of space to the exploitation of technologically modified worlds of color.

Not even the space occupied by a picture can be regarded as a closed book, as is shown by the photographs of Pertti Kekarainen (b. 1965), who employs subtle means to create spaces that are nested inside each other or superimposed on top of each other, thus problematizing the viewing of pictures and the relation of the viewer to what he sees.

Most prominent among the reformers of the art of painting are Marianna Uutinen (b. 1961) and Nina Roos (b. 1956). Uutinen sought to diffuse the traditional role of the painter by extruding strands of acrylic paint over canvasses and other objects. By enveloping one of Alvar Aalto's famous three-legged stools in green bands of acrylic, she symbolically did modernism to death and proclaimed the triumph of post-modernism.

Nina Roos' paintings in acrylic are exceedingly subtle studies of light and transparency in which the significance of color as a material component virtually disappears.

Perspective, space, reflection and transparency are the elements of which Susanne Gottberg's (b. 1964) dream-like paintings are composed. She has sometimes been regarded as a surrealist, her technically dazzling paintings are rather a matter of a conscious questioning of what one sees, as if it were a falsification of the real world brought about by subconscious stimuli. In some of her works she constructs a space trap: the spectator is looking at a scene which, thought about logically, is behind him.

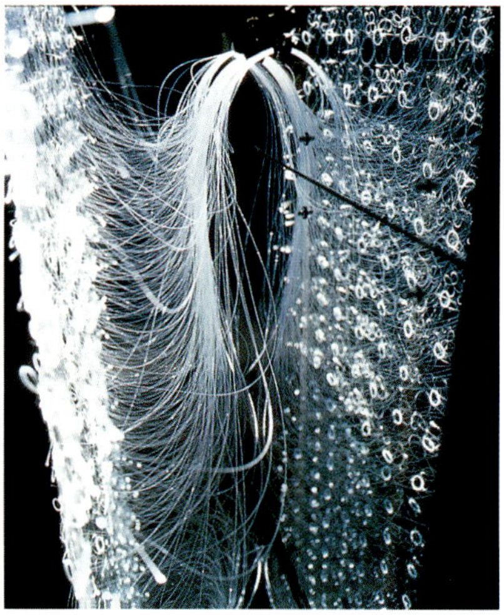

Helena Hietanen:
Technolace light sculpture. 1997.
Optical fibres, light projectors, reflective glass, aluminium strips, light moves inside the fibres, 200 x 320 x 400 cm.

Pertti Kekarainen:
Intensification. 1998.
Chromogenic color print, 185 x 230 cm.

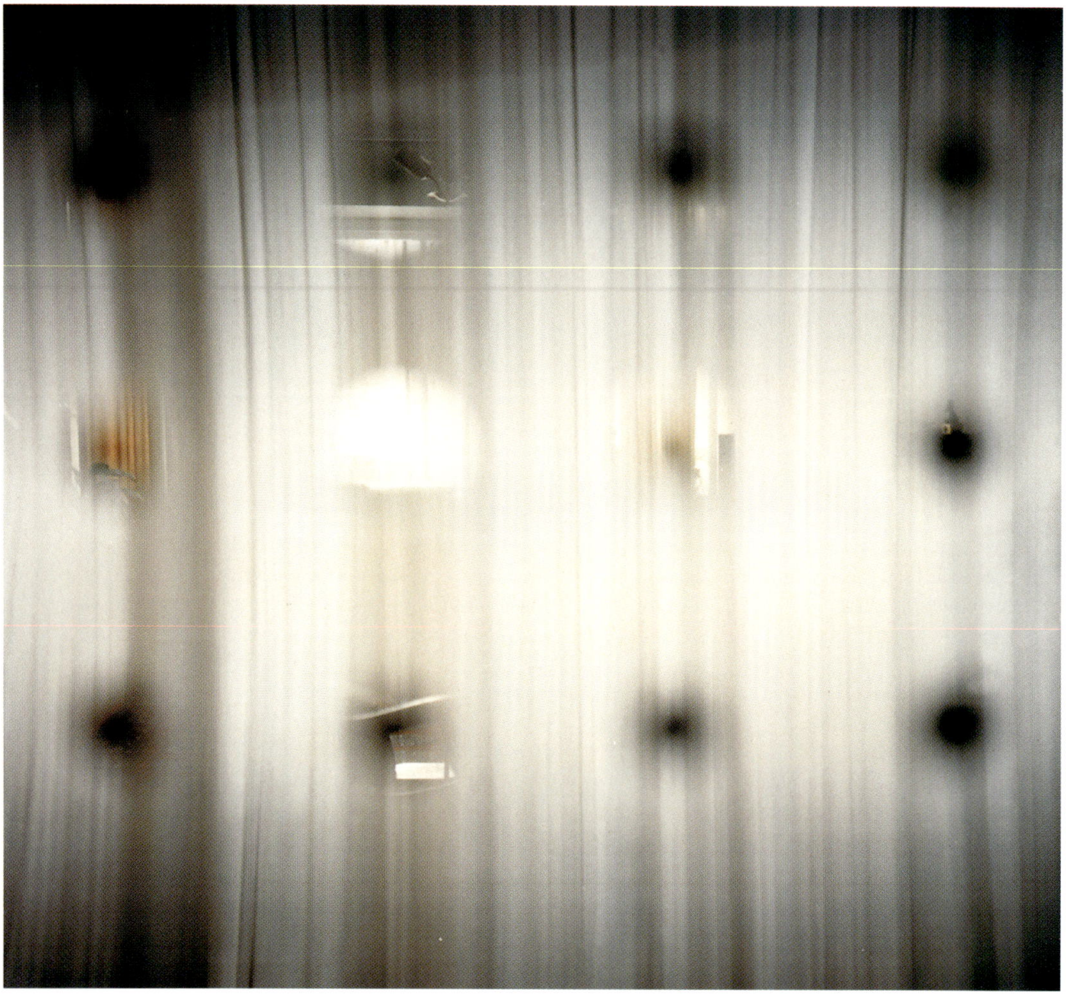

Susanne Gottberg:
In Mid-Movement. 1997.
Oil, 60 x 57 cm.

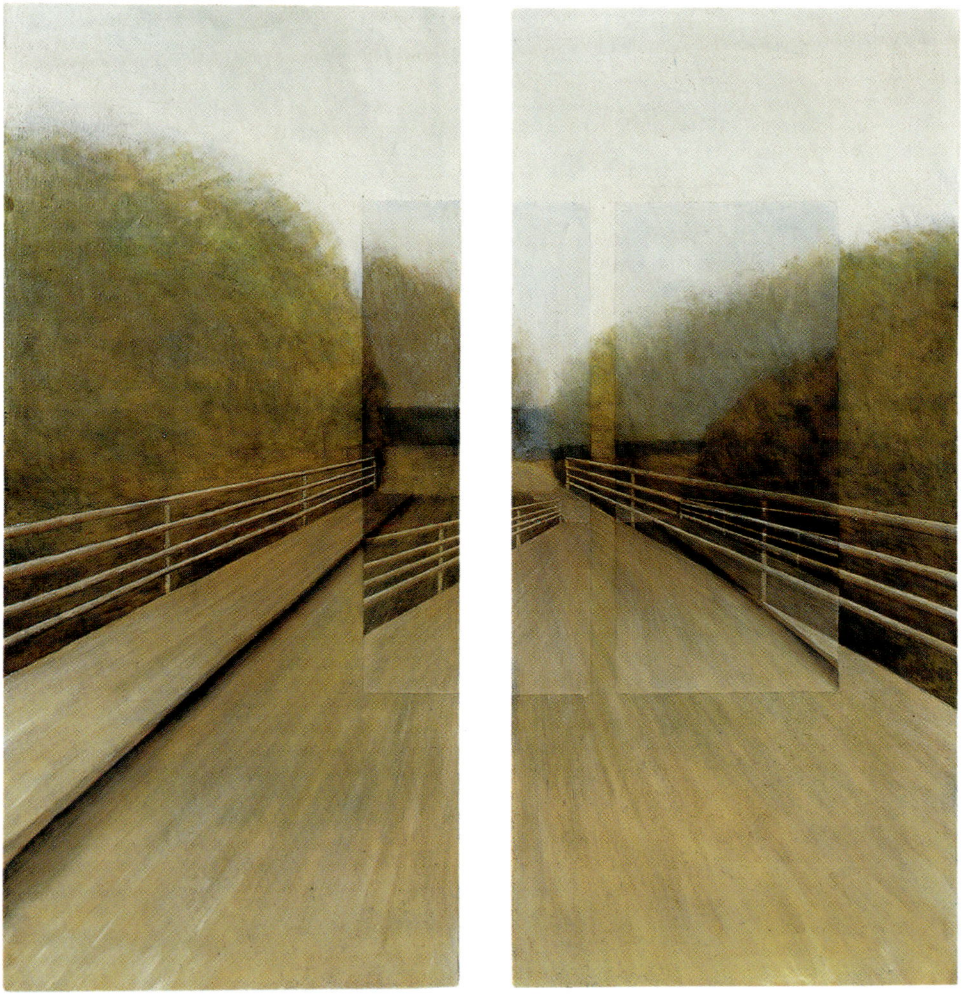

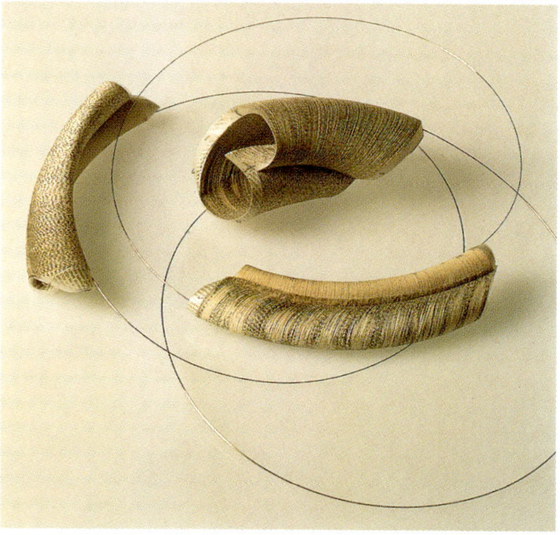

Janna Syvänoja:
Necklaces. 1996.
Telephone directory paper, steel.

The natures of a sculpture

The sculptress Kirsi Mikkola (b. 1959) has attempted in her faintly humorous, stylized cartoon-like works to crack the stereotypes associated with the new female image:

"The way the women's magazines keep up the beauty queen cult makes me sick. Almost any idea or opinion has to be bound up with a female body. I am more interested nowadays in the essence of being human and what I would like it to be. Even feminism can be a chain round one's neck."

Janna Syvänoja (b. 1960) and Stefan Lindfors (b. 1962) are both industrial designers by training, but they have also had substantial careers as graphic artists. Syvänoja has developed the paper creations that she first planned as decorations into a whole art form of their own, while Lindfors has made use of his knowledge of materials and structures to create whole dramatic interiors.

The performance artist Irma Optimisti (b. 1952) is a philosopher by profession, and attempts in a provocative way to expose the ridiculous elements in role models. Virve Hirvensalo's description provides some idea of the techniques that she employs:

"Irma Optimisti is about to perform. First she will tape a fishing rod down onto the table. Then she will inflate a few condoms and squirt them full of shaving foam. Then she will scrape the foam out and put on shiny red boxing gloves, and then... and then..."

Helena Hietanen (b. 1963) has taken optical fibres and woven them into huge pieces of techno-lace that possess a fascinating romantic beauty that is at its best at night. One of her main works, "Tecnopizzo a Venezia", she produced for the Venice Biennial in 1997, on the façade of the Palazzo Troni that faces the Grand Canal.

One point of departure for her works is the justification of women's traditions:

"I have consciously wanted to find a 'ladylike' way of doing things. My mother would always sew things, while I have always favoured weaving, making things with my hands."

Both the works of the sculptor Lauri Astala (b. 1958) and the sound and installation art of Tommi Grönlund (b. 1967) and Petteri Nisunen (b. 1962) have been inspired by the world view generated by the natural sciences and the challenges of technology. The latter have been working together since 1992 and have been particularly interested in systems that react to unseen changes in their environment, such as variations in background radiation.

Select bibliography

Ahtola-Moorhouse, Leena; *Suomalaista veistotaidetta – Finnish Sculpture.* Helsinki 1980.

Appelberg, Hanna och Eilif; *Helene Schjerfbeck. En biografisk Konturteckning.* Helsingfors 1949.

Art in Finland. Survey of a Century (ed. A. Krohn). Helsinki 1953.

Bästbacka, L; *T. K. Sallinen. Hans studieår och koloristiska genombrott 1905–1914.* Helsingfors 1960.

Boulton Smith, John; *A Century of Finnish Graphic Art.* Catalogue of Exhibition at the Morley Gallery. London 1975.

Boulton Smith, John; *The Golden Age of Finnish Art. Nouveau and the National Spirit.* Second revised ed. Helsinki 1985.

Hertzberg, Rafael; *Finska konstnärer.* Helsingfors 1911.

Holger, Lena; *Helene Schjerfbeck. Liv och Konstnärskap.* Stockholm 1987.

Juhani Harri. (Catalogue of an Exhibition, ed. Bhupendra Karia). New York 1992.

Kent, Neil; *The Triumph of Light and Nature. Nordic Art 1740–1940.* London 1987.

Konsten i Finland från medeltid till nutid. (ed. Sixten Ringbom). Helsingfors 1978.

Konttinen, Riitta; *Totuus enemmän kuin kauneus. Naistaiteilija, realismi ja naturalismi 1880-luvulla. Amélie Lundahl, Maria Wiik, Helena Westermarck, Helene Schjerfbeck ja Elin Danielson.* (English summary). Helsinki 1991.

Nervander, E; *Ett konstnärslif. Till minne af Severin Falkman.* Helsingfors 1902.

Nordisk 60-tal, uppbrott och konfrontation. Pohjolan 60-luku, murros ja vastus. The Nordic '60s, Upheaval and Confrontation. (Catalogue of an Exhibition organized by the Nordic Arts Center 3.3.–31.12.1990.

Nordman, C. A.; Medeltida skulptur i Finland. *Finska Fornminnesföreningens Tidskrift 62.* Helsingfors 1964.

Northern Light: Realism and Symbolism in Scandinavian Painting 1880–1910. (Ed. Kirk Varnedoe). New York 1982.

Olli Lyytikäinen 1949–1987. Nelivärinen uni/Fyrfärgad dröm/ 4-Colored Dream. (Ed. Eeropekka Rislakki). Helsingfors 1989.

Pearson, Paul David; *Alvar Aalto and the International Style.* New York 1978.

Punainen huone. Röda rummet. (Eds. Erik Bergh och Päivi Hovi). Turku 1988.

Puokka, Jaakko; *The Development of Graphic Art in Finland.* Helsinki 1953.

Rácz, István; *Treasures of Finnish Renaissance and Baroque Art.* Introduction and notes by Nils Cleve. Helsinki 1967.

Ringbom, Sixten; *Art History in Finland before 1920.* Helsinki 1986.

Sarje, Kimmo; *Realismi ja utopiat. Yhteiskunnallinen realismi Suomen 1970-luvun kuvataiteessa. Realism and Utopias. Social realism in 1970s Finnish Art.* Helsinki 1989.

Stjernschantz, Torsten; *Alexander Lauréus. En konsthistorisk studie.* Borgå.

Tanttu, Erkki; *Puupiirroksia. Träsnitt. Woodcuts.* Helsinki 1967.

Tikkanen, J.J.; *Finska konstföreningen 1846–1896.* Helsingfors 1896.

Tolvanen, Jouko; *Graphic Art in Finland.* Helsinki 1956.

Valkonen, Markku; *The Golden Age. Finnish Art 1850–1907. Helsinki 1992.*

Valkonen, Olli; *Maalaustaiteen murros Suomessa 1908–1914. uudet suuntaukset maalaustaiteessa, taidearvosteluissa ja taidekirjoittelussa.* (English summary). Jyväskylä 1927.

INDEX

Aalto, Aino 127
Aalto, Alvar 120, 123, 126, 127, 128, 134
Aalto, Ilmari 109, 110
Aaltonen, Wäinö 109, 113, 116, 117, 122, 123
Aalto, Timo 146
Aarnio, Pekka 136
Aarras, Raimo 119
Åberg, Viktoria 38
Achenbach, Andreas 37
Acke, J.A.G. 70
Adlercrantz, Carl Fredrik 21
Agricola, Mikael 12, 31
Ahlgrén, Lauri 141, 142
Ahlstedt, Fredrik 70
Ahlstedt, Nina 70
Aho, Juhani 72, 73
Ahola-Valo, Aleksanteri 123
Ahrenberg, Jac. 43
Ahtela, H. (Reuter, Einar) 120, 121
Ahtila, Eija-Liisa 158, 159
Aiha, Martti 153
Akiander, M. 45
Ala-Lääkkölä, Sirpa 156
Alanko, Uuno (Uno Alanco) 109, 124
Albert-Lazard, Lou-Lou (Lou Andreas Salomé) 119
Alexander I 21, 22, 23, 37
Alexander II 34, 52
Alexander III 73, 74
Alexander, Heir Apparent 27
Andersson, Axel 70
Angelico, Fra 96
Antell, Herman Frithiof 57, 69
Anttila, Lauri 156
Arman 143
Arne, Tor 136
Arwidsson, Adolf Ivar 28
Aschenbach, Oswald 40
Aspelin, Eliel 20, 52
Astala, Lauri 164
Åström, Emma Irene 60
Åström, Werner 108, 123
Augustson, Göran 146
Bäck, Yngve 129, 130, 132, 134
Backman, Johan 17
Barbarus, Antti 33
Bastien-Lepage, Jules 48, 49, 51, 62, 68, 77
Becker, Adolf von 38, 43, 46, 49, 59
Berndtson, Fredrik 29
Berndtson, Gunnar 48, 79
Bernini, Lorenzo 57
Bissen, Herman Vilhelm 34, 54
Bissen, Vilhelm 54
Blackstadius, Johan Z. 32
Blomstedt, Juhana 146, 147
Blomstedt, Väinö 78
Bobrikov, Nicholas Ivanovich 89, 90, 100
Böcklin, Arnold 38, 87, 126
Bodom, Erik 36
Boehm, Tuomas von 134
Bonnard, Pierre 108, 127
Bonnat, Léon 51, 57, 62
Bourguerau, William 68
Brahe, Per 14
Brandes, Georg 69
Braque, Georges 126, 127
Brenner, Elias 17
Breton, Jules 51
Broms, Arvid 127
Brut, Jack Hellen 156
Bryggman, Erik 126
Burljuk, David 110
Burljuk, Vladimir 110
Burri, Alberto 141, 143
Cage, John 143, 145
Cainberg, Erik 21, 22, 23, 25, 33
Calder, Alexander 127
Campendonck, Heinrich 110
Canogar, Rafael 141
Canth, Minna 60
Capsia, Margareta 17
Carlstedt, Birger 124, 126, 132
Carlstedt, Mikko 109
Carpeaux, Jean-Baptiste 57
Carrá, Carlo 126
Cavelier, Jules 57
Cavelier, Pierre Jules 57
Cawén, Alvar 105, 108, 109, 110, 113, 117, 118
Cavén, Kari 156
Caz, Jean 51
Cedercreutz, Emil 100
Cederström, C.G. 43
Cellini, Benvenuto 46
Cézanne, Paul 96, 108, 109, 113, 117, 127
Chagall, Marc 116, 126, 127
Chapman, Fredrik Henrik af 20
Chardin, Jean-Baptiste 43
Charles X Gustavus 14
Charles XII 17
Chavannes, Puvis de 60, 78, 81, 82, 95
Chirico, Giorgio de 126
Christina, Queen 14
Churberg, Fanny 39, 40, 41, 43, 44, 48, 59, 62, 63, 69, 98
Claeszon, Aris 15
Colliander, Ina 141
Collin, Marcus 104, 105, 109, 118, 123
Copper Markus 158
Cormon, Fernand 68
Cornell, Joseph 145
Corot, Camille 40
Courbet, Gustave 39, 43, 68
Courtois, Gustave 62
Craig, Gordon 102
Crippa, Roberto 141
Cunningham, Merce 143
Cygnaeus, Fredrik 30, 32, 33, 34, 45, 46, 59
Dagnan-Bouveret, Pascal-Adolphe-Jean 49
Dahl, Johann Christian 37
Dahlman, Helge 130
Dahlström, Hampus 55
Danielson-Gambogi, Elin 70, 71
Daubigny, Charles-François 40, 43
Daumier, Honoré 105
Delacroix, Eugène 68
Delaunay, Robert 119
Denis, Maurice 82, 105
Derain, André 127, 128
Diaghilev, Sergei 102
Diehl, Gösta 130, 134
Dietrichson, Lorentz 33, 55
Dongen, Kees van 107
Donner, Henrik Otto 145
Dörnberger, Adam 68
Duchamp, Marcel 145
Dupré, Jules 43
Dürer, Albrecht 88
Edelfelt, Albert 43, 46, 47, 48, 49, 51, 52, 60, 62, 68, 69, 70, 72, 74, 75, 77, 82, 89, 90, 91, 100
Ehrensvärd, Carl August 18, 20, 25, 26
Ehrensvärd, Augustin 18, 20
Ehrström, Eric O.W. 87, 92
Ekelund, Ragnar 108, 109, 118, 134
Ekman, Fredrik 25
Ekman, Robert Wilhelm 24, 27, 31, 32, 34, 45, 58
Elfgren, Gunnar 134
Elizabeth, Czarina 22
Elmgren, Sven Gabriel 34
Enckell, Magnus 78, 79, 80, 81, 90, 91, 96, 97, 102, 104, 105, 108, 113
Enckell, Torger 132, 134
Engblom, Alma 59, 60
Engel, Carl Ludvig 22, 46, 123
Enroth, Erik 128, 131
Ericsson, Henry 123
Erik XIV 39, 46
Ervamaa, Jukka 30, 31
Eskolin, Veikko 136
Essen, Werner von 108
Estlander, Carl Gustaf 45, 51, 58, 63, 71
Falkman, Severin 48, 49, 96
Fautrier, Jean 141
Favén, Mauri 141
Favorin, Ellen 60
Federley, Alexander 70
Finch, Alfred William 101, 102, 108
Finnberg, Gustaf Wilhelm 20, 24, 25
Finne, Gunnar 123
Flaubert, Gustave 51
Flaxman, John 57
Fleming, Henrik 15
Flodin, Hilda 100
Fontana, Lucio 143
Forselles, Sigrid af 60, 100
Forsman, Aline 58
Forsström, Wiking 138
Forstén, Lennart 29
Franzén, Franz Michael 23
Friedrich, Caspar David 38
Frosterus, Sigurd 101, 102, 105, 127
Frosterus-Soltin, Alexandra 38, 39
Gallén, Axel (Gallen-Kallela after 1907) 52, 60, 66, 67, 68, 69, 72, 73, 74, 82, 83, 84, 85, 87, 88, 89, 90, 91, 95, 96, 101, 102, 108, 114, 122, 156
Gallén, Jorma 91
Gallén, Mary 72
Gallén, Mathilda 85
Gallénius, Lars 17
Gauguin, Paul 78
Gebhard, Albert 95
Geet, Jacob Sigfridsson 13
Gegerfelt, Wilhelm von 43
Geitel, Johan Georg 18, 19
Gemito, Vincenzo 58
Geffroy, Gustave 92
Géricault, Théodore 57, 68
Gérôme, Jean Léon 43, 48, 51, 62
Gesellius, Herman 90, 101
Gezelius, Juhana 14
Ghirlandaio, Domenico 96
Giotto di Bondone 96
Gjörwell, Carl Christoffer 21, 23
Gobineau, Arthur de 33
Godenhjelm, Berndt Abraham 24, 27
Gogh, Vincent van 96
Gontcharova, Natalia 110
Gorky, Maria Andreyevna 101
Gorky, Maxim 101
Gottberg, Susanne 161, 163
Granberg, Emanuel 18, 19, 20
Grönlund, Tommi 164
Grönvall, Sven 126, 132
Gude, Hans 36, 37, 40
Guerin, Charles 108
Gullichsen, Maire 127, 132, 134, 141
Gustavus II Adolphus 13, 17
Gustavus III 18, 21, 23
Gustavus IV Adolphus 22
Gustavus Vasa 31
Gyldén, Nils Abraham 26
Haapasalo, Johannes 123
Haapasalo, Kreeta 31
Haarala, Olavi 138
Haarla, Rafael 117
Haartman, Axel 25
Haartman, Lars Gabriel von 38
Hadrian 79
Hahl, Nils Gustav 127
Häiväoja, Heikki 142
Halonen, Eemil 90
Halonen, Pekka 73, 78, 89, 90, 94, 95, 114
Hämäläinen, Helvi 132
Hämäläinen, Kauko 136
Hanotaux, Gabriel 58
Harri, Juhani 143, 144, 145
Hartman, Mauno 142
Hartung, Hans 141
Hautala, Jorma 146
Hedeman-Gade, H. 117
Hegel, Friedrich 45
Heikel, Rosina 60
Heikkilä, Erkki 141, 142
Heiskanen, Outi 152, 153
Hellaakoski, Aaro 116
Hellaakoski, Elsa 116
Helmholtz, Hermann von 102
Hienonen, Erkki 136
Hietanen, Helena 162, 164
Hildén, Kaarlo 123
Hiltunen, Eila 138, 141, 142
Hintze, Bertel 120
Hirn, Yrjö 73
Hirvelä, Erkki 146
Höijer, Carl Theodor 45, 46
Holbein, Hans Jr. 88
Holmberg, Werner 34, 36, 37, 38, 39, 40, 46
Hårleman, Carl 20
Hovi, Mikko 134
Hütt, Wolfgang 36
Ibsen, Henrik 60
Ilmoni, Einar 107
Ilvas, Juha 55
Ingres, Jean 120
Isto, Edvard 90

Jacobsen, Arne 134
Jaeger, Hans 69
Jalavisto, Mikko 146
Jansson, Edla 31
Jansson, Karl Emanuel 38, 39, 43
Järnefelt, Aino 73
Järnefelt, Arvid 77
Järnefelt, Eero 73, 76, 77, 78, 90
Jawlensky, Aleksi von 110
John, Duke 13
Josephson, Ernst 87, 124
Jung, Valter 92
Junno, Tapio 152, 153
Jürgensburg, P. Klodth von 54
Jusélius, F.A. 91
Jylhä, Kari 146
Kaijala, Ilmari 118
Kaivanto, Kimmo 148
Kajander, Ismo 145
Kajanus, Robert 82, 114
Kamppuri, Väinö 118
Kandelin, Ole 132
Kandinsky, Wassily 102, 110, 120
Kanerva, Aimo 131, 132, 150
Kanervo, Marja 156
Karin Magnusdotter 46
Kärkkäinen, Seppo 136
Kaskipuro, Pentti 139, 141
Kauhanen, Pekka 153
Kekarainen, Pertti 161, 162
Kekkonen, Urho 153
Kivi, Aleksis 116, 117
Kivijärvi, Harry 136, 141, 143, 153
Kivimäki, T.M. 122
Klee, Paul 110, 119
Kleineh, Oscar 40, 43
Klinckowström, O.W. 27
Klinge, Matti 22, 24
Knutson, Johan 29, 37
Koistinen, Unto 132
Kojo, Viljo 109
Konttinen, Riitta 59, 60
Kooning, Willem de 131
Koskinen, Harro 145
Kothen, Casimir von 45
Krohn, Ernst 126
Krohn, Kaarle 12
Kruskopf, Pehr Adolf 25, 29, 37
Kügelgen, Carl von 37
Kujasalo, Matti 156
Kulovesi, Erkki 123
Kunnas, Väinö 120, 121, 122
Kuutola, Kalle 110, 124
Kylberg, Karl 131
Laine, Lauri 153, 156
Laitila, Atte 124
Lampi, Vilho 122
Landström, Björn 128
Lanu, Olavi 150
Laurencin, Marie 128
Laurens, J.P. 43
Lauréus, Alexander 20, 21, 25
Le Fauconnier, Henri 109
Léger, Fernand 127, 136
Lehtinen, Kauko 145
Lehtonen, Henrietta 159
Lehtonen, Joel 109
Leino, Eino 114
Leino, Kasimir 72, 81
Lessing, Johan Christian 40, 41
Lhôte, André 120, 124, 127, 136
Lieto, Master from 12, 13
Liipola, Yrjö 122, 124
Lilius, Carl-Gustav 141
Liljelund, Arvid 39, 40, 43
Lindfors, Anton 109
Lindfors, Stefan 164
Lindgren, Armas 90, 101
Lindh, Johan Erik 25, 31
Lindholm, Berndt 38, 39, 40, 41, 43
Lindsten, Leo 146
Lindström, Aune 41
Linnilä, Kai 148
Linning, C.A. 25
Liulia, Marita 159
Löfgren, Erik Johan 31, 38, 39
Lönnberg, William 108, 127
Lönnrot, Elias 32, 33, 98
Ludwig, Carl 41
Lumikangas, Pentti 139, 141
Lundahl, Amélie 60
Luostarinen, Leena 153, 155
Lydén, Edwin 118, 119, 120, 126
Lyytikäinen, Olli 150, 151
Lyytinen, Pentti 31
Maarni, Elvi 132
Magnus II Tavast 13
Mäkelä, Juho 104, 105, 107, 108
Mäkelä, Marika 153
Mäki, Martti S. 146
Mäki, Teemu 159
Mäkilä, Otto 125, 126, 127, 130, 132, 134
Männikkö, Esko 160, 161
Mäntynen, Jussi 123
Mallander, Jan Olof 150
Malling, Otto 119
Malmberg, Viktor 100
Manet, Edouard 40, 63, 96
Mannerheim, C.G. 114
Manni, Tarmo 142
Mantegna, Andrea 96
Marc, Franz 110, 119
Markkula, Mauno 131
Martin, Elias 20, 25
Martos, Ivan 23
Masaccio 96
Masreliez, Louis 23
Masson, André 128
Matisse, Henri 107, 126, 128
Matson, Alex 109
Mattas, Åke 131, 132
Mechelin, Leo 45, 74, 100
Meissonier, Ernst 48
Mennander, C.F. 18
Menshikov, Alexander Sergeievich 30
Merian, Matthäus 18
Merikanto, Oskar 82
Mether-Borgström, Ernst 136, 137, 146
Meurman, Agathon 52
Michelangelo 46
Miettinen, Olli 124, 132
Mill, John Stuart 60
Mikkola, Kirsi 164
Minguzzi, Luciano 141
Miró, Joan 132
Mitjens, Martin the Elder 17
Moholy-Nagy, Laszlo 119
Møllerum, Diedrich 17
Monet, Claude 70
Montesquieu, Charles Louis 21
Montgomery, Robert 52
Moore, Henry 132
Morand, Paul 126
Morris, William 91, 92
Moss, Jacob 17
Munch, Edvard 82, 85, 105
Munsterhjelm, Hjalmar 38, 39, 43
Myller, Veikko 153
Münter, Gabriele 110
Myntti, Eemu 126
Napoleon I 21
Näsänen, Perttu 148
Neiman, Jochim 15
Nelimarkka, Eero 109, 110
Nevalainen, Pekka 156
Nicholas I 22, 27
Nicholas II 89, 100
Nietzsche, Friedrich 118
Nisunen, Petteri 164
Niva, Jussi 161
Nolde, Emil 131
Nopsanen, Aarne 128
Nordensvan, Victorine 40
Nordström, Lars-Gunnar 132, 133, 134, 136
Nordström, Vilhelmina 38
Nylund, Felix 123
Nyman, Gunnel 134
Oinonen, Mikko 107, 123
Oja, Marjatta 156
Okkonen, Onni 69, 116, 117, 122, 124
Oldenburg, Claes 150
Ollila, Yrjö 105, 108, 120, 128
Optimisti, Irma 164
Osipow, Paul 146, 152, 153
Oxenstierna, Axel 14
Paasikivi, J.K. 153
Paatela, Oskari 105
Paavolainen, Olavi 120, 122, 130
Palmgren Raoul 127
Palomeri, R. 127
Paraske, Larin 77
Parviainen, Oscar 123
Pasch, Johan 20
Pasteur, Louis 51
Paul, Adolf 82, 85
Péladan, Joséphin 79
Peña, Diaz de la 43
Peter I 18
Petterson, Jonas 108
Picasso, Pablo 126, 128, 130, 145
Pietilä, Tuulikki 141
Pillet, Edgar 136
Pirtola, Erkki 156
Pissarro, Camille 40, 49
Plato 79
Porthan, Henrik Gabriel 19, 23, 33, 34
Preidelsberger, Marianne 62
Pullinen, Laila 138, 142
Pusa, Unto 130, 132, 134, 135, 136
Qvanten, Emil von 82
Raittila, Tapani 134
Rajulin, Erkki 150
Ramstedt, Yrjö 105
Ranta, Viljo 132
Rantanen, Silja 153, 155
Rantanen, Ulla 140, 142
Ranttila, Martti 120
Raphael 46
Rappo, Charles 26
Räsänen, Kauko 136, 137, 141
Rauschenberg, Robert 143
Rautala, Emil 118
Rehbinder, Robert Henrik 22, 28
Reiman, Matias 17
Reinholm, H.A. 29
Reinikainen, Raimo 146
Rein, Th. 72
Reitala, Aimo 36, 40, 46, 48, 73, 95, 126
Renoir, Auguste 51
Repin, Ilja 95
Richter, Edvard 124
Rilke, Rainer Maria 119
Rinne, Antero 126
Rissanen, Juho 90, 92, 94, 95, 96, 98, 105, 108, 109
Robert-Fleury, Tony 68
Rodin, Auguste 58, 100
Rönnberg, Hanna 70
Roos, Nina 161
Rosenberg, Valle 108
Rossetti, Dante Gabriel 81
Rothovius, Isak 17
Rousseau, Jean-Jaques 68, 120
Roussel, Ker-Xavier 108
Rubens 18
Rude, François 58
Runeberg, Johan Ludvig 24, 27, 28, 33, 34, 46, 54, 55
Runeberg, Walter 43, 52, 54, 55, 57, 60
Rung, F.L. 18
Ruokokoski, Jalmari 105, 106, 108
Ruotsala, Maria 158
Ruutsalo, Eino 138, 141
Rydberg, Viktor 82
Rydeng, N.P. 108
Ryti, Risto 153
Saabye, A.V. 58
Saari, Lauri 120
Saarinen, Eliel 90, 101, 114
Saarinen, Yrjö 129, 130, 131
Saglio, André 102
Salama, Hannu 146
Salla, Irja 113
Sallinen, Tyko 106, 107, 108, 112, 113, 126
Salokivi, Santeri 118, 123
Sandberg, J.G. 31
Sarajas-Korte, Salme 68
Särkelä, Eveliina 58, 59
Sattler, Josef 85
Schauman, B.O. 56
Schauman, Eugen 100
Schauman, Sigrid 100, 107, 134
Schillmark, Nils 18, 21
Schjerfbeck, Helene 46, 47, 48, 59, 60, 62, 63, 64, 67, 87, 96, 97, 98, 107, 114, 115
Schultz, Peter 14, 15
Sedmigradski, F.F. 25
Segerstråle, Lennart 123, 128
Sergel, Johan Tobias 21, 23
Serlachius, G.A. 69
Sérusier, Paul 79
Seseman, Elga 132
Seurat, Georges 101
Shelesnov, Jakov 23
Sibelius, Jean 10, 73, 82, 85, 100, 114, 142
Sievänen, Jaakko 140, 141, 142

Signac, Paul 105
Sillanpää, F.E. 122
Simberg, Hugo 86, 87, 88, 90, 91, 92
Sim, Filadelfio 96
Sipilä, Sulho 116, 120, 122
Sirén, J.S. 122
Sjöstrand, Carl Eneas 32, 33, 34, 46, 52
Sjöström, Wilho 104, 105
Sköldebrandt, A.F. 37
Slöör, Mary 73
Snellman, Johan Vilhelm 29, 30, 33, 59
Söderstrand, Carl Gustaf 26
Sohlman, August 32
Soisalo, Juha 146
Soldan, Augusta E. 38
Soldan, Venny 90
Somersalo, Jaakko 141
Somma, Ossi 153
Sonck, Lars 91, 92
Soulanges, Pierre 141
Sparre, Louis 72, 73, 87
Speitz, Hartikka 15
Speranski, Mihail 22
Staffanson, Henrik 13
Staffanson, Sigfrid 13
Staudiger, Uno 98
Stenbäck, Josef 91
Sten, John 109
Stenman, Gösta 107, 114
Stewen, Riikka 88
Stigell, Robert 52, 57, 89, 90
Stigzelius, Julia 43
Stjernschantz, Beda 79, 80, 81, 82
Ståhlberg, K.J. 114
Stokes, Adrian 62
Strengell, Gustaf 101, 105
Strindberg, August 44, 68
Summanen, Arvo 138
Suomalainen, Kari 128
Syvänoja, Janna 164
Takalo-Eskola, Juhani 150
Takanen, Johannes 43, 52, 54, 55, 56, 57, 58
Tamminen, Maria 120
Tandefelt, Heikki 107
Tanttu, Erkki 128
Tapiola, Marjatta 153, 155
Tapiovaara, Tapio 123
Tapper, Harri 143
Tapper, Kain 136, 138, 141, 142, 143
Tawaststjerna, Erik 85
Tengström, Jakob 23, 29
Thelning, Emanuel 24, 45
Thersner, Ulrik 29, 37
Thesleff, Ellen 79, 80, 81, 102, 103, 105, 108
Thiis, Jens 110
Thilén, Ada 60
Thomé, Verner 96, 103, 105, 108, 109
Thorvaldsen, Bertel 54
Tikkanen, Henrik 128
Tikkanen, J.J. 27, 98
Tirronen, Esko 141, 142
Tohka, Sakari 126
Toivola, Hilkka 132
Tollet, A.M. 107
Tolonen, Kari-Juhani 146
Tolstoy, Leo 77
Topelius, Eva 70
Topelius, Zachris 25, 27, 29, 30, 36, 41, 52, 70
Toppelius, Mikael 17, 19, 20
Toppila, Heikki 150
Tott, Christina 14, 15
Tott, Åke 14, 15
Traini, Francesco 96
Tudeer, O.E. 71
Tuhka, Aukusti 123
Tukiainen, Aimo 130, 138, 141
Tuukkanen, Bruno 110
Tynys, Arvi 138
Uhde, Fritz von 74
Uljaska 72
Ullberg, Uno 123
Ungern, Ragnar 118
Uotila, Aukusti 51, 52, 60
Utriainen, Raimo 147, 148
Utrillo, Maurice 128
Uutinen, Marianna 161
Vallgren, Ville 44, 46, 52, 57, 58, 60, 90, 98, 100
Valtonen, Osmo 149, 150
Vanninen, Antti 109
Vanni, Sam 132, 134, 136, 137, 146
Vasarely, Victor 134, 136, 146
Vasström, Eric 107
Vehmas, E.J. 131, 138
Velázquez, Diego 96
Velde, Henry van de 101
Vigeland, Gustav 82
Vihanta, Ulla 126
Vilhunen, Risto 146
Viljo, Eeva Maija 45
Vionoja, Veikko 150
Virolainen, Heikki W. 146
Vischer, Friedrich Theodor 45
Vuillard, Jean Edouard 128
Wacklin, Isak 18, 20
Waenerberg, Thorsten 40
Waldin, Petrus 14
Wallenius, Johan Fredrik 23
Walter, Arthur 45
Wargh, Carl 120, 127
Wasastjerna, Torsten 70
Weckström, Marjatta 141
Wehmas, Einari 120
Wennervirta, Ludwig 57, 87, 102, 105, 124
Westerholm, Victor 70, 90, 92, 95
Westerlund, Sven-Olof 148
Westermarck, Helena 60, 62, 63, 67
Westman, Edvard 70
Whistler, James McNeill 96, 98
Wiik, Maria 41, 60, 61
Wikström, Emil 73, 74, 90, 98, 122
Wilhelms, Carl 122
Willbrandt, Christian Hendhersson 14
Winckelmann, Johann Joachim 19
Wirkkala, Maaria 156, 157
Wirkkala, Tapio 134, 153
Wrede, Rabbe Fabian Gustaf 24
Wright, Ferdinand von 28, 29, 31, 36
Wright, Karl Magnus von 56
Wright, Magnus von 28, 29, 37, 38
Ylikangas, Heikki 30
Young, Thomas 102
Zola, Émile 51
Zorn, Anders 74